18.00 xx

Corner House

P9-DFM-328

DATE DUE

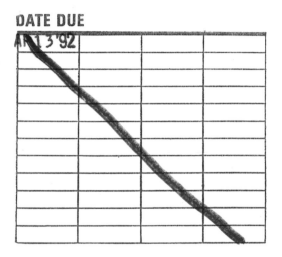

APR 13'92			

DEMCO

Corner House Publishers

SOCIAL SCIENCE REPRINTS

General Editor MAURICE FILLER

CHILD OF CHARLES I
VANDYCK

ENGLISH CHILDREN
IN
THE OLDEN TIME

BY

ELIZABETH GODFREY

WITH THIRTY-TWO ILLUSTRATIONS

SECOND EDITION

CORNER HOUSE PUBLISHERS

WILLIAMSTOWN, MASSACHUSETTS 01267

1980

First Published . . September *1907*

Second Edition . . December *1907*

REPRINTED 1980

BY

CORNER HOUSE PUBLISHERS

ISBN 0–87928–104–9

Printed in the United States of America

TO
THREE HAPPY CHILDREN
OF TO-DAY,
ENID, ARCHIBALD, ERIC
LINDSEY

CONTENTS

CHAPTER VIII

SOME ROYAL CHILDREN

CHAPTER IX

CONCERNING PEDAGOGUES

CHAPTER X

PLEASANT PASTIMES

CHAPTER XI

THE GOLDEN AGE

LIST OF ILLUSTRATIONS

xiii

PREFACE

O N first entering on the study of this subject it seemed it would be difficult to discover information enough for the earlier centuries; records of childhood are so scanty until almost the Stuart times: later it proved only too abundant, and the task was rather to select the most characteristic features of different periods and combine them into a coherent picture. Gleanings, sometimes sparse, had to be made over a very wide field: not history alone, but still more biography and domestic letters must be laid under contribution. History indeed yields but little to the purpose, except in such works as Green's *Short History of the English People*, or Traill's *Social England*, where the domestic side is brought forward. Letters are frequently disappointing, as when a survey of the bulky volumes of the *Paston Letters* results in two or three brief references to the children; while those of the seventeenth century, notably the Verney correspondence, the Lismore Papers, and various letters and memorials of the Sydney family and the Memoirs of the Norths, yield a rich harvest.

This makes it impossible to indicate in detail the sources from which this sketch of the development of child life in England has been drawn, but to certain modern writers I should like to acknowledge my indebtedness. First and foremost, to Mr. de Montmorency, who most generously placed a precious store of notes he had gathered on early education at my disposal, extending widely the debt I owed to his two books on the subject, *State Intervention in English Education* and *The Progress of Education in England.*

Hardly less am I indebted to Mrs. Field's admirable work, *The Child and His Book,* which affords not only a comprehensive view of child literature, but also gives incidentally many valuable details of child life.

The Rev. Dr. Macintosh contributed many most useful suggestions as to sources of information, especially with respect to children as dealt with by the dramatists and the poets. To these and to others who have helped by hints or loans of books I tender sincere thanks.

Much of the same ground as in the later portion of the book is covered by Mrs. Earle's *Child Life in Colonial Days,* but I did not meet with her book until my own gleanings were almost completed, so that similarities are caused by having gone to the same fountain head, each drawing in her own pitcher.

Available illustrations are inevitably somewhat meagre for the earlier part and embarrassingly abundant for the later ; more especially for the eighteenth century, when both painters and engravers seem to have delighted in child subjects ; children working, children playing, children quarrelling offered inexhaustible themes for their pencils. Much help in finding suitable matter was afforded by the courtesy of the custodians in the Print Room at the British Museum. Leave also has been kindly granted by the authorities to reproduce the Villiers family group from the National Portrait Gallery and the baby holding a coral from the Royal Collection at Kensington Palace. Thanks are also due to the Proprietors of the Leadenhall Press for kindly permitting reproduction of the portrait of Miss Campion from the *History of the Horn-Book* by the late Andrew Tuer, and one of the *Six Charming Children* from *London Cries*, by the same author.

The delight in little children which the eighteenth century testified in its pictures is even intensified in the twentieth, so this little study goes forth sure of a sympathetic interest in its subject, however far short the execution may have fallen of the completeness of which it deserves.

E. G.

THE AGE OF INNOCENCE
JOSHUA REYNOLDS

ENGLISH CHILDREN IN THE OLDEN TIME

CHAPTER I

BABIES IN BYGONE DAYS

GAZING back to the far distance from which we have travelled, we may see the crests of the tall forest trees rearing themselves against the horizon, some far overtopping the rest ; but of the saplings at the foot we can discern nothing, unless it be as a mist of green. So as we look across the hills of time, heroic figures—an Arthur, a Bede, an Alfred— arrest the eye ; we seek almost in vain for the little children. But in these days, when we have come to think so much of children and to study them so deeply, we want to know how the little ones of old lived, how they were nursed and taught.

Because children are so rarely and so briefly mentioned in old chronicles, some have fancied they must have been looked on with indifference. Not so : childhood in itself, it may be, was made less of than now ; but it was because of the eagerness of our fore- fathers about their offspring, not their indifference ; they were not content to prolong the days of dandling the baby; they wanted to see stalwart sons ready to follow them to the field, fair daughters early ripe to be matched with bold sons-in-law. Truly, in those far-off days, "Like as the arrows in the hand of the giant even so were the young children."

Their nurture was hard and rude. Tacitus records how the Saxon tribes early inured their babies to the sights and sounds of warfare, the camps for the women and children being pitched close to the battlefield. Almost the earliest thing we learn about infants is that, newly born, they were plunged over head and ears into extreme cold water to harden them. This is stated by Galen to have been the practice of the Saxon tribes of Germania, and since our Saxon ancestors were of the same race, they had, in all probability, similar customs. Moreover, the Britons are believed to have done the same thing; so it is asserted by Traill in his *Social England*. The babe was then dressed, not in the little garments of fine lawn and lace that came into use later, but, like the infant Saviour, in swaddling clothes, as may be seen in an illuminated manuscript of the ninth century, given in Strutt's *History of Costume*. This represents a high-born lady in a coronet handing her infant to a young girl—the nursemaid presumably, who wears her hair in two long plaits down her back. The baby is depicted in swaddling bands, and looks the shape of a cocoon; the end of the swathing-cloth is brought over the head like a little pointed hood, and all is kept in place with green ribbons wound round and round. This custom lasted long, for a manuscript of the fourteenth century shows a baby similarly wound up. In a drawing by Matthew Paris of the little Prince Edmund, son of Henry III., the baby is seen wound round with the same crossway bands, lying in a little cot on legs with curtains like a miniature four-poster.

The earliest known lullaby points to a little furry garment for winter babies; this may have been put on outside the swaddling bands, or may have been taken to when these were left off. The lines are still familiar—

> "Bye, baby bunting,
> Father's gone a-hunting
> To fetch a little rabbit-skin
> To wrap the baby bunting in."

It is impossible to say when swaddling clothes went out in favour of the dainty little shirts and robes of fine cambric, with wonderful delicate stitchery, in which seventeenth-century babies were pranked. These may have come in in the previous century, when all the arts of the needle were so much cultivated, or possibly earlier still. The oldest I have seen are those preserved in the South Kensington Museum, having adorned the babyhood of Charles II.; they are exquisitely hem-stitched and feather-stitched, the outfit being completed by little lace mittens for the tiny hands. It is evident, however, that the Saxon baby did not rejoice in anything so fine.

Before the child could toddle, it seems to have been put into a little frock or tunic down to the feet, tied in

round the waist. In an early manuscript there is a
baby still in arms in such a blue tunic, with bare feet,
and this garment, though it must have been very awkward for the child to play in when he could run about,
seems to have held its ground for some time. The
baby king, Henry VI., at about nine months old is
represented, in an old painting, in the arms of his
guardian, the Earl of Warwick, wearing just such a
little gown, with a crown on his bald head ; and as late
as the seventeenth century the small Duke of York
wears petticoats down to his toes like a little girl,
according to the well-known group by Vandyck, though
he must have been quite six years old.   There are two
baby portraits of children unknown, attributed to Milani,
which appear to represent babies from eighteen months
to two years old.   Both are dressed in long frocks with
little caps on their heads ; one grasps a rattle, the
other a coral and bells. These now hang in Kensington
Palace. If by Milani, they must be of the seventeenth
century; but they have the air of being considerably
older—possibly of the time of Holbein.

To return to the infant Saxons ; they, in the earliest
times, probably wore but little, their swaddling clothes
being discarded, for Tacitus says, " In every house you
may see little boys, sons of lords or peasants, equally
ill-clad, lying about or playing among the cattle." They
were early encouraged to run, jump, wrestle, climb, or
swim, and tradition says that the first morsel of solid
food was put into the boy's mouth on the point of his
father's sword that he might be a valiant warrior and

WINTER

AFTER HAMILTON

die on the field of battle. The mother then, and for long after, always suckled her infant; and failing the mother, a foster-mother would be resorted to. Patent foods were unknown, and bringing up by hand only tried in cases of dire necessity. When the child was weaned, it would be fed with spoon or pap-boat. The earliest mention of a sucking-bottle is in the seventeenth century, when one was tried to feed Master Marmaduke Rawdon, he having severely burnt his mouth by playing with fireworks. Ancient silver pap-boats have come down in many families, some probably far earlier than the historic one at South Kensington, out of which Oliver Cromwell is supposed to have been fed.

The babies were certainly washed, and washed by a fire, in very early days. How else could the fairy-wife have insisted that clean water and towels be left by the fire for her to come and wash her own imp-baby, according to the old legend? Dressed in front of a good fire too, probably, for in one of the old Breviaries of Health that were almost as popular as the Books of Nurture, the importance of dressing as well as undressing by a good fire, and warming the clothes before they were put on, is strongly insisted on. In a most comfortable picture of a lady's bedchamber, from a Harleian manuscript of the middle of the fifteenth century, we see a nurse dressing a baby in front of a blazing wood fire.

The nurse so often figures in old tales and ballads, she must be as old as civilization—or older—with her crooning lullabies, her marvellous stories, her physic of simples; her skill in charms and magic too, which may now be counted to her for ignorance rather than for learning. She very often began as foster-mother, as the many tales of infants changed at nurse may testify, and in many cases brought up the child at her own home, amongst her own little ones; but in earliest times would be more often a member of the castle household, the wife, maybe, of some retainer, or widow of one who had lost his life in his lord's service. In royal households, or those of the higher nobility, she would usually be a gentlewoman of some position. Frequently she developed into a kind of chaperon to the girls—in which capacity she was not always a success—like Juliet's nurse or the "ancient gentlewoman" who did such dis-service to poor Venetia Stanley, Sir Kenelm Digby's sweetheart, whose orphanhood she mothered. She might be a strict disciplinarian and earliest instructor in manners and morals, but her discretion was not invariably to be relied on—at least, as her nurselings grew up; her experience with the babies and their ailments was, at the worst, equal to that of their mothers. The bringing up of children in those early days was, in any case, a curious mixture of wisdom and ignorance, of sound common sense and superstition.

At seven years old the little boys were usually withdrawn from her charge, for fear of too much "dallying and fond cokkering," but over the girls her sway would extend until their marriage—sometimes was carried to the second generation, as in the case of the delightful Nan Fudd of the *Verney Letters*, who not only brought

up the eleven children of Sir Edmund and Dame
Margery, but those of their eldest son Ralph and his
youthful wife, hardly more than a child herself when
she had—and lost—her first two babies. When the
young couple were in exile in France their second boy
was left in Nan's charge, his grandparents being dead ;
but with this little fellow Nan was not always judicious,
since he grew up with crooked legs, though otherwise a
fine child, and his mother, when she visited him, attributed it to his keeping "a very ill diet," being allowed
to eat anything he had a mind to. Nurse had, however,
taught him to sing prettily, and his mother declared
him to be "an extreme witty child." Spite of this
early spoiling, he was a very good boy, as was testified
by another nurse who had charge of him in France, and
wrote to his father: "Mr. John hath keept his clothes
in such good order, I have not had to buy anything
for him : next week I will send him again to school
though we are great gainers by his sober company."
This little Master Jack must have been an example to
his younger aunts, Molly and Betty Verney, whom Nan
spoilt so outrageously that neither elder sisters nor
sister-in-law could do anything with them.

Likewise we may fancy that the "old Joan" who
figures in the charming letters of Anne, Lady North,
may have been in that family for at least two generations, being the indulgent nurse of her earlier nurseling's
children, when in their grandmother's charge. A tanta-
lizingly brief message, in a letter from Dorothy Osborne,
begs that a certain "Nan" may cut a lock of Sir

William Temple's hair for her, suggesting that that
grave statesman may have kept his old nurse as a pen-
sioner in his household.   It is good to see that these
faithful women were not forgotten by their royal or
noble nurselings.   One of the first things Henry V. did
on succeeding to the throne was to bestow a pension of
£20 (equal to about £300 now) on Johanna Waring,
who had had charge of his sickly infancy, and Henry
VIII. did the same thing for his nurse, Anne Luke.

We have travelled a long way from Saxon nurseries,
but we may be sure the nurse was, as she has ever been,
prime solacer of the woes of infancy, its sorrows or its
sicknesses ; her lap the refuge from the teasing tyranny
of small brothers or the terrors of "Bogey" ; her skill
at the service of cuts and bruises, of broken knees or
broken dolls.   She had considerable lore in herbs and
in domestic surgery, as well as charms at her tongue's
end for warts, hiccups, toothaches, or earaches.   There
she sits, an antique figure, her lap the background for
all nursery pictures, and at her feet the cradle.

The oldest known cradles are of wood, those that
have survived the wreck of time often of oak richly
carved.   It is, however, extremely likely that osier
baskets were also used, especially by the peasantry ; but
these being so perishable, would naturally disappear
unrecorded.   A very queer form of cradle seems to have
been in use in Ireland, for Robert Boyle, in his autobiography, says that he and all his brothers and sisters
were brought up in an Irish cabin by a foster-mother,
as the old Earl of Cork had a great idea of hardening

CHILD WITH CORAL AND BELLS
ATTRIBUTED TO MILANI

children, and were put into a kind of "pendulous satchel," with a slit for the child to look out of, which seems to have been hung up like a hammock or the cradle of an Indian papoose. This, no doubt, swung; but rockers do not seem to have been an invariable feature of the cradle, as in the picture of Prince Edmund, referred to above, there were none, but most early manuscripts show them. In one, given in Green's *Short History*, a cradle by the bedside of the mother is being rocked by an attendant. Also Smith, writing in the eighteenth century, speaks of cots coming in instead of cradles with rockers as quite a new departure. Rocking as a method of soothing infancy is traditional and instinctive; it was reserved for the twentieth century to discover—or fancy—that it is not good for babies.* And to the cradle belong the rocking tunes that the nurses used to chant. But before we go into the history of these we must speak of some other bits of nursery equipment.

The rattles depicted in the two baby portraits described above are of quite an advanced type; but some form of rattle was probably in existence from the first. I have somewhere met with mention of one made of an inflated bladder with dried peas inside it, a primitive form which was no doubt found very gratifying The coral would, I suppose, be later; and I dare say our Saxon forefathers cut their teeth upon a crust of bread, always handy for the purpose. A bit of nursery furniture which is of considerable antiquity, though I

* The rocker held a distinct office in the households of infant princes and princesses.

cannot assert that it was known in Saxon nurseries, was the go-cart, a frame of wood fixed at the height of the child's armpits, in which he was securely fastened, his feet touching the floor, but without letting the weight of the body rest upon them. It was furnished with little castors at the four corners, so that it would go easily, and in this the child learned to walk without risk of bandy legs. A contrivance which kept it from straying, and perhaps saved a fall, but gave no support, was a band passed round its waist, or rather just under its arms, with long ribbons like toy reins, held by the nurse. A crimson pair, embroidered by Mary Queen of Scots for her little son, was exhibited amongst the Stuart relics shown in London some few years ago.

A very curious device, mentioned in Smith's *Book for a Rainy Day*, as of antiquity in his time, was called a black pudding. It was a round, thickly wadded cap of black velvet, put upon the child's head when he began to go alone to save it from bumps in falling. An ingenious method of carrying children, when there was more than one unable to walk, was a long double pannier, shaped like a canoe, holding a child at each end, and carried by a handle in the middle. This is depicted in Green's *Short History;* it must have been a great boon to the wayfaring class, which was in the Middle Ages so numerous.

At seven years old little boys left the nursery ; they then wore tunics to the knee, with long hose, sometimes only shoes and bare legs, or, in some cases, leg-bands wound round, such as our soldiers used in South Africa.

A short, full mantle was often worn, fastened on the shoulder with a gold brooch or clasp. At a little later age the tunic is shorter, and breeches are added. The cap, setting close to the head, with a little peak at the top shaped like a cockscomb, was usually of leather, sometimes of velvet, and occasionally for winter has an edging of fur. Shepherd boys or other peasants are depicted with longer tunics and a hood ; the cap seems to belong to the page, or at least to the boy of the upper class. The hair was worn to the poll, and cut straight across the forehead. The little girls were not so fortunate, as they never got out of their long petti-coats ; their dress was that of their mothers in miniature. A little Saxon princess is seen in a long train, lined with ermine, with hanging sleeves, and a little flat cap on her head. The hair usually hung down until marriage, either in two long plaits or combed straight down each side. The hanging sleeves must have been as tiresome for a game of play as the train ; however, as little girls certainly did play, these garments may only have been donned for occasions of ceremony, and some useful smock or overall worn in the nursery. This kind of costume, with slight modifications, seems to have been worn from the earliest days of a civilization sufficient for the production of illuminated manuscripts down to comparatively modern times—say the middle of the seventeenth century.

If we want to form a mental picture of these children of old, I think we may conclude they were not unlike the children of to-day, probably even fairer before the admixture of Norman blood, with the same golden curls and fresh pink cheeks that the child-lover delights in now. For in the well-known story of the sending of the English Mission, Pope Gregory is represented as being struck with the fairness of the little Saxon children in the slave-market, and being told they were Angles from the kingdom of Ælla, answered, "Not Angles, but angels, and they shall be taught to sing Alleluia."

CHAPTER II

NURSERY LORE

WHEN the small mind began to awake, the
small character to unfold, the nurse was the
first person to develop the dawning intelligence. She was the prime repository of the legendary
tales, the ballads, the rhymes which the babe sucked in
in his cradle before he could speak. It was the nurse
quite as much as the minstrel who handed down these
things from no man can say how far back with marvellously little change ; for what we listen to in infancy
takes firmer root in the memory than any later lore,
and children are such conservatives, they are the last
to permit any liberties to be taken with the stories they
are used to. Let the teller of tales in the nursery
attempt to embroider with any flowers of fancy of his
own, and he is sure to be pulled up with, " No, no, that
isn't the way it goes." At his peril let him vary a
phrase. So we get even now the same old tales.

Doubtful as we may be as to the antiquity of the
rattle, the go-cart, or the black pudding, about that of
the old lullabies to which the children listened there
is no doubt at all. Of some of them we may say with
certainty that they were sung to Saxon babies, for this
reason, that they are found by those who have made

14 ENGLISH CHILDREN IN THE OLDEN TIME

study of such things in old Swedish, Danish, or German
form, and as these peoples are of like ancestry with
ourselves, the natural inference is that the Saxons
brought them over. Among these are "Lady-bird,
lady-bird, fly away home!" and the story of the old
wife and her piggy Fick, which runs, "There was once
upon a time an old woman who had a little pig hight
Fick, who would never go home in the evening. So
the old woman said to her stick, 'Stick, beat Fick, I
say. Piggy will not go home to-day!'" A chant that
may have been found efficacious with a recalcitrant
infant who would not be put to bed. Of like antiquity
is the rhyme of "Humpty-Dumpty," which is found
in Danish in a version which is thus translated by
Mr. Halliwell Phillips, from whose book on *Nursery
Rhymes* these notes are taken—

> " Lille Trille lay on a shelf,
> Lille Trille thence pitched himself ;
> Not all the men in our land, I ken,
> Can put Lille Trille together again."

Other versions are quoted from the Swedish.

As ancient as any of these are the old lullabies ; as
old as the hills many of them seem. Patient Grizzel
dandles her babe to the monotonous chant—

> "Hush, hush, hush !
> And I dance mine own child,
> And I dance mine own child ;
> Hush, hush, hush !"

"Hush-a-bye, baby, upon the tree-top" is believed,
according to the same authority, to be of later date
than—

> " Rock-a-bye, baby, thy cradle is green,
> Father's a nobleman, mother's a queen."

But he cannot tell, nor, I suppose, can any one, the origin of the latter, nor to what queen's child it first was sung. The soothing and drowsy rhythm of " Ding, dong, bell; Pussy's in the well," suit it admirably for putting a baby to sleep. Its antiquity is considerable; it can be traced as far back as the reign of Elizabeth, for the first line is quoted both in the *Merchant of Venice* and in the *Tempest*, and that usually implies that the lines were already old and familiar. The age of " Handy Spandy Jack a Dandy" who "loved plumcake and sugar-candy" is at least as well established. Lear's Fool alludes to it, and it is mentioned in one of Florio's collections of words or ancient sayings, which were published towards the end of the sixteenth century. It has been used in nurseries up to this day for giving children shares of some dainty, making them choose without seeing, so that there might be no unfairness— a thing which the child instinctively resents. The two apples or pieces of cake, or whatever it might be, were quickly passed from the right hand to the left behind the back while the rhyme was said, ending up with "Which good hand will you have?"

The dandling songs, or those for riding the child upon the knee or foot, are many. It might be tossed up and down upon the arm to—

> " Here we go up, up, up !
> Here we go down, down, downy !
> Here we go backwards and forwards,
> And here we go round, round, roundy !"

Or tipped backwards by its arms to the tune of " Titty cum Tawty, the duck's in the wawty," or " See-saw, Margery Daw." " Ride a cock-horse to Banbury Cross," " To Market, to Market to buy a plum bun," and " Johnny shall have new bonnet, and Johnny shall go to the fair," were all used as riding ditties, the child being perched astride the leg, which was swung up and down, faster and higher, to suit the words. *To Market* is certainly very ancient ; a version is quoted as a great antiquity in a curious ballad written in 1720. The oldest version runs—

> " To market ride the gentlemen,
>   So do we, so do we !
> Then comes the country clown
>   Hobble-de-gee, hobble-de-gee !

> " First go the ladies, mim, mim, mim ;
>   Next come the gentlemen, trim, trim, trim !
> Last come the country clowns, gallop-a-trot ! "

The more familiar version begins, " This is the way the ladies ride ; tre, tre, tree ! tre, tre, tree ! " " I had a little pony, and called it dapple-grey " may have been used in the same way.

The game of Bo-peep is, as Mr. Halliwell Phillips says, probably as old as the race, hiding and peeping at a baby to teach it to recognize mother or nurse, but how it became connected with sheep and the loss of their tails is shrouded in mystery. There is a reference to it in a very old manuscript in the library of Corpus Christi, Cambridge ; it runs—

> " Halfe England ys nowght now but shepe,
>   In every corner they play boe-pepe."

This, too, comes into *King Lear*. One of the pathetic speeches of the Fool is—

> " Then they for sudden joy did weep,
>   And I for sorrow sung,
> That such a king should play Bo-peep,
>   And go the fools among."

Little Boy Blue and *Baa, baa, Black Sheep* are also traditional.

Then we have the venerable rhymes by which the babies learned to know their fingers from their toes. *This little pig went to market* is the one that has survived in most nurseries, but there is another quite as old, and less familiar—

> " ' Let us go to the wood,' says this pig.
> ' What to do there ? ' says that pig.
> ' To look for my mammy,' says this pig.
> ' What to do with her ? ' says that pig.
> ' To kiss her, to kiss her, to kiss her ! ' says this pig."

The names of the toes were Harry Whistle, Tommy Thistle, Harry Whible, Tommy Thible, and little Oker Bell. The fingers, too, all had their nursery names : Tom Thumbkin, Bess Bumpkin, Bill Winkin, Long Linkin, and Little Dick. But grown-up people as well as children had their names for the fingers. In very old works they are called thumb, toucher, longman, leche-man, little-man ; leche, because the third finger was always used by the apothecary to taste his mixtures. Several face rhymes are given by Phillips ; some were quoted in *Home Life under the Stuarts*. Here is another, which cannot be more than eight hundred years old, as earlier than that mayors were not—

" Here sits the Lord Mayor (*forehead*) ;
Here sits his two men (*eyes*) ;

" Here sits the cock (*right cheek*) ;
And here sits the hen (*left cheek*) ;
Here sit the little chickens (*tip of nose*) ;
And here they run in (*mouth*).

" Chinchopper, chinchopper,
Chinchopper, chin ! "

For putting on the first pair of shoes was " Shoe the
horse and shoe the mare," accompanied with a slap on
the sole of the little foot. For consolation in the
tumbles that were not infrequent when the go-cart was
dispensed with, and the first unsupported footsteps
attempted, there was *Jack and Jill*, equally suitable for
the tumble of a bigger child downstairs.

In the lap of some good woman, dandled up and
down, or lying in the carved wooden cradle with deep
rockers, gently swayed by the motion of her foot, the
babies would make their first acquaintance with the
world of fable. Perhaps it was *The Babes in the Wood*,
an o'er-true tale, for it is believed to have been founded
on a real event, though fancy ended it with the covering
of the little bodies with leaves by Robin Redbreast.
However, the veracity of the story had little to do with
its charm for children. The honour in which Cock-
Robin has always been held goes very far back ; nursery
lore is full of his praise from this tale of his deed of
pity down to *Who killed Cock Robin?* A saying
was current with children, " The robin and the wren
are God Almighty's cock and hen," and the little
friendly bird with his red waistcoat and his bright black

eyes, so tame that he would hop into the nursery for crumbs, has ever been beloved of the children. A sleepy little rhyme about him may have been used as a lullaby—

" Little Robin Redbreast
Sat upon a rail.
Niddle noddle went his head,
Wiggle waggle went his tail."

Another better-known Robin song is—

"The north wind doth blow
And we shall have snow,
And what will the robin do then,
Poor thing?

" He will sleep in the barn
To keep himself warm,
And hide his head under his wing,
Poor thing ! "

Perhaps the favourite may have been the story of the teeny-tiny woman who lived in a teeny-tiny house, and put on her teeny-tiny bonnet to go for a teeny-tiny walk. Very little children like these repetitions, and will follow with breathless attention to the appalling growl at the end of "Give me my bone!" They generally enjoy, too, such oddities as *The Cat and the Mouse*, a cumulative story after the manner of *The House that Jack built*. This last is of an antiquity that reaches far beyond our own country.* The original is found in the Chaldean language, in an ancient Hebrew manuscript, and begins, "A kid, a kid my father bought for two pieces of money." When our own version found its way to England it is impossible to say : perhaps the

* On the authority of Mr. Halliwell Phillips in his *Nursery Rhymes*.

Crusaders may have brought it, as they did so many other things and fashions from the East. There is an old thing of the same class belonging to the reign of Richard II., beginning, "John Ball shot them all." Another, less familiar than *The House that Jack built*, is, "I sell you the key of the King's garden: I sell you the string that ties the key of the King's garden: I sell you the rat that gnawed the string, etc., and the cat that eat the rat that gnawed the string," and so forth through a long succession, a good exercise in memory for the little ones who were beginning to learn by heart. A similar one, whether imitation or traditional I cannot tell, was included in a delightful child's book of fifty or sixty years ago, called *The Charm*. It was about a sausage, a mouse, and a dried pea.

An ancient forbear of *Miss Peck*, a favourite of about the same date, was Chicken-licken, who went to walk in the wood one day when an acorn fell upon her poor bald pate, so she started off to London to tell the king that the skies were falling. She was joined in succession by Hen-len, Duck-luck, Drake-lake, Goose-loose, Gander-lander, and Turkey-lurkey; only, unfortunately, the party was joined by Fox-lox, who kindly offered to show them the way, in consequence of which they never reached the palace, and the king never learned the remarkable fact that the skies were falling. This is the kind of humour that appeals to small children; they think it very funny, and will laugh aloud at it, whereas the jokes and chaff of their elders leave them perfectly solemn. "Little Mary Ester, who sat upon a tester" (probably a tester bed or canopied sofa), with her successor, " Little Miss Muffet, who sat on a tuffet," and who were both alarmed by a spider, also seem to them exquisitely comic. So, too, does the man who "jumped into a quickset hedge and scratched out both his eyes." " Tom, Tom, the Piper's son " is another jest they can enter into. Mirth is invariably provoked when—

> "The pig was eat, and Tom was beat,
> And Tom ran squealing down the street."

At the same time, even more than funny things, children relish tales about grown-up people. I can remember my own delight in an old song an old-time nurse used to sing ·to me about *Richard of Taunton Dene*. In an earlier version he figures as *Richard of Dalton Dale;* but the story is the same. His wooing pleased me far better than the doings of any good little Tommies or Marias. It relates how Richard donned his "roast-beef clothes"—delightful expression for Sunday best—and went courting the parson's daughter, Mistress Jane. His wooing did not speed, however, for when he informed her, "I addle my ninepence every day," she turned on him with—

> "Oh, ninepence a day will never do,
> For I must have silks and satins too !"

The other suitors who stood round laughed him to scorn, and he was obliged to beat an ignominious retreat.

These little folk, who were to be married so early, were soon introduced to songs of courtship. Long before *A Frog he would a-wooing go* there was *Here comes a Lusty Wooer*, and—

> " ' Where have you been all the day,
> My boy Willy?'
> ' I've been all the day
> Courting of a lady gay,
> But, oh, she's too young
> To be taken from her mammy.' "

Then there was the " little man who wooed a little maid," and "Curly locks, curly locks! wilt thou be mine?"   I wonder if Kenelm Digby had any of these on his tongue when, at four years old, he made love to the lovely little Venetia Stanley, who was six.

Little children began to learn their letters very early, and in the nursery acquaintance was first made with the A, B, C, in the form of A—Apple-pie, which being quoted in the seventeenth century as an almost obsolete antiquity, goes back, we may take it, pretty far. Its successor, A was an Archer and shot at a frog, seems to have been coming into fashion in that century, as it is included in several little books published then. The three last letters of this are rather fascinating—

> " X was Xpensive, and so became poor :
> Y was a youth who did not love school :
> Z was a Zany, a silly old fool."

The teacher would be at pains to point out that this last line was the direct consequence of the preceding. If the spelling does not quite meet our modern notions of orthography, it was at least an improvement on the earlier method of evading the difficulty by lumping together X, Y, Z, and Amper's and or &, as the old

MISS CAMPION

version did. The Horn-book, so far as can be traced, did not come into existence until after the invention of printing. A large volume—a very interesting one too —has been written by Andrew Tuer on its history and developments. Suffice it here to say that to avoid the risk of tearing in days when books could not easily be replaced, it was the custom by the middle of the fifteenth century to paste the alphabet, in black-letter and Roman, the numerals, the Ave and Paternoster, upon an oblong piece of wood, covered with a sheet of thin horn, through which the lettering could be plainly seen. This was bound round with brass to make it strong, and had a wooden handle like a battledore, with a hole for a piece of string, to tie it round the child's neck or to his waist, that he might not lose it. The alphabet had a little cross at the beginning and end, and some early horn-books have the rhyme—

" Christës Cross be my speede
In all vertue to proceede."

From this children often called it their criss-cross row. Some, made for the children of the well-to-do, had beautifully embossed and gilded leather backs with a picture, sometimes of the reigning monarch on a prancing steed. Very, very few have come down. When done with, they were no doubt cast aside by the child as of no account. The prices they fetch in these days are enormous.

It was at the nurse's knee that the horn-book was first conned, for children began to learn their letters at

two years old, and one educational expert recommends
that they be taught to read at the same time as to
speak. It was not until late in the sixteenth century
that they had blocks to play with with letters upon
them, for these were the invention of a certain Sir Hugh
Plat, who seems to have been a kind of Mrs. Beeton, for
his *Jewell House of Art and Nature* is quite an *Enquire
Within*, affording instruction on anything from the
making of pot-pourri to devising a perspective glass to
see what cards your adversary held, from curing a
smoky chimney to teaching children their A, B, C. His
idea was that playing with these dice, as he called them,
the little ones would learn their letters " by way of sport
and pastime."

Counting was taught by "One, two, buckle my
shoe," as well as by the instinctive pastime of counting
one's fingers and toes. A very curious device for
teaching children numbers, which was still used in
nurseries in the last century, is said by some to be of
great antiquity ; this was a wooden frame, the size of
a slate, with wires fixed across it, on which were loosely
strung beads in tens of different colours. This impresses
a decimal reckoning vividly on the child's mind.*

Nan Fudd, as we learn from the *Verney Letters*,
had not only to hear little Betty her book, but also to
teach her her work, and this was a very elaborate
business, done on a sampler of fine canvas in delicate
cross-stitch, to be followed up by many more difficult

* Invented by the Greeks, and called "abacus." These are still in use
in Scotland and also in Germany.

stitches as the little fingers grew more expert in wielding the needle. This would be occasionally varied by sewing a long white seam. Often the seam was beguiled by song or story. Singing was one of the earliest things taught; little Jack Verney was not the only one who learned to sing prettily at three years old, for writers of far older date urge singing as a most healthful and cheerful thing for children to practise.

To name half the songs the old-time children loved would swell this chapter to too great length. I think we may be sure that *Tom, he was a Piper's Son* was an old favourite, for part of it comes into *Jockey's Lamentation* in a curious old book called *Pills to Purge Melancholy*. This is not that hero who "ran squealing down the street" after the theft of a pig, but one whose story recalls that of Orpheus, for none who heard him could keep still. "Pigs on their hind legs would after him prance," Dolly upset her milk-pail, for the cow would start frisking when she heard, and Dame Trot, who was impelled to attempt a jig, threw down her basket and broke all her eggs. The long tale is almost forgotten now, but one verse lingers still in the memory—

> "But all the tune that he could play
> Was 'Over the hills and far away;'
> Over the hills and a great way off,
> And the wind will blow your top-knot off."

Of greater antiquity, and of a very different type, was *Old King Cole*. This cheerful old person legend relates to have been a British king or tribal head in the third century, whose daughter Helena married the

Emperor Constantine, according to the chronicle of Robert of Gloucester. There was an old earthwork at Colchester traditionally called King Cole's kitchen. Quite possibly the rhyme may be older than the chronicle.

Songs of Arthur's court were early current, and songs of Robin Hood and the greenwood were always popular. One of the prettiest, as well as earliest, was—

> "Robin Hood, Robin Hood is in the mickle wood !
> Little John, Little John, he to the town is gone.
>
> "Robin Hood, Robin Hood is telling his beads
> All in the greenwood among the green weeds.
>
> "Little John, Little John, if he comes no more,
> Robin Hood, Robin Hood, he will fret full sore."

Possibly "'I'll go to the wood,' says Richard to Robin," may belong to these, but in an old book of nursery songs, published by Darton and Clarke early in the last century, is reckoned with those belonging to Robin Goodfellow. The same collection puts Puck's song from *A Midsummer-Night's Dream* as though it were traditional, calling it Robin Goodfellow's, and also the " Ho, ho, ho !" song. This may well be, as Shakespeare took his material wherever he found it, though I find no mention of the source in Gollancz's edition.

Another favourite ditty was "Three children, sliding on the ice, all on a summer's day." This Mrs. Earle, in her book on *Child-Life in Colonial Days*, ascribes confidently to Goldsmith ; but, on the authority of Halliwell Phillips, it appears in a collection, printed in 1652, called *Choyce Poems*, and was probably not new then. We may, therefore, take leave to doubt her assertion that he was the real author of *Goody Two-shoes*. Charles Lamb evidently did not think so; but he was the re-teller of many an old tale, which, being unfathered, he did not think it necessary to disclaim, unless as, in a joking way, when he said the manuscript of *Goody* was in the Vatican with drawings by Michael Angelo! He wrote numbers of these tales for Newberry, to whose little books we shall come later on.

Two very old songs are *The Six Horses* and *Sing a Song of Sixpence*. The former is supposed to belong to the time of the Jack Straw rebellion in the reign of Richard II., but I would suggest with all humility that it may be of still greater antiquity, and being caught up as a chorus by the rebels, they may have named their leader from it, rather than the song from him. The refrain lends itself well to a marching song—

" With a whim, wham, whommy lo ! Jack Straw blazey, boys !
Whimmy lo ! whommy lo !   Wob, wob, wob ! "

The *Song of Sixpence* finds mention in a play by Beaumont and Fletcher, and is also alluded to in *Twelfth Night*. The line, "When the pie was opened the birds began to sing," alludes to a real practical joke for in *Epularius ; or, the Italian Banquet*, is a device how to introduce live birds into a pie for a jest. They must have been less astonishing to the guests than the dwarf, Sir Geoffrey Hudson, who was similarly "baked in a pie." Other very old songs are *The Misty Moisty*

Morning, The Carrion Crow, and *Kitty Alone.* The
song about the fox, which begins—

> " The fox jumped up on a moonlight night,
> The stars they were shining, and all things bright,"

is found in a fifteenth-century manuscript, and *The
White Dove sat on the Castle Wall* is out of a black-
letter play of the same century.

Riddles, too, were held in high honour in the
nursery, and were considered a valuable sharpener of
young wits. The Jester, or Fool, who was a regular
functionary of all great houses in the olden time, had
always a store of them at his tongue's end, and a very
popular collection was printed in 1511 by Wynkyn de
Worde in black-letter, under the title of *Demaundes
Joyeuses.* Some of the children's favourites were very
simple, such as " There was a little green house, and
inside it a little brown house, and inside that a little
yellow house, and inside that a little white house," the
answer being " A walnut." Another of the same sort
was " A house full, a yard full, and ye cannot catch a
bowl full "—" Smoke." For the going out of a candle—

> " Lilly lo, lilly lo, set up on end,
> See little baby go out at town end."

Together with such lore the nurse would have a
store of charms. " Robert Rowley rolled a round roll
round " was considered a specific for hiccups; and for
stammering children and such as spoke in too great a
hurry, " Peter Piper picked a peck of pickled pepper,"
or " When a twister a-twisting will twist him a twist,"

must have been a sovereign remedy. While for little lispers, "Swan swam over the sea, swim, swan, swim," might be tried, though whether it would succeed or only increase the mischief may be questioned.

When the children were put to bed, they doubtless said their Paternoster and Hail Mary! at the nurse's knee, and not improbably added the traditional charm which lingers yet—

> " Four corners to my bed,
> Four angels round my head,
> One to watch and two to pray,
> And one to bear my soul away."

"Matthew, Mark, Luke, and John" probably crept in later as a corruption, the four evangelists conveniently matching the four bed-posts.

As the little ones dropped asleep, we may picture them peeping, half frightened from their cribs, to see if the fairy-wife had brought her baby to wash in the bowl of clean water nurse had carefully set, and dry it on the clean towel left hanging over the airing horse by the fire ; for if these preparations were not made, there was no telling, nurse averred, what mischief the fairies might not do in the nursery before morning. But the little eyes were always closed before the fairy-wife came, for she was as hard to catch sight of as Santa Claus himself.

CHAPTER III

THE CHURCH AND THE CHILDREN

DIM tradition points to the Druids as the pioneers of education in these islands, but whether, as Traill asserts, in his *Social England,* only those children who were intended for the priesthood were placed in their hands, or, as some other writers have thought, all British children were taught by them to sing, dance, and recite hymns by heart, remains obscure. More certain is it that the Roman Provincials would introduce schools, as they did all other customs of civilization ; but these, of course, were swept away by the Saxon invasion, together with the settlements of the early British Church. Until Christianity came in again there is no record that any but the parents concerned themselves for the young children. The religion of Christ, with its devotion to the Mother and the Divine Child, put childhood on a higher level of importance, and the new preachers, mindful of the command " Feed My lambs," quickly opened schools for the little ones. The Mission of Augustine established itself in Canterbury in 595, and soon a school arose there. In 668, under Archbishop Theodore, one appears in full activity, in which the good Archbishop himself, with the Abbot Adrian, did not disdain to teach.

Here, for about four centuries, the little Saxons were studying the seven liberal arts : the Trivium, consisting of grammar (which included reading and writing), logic, and rhetoric ; the Quadrivium, comprising music, arithmetic, geometry, and astronomy. For little children the primary instruction was in music and getting by rote simple religious lessons and portions of the Church service. In those early days reading almost of necessity involved learning by heart, for books were so scarce and precious, they would hardly be trusted in the hands of young children ; the master wrote words and sentences on a board in sight of the class, and the pupils had either to commit them to memory, or if they had mastered the art of writing, to write them on their tabulæ or slates. These tabulæ were probably of wax, like those used by the Romans. Mrs. Field, in *The Child and his Book*, says "or slates ; " but another authority, Mrs. Earle, in *Child-Life in Colonial Days*, asserts that the use of slates for writing was not known until 1737.

Quite little children learned to recite the Psalms in Latin, and to chant the Gloria in Excelsis, the Nicene Creed and the Paternoster, both in Latin and, it is believed, in Greek. Mr. de Montmorency, who has written much on this subject, says, in a valuable Note from which he kindly allows me to quote: "An examination of the early Saxon Psalters and Antiphonals, shows us that Greek was in use. Indeed, we also find the Gloria, the Litany of the Saints, the Apostles' Creed, and the Sanctus, in their Greek dress in some early Saxon Service-books. The children in the monasteries must have sung from these, and so we have an early and learned beginning of child-life in England."

It is often supposed that because the accomplishments of reading and writing were scarce amongst grown folk, except in monasteries, that the laity received little or no education, but this was not so ; the notion arose from our having come to associate the idea of education exclusively with books since the invention of printing. All classes, however, attended school, the first reading lessons being the Paternoster, Ave, and Credo, all which they got by heart, and besides, committed to memory a considerable amount of Latin, as well as of their mother-tongue. But it may be well understood that unless, showing a distinct vocation or a leaning towards letters, they embraced the monastic life, they would very soon, in the dearth of books, in a life spent in camp, in the workshop, or at the plough, forget how to read ; for, of course, precious manuscripts were hardly to be found except in the cloister or in rich men's houses. What they had by heart, however, would rarely be lost.

In later days a petition was addressed to King Richard II., demanding that villeins be restrained from sending their children to school, because the ambition to rise in life by becoming a " clerk " was taking so many workers from the land ; but the request was refused, and, further, in 1406, a new enactment was made that every villein should have the right to send either son or daughter to school if he pleased, showing that girls shared, the advantages of education equally with boys. Parents, however, did not always please. Then, as now, eagerness for the earnings of the child would obscure the desirability of scholarship for him, and he was too often put to the plough before he had mastered more than the rudiments of learning.

The village children had to be day scholars perforce, because without a licence the child of neif or villein might not leave the land, as it would have been an infringement of the rights of the Lord of the Manor : permission was granted in certain cases. On the other hand, Mr. de Montmorency's researches seem to show that in many Manors, before the statute of 1406, the Lord of the Manor had it in his power to deprive the children of his serfs of education altogether ; this, however, cannot have been universal, or there would have been no occasion for the petition to King Richard, which indirectly led to that statute.

The Church from the first championed the children in this matter. As early as 747 the English Provincial Synod at Cloves-Hoo enacted in its Seventh Canon that " Bishops, Abbots, and Abbesses do by all means take care and diligently provide that their families (*i.e.* households) do incessantly apply their minds to reading, and that it may be made known by the voices of many to the gaining of souls and to the praise of the Eternal King. For it is sad to say how few nowadays do heartily love and labour for sacred knowledge, and are willing to take any pains in learning ; but they are from their youth up rather employed in diverse vanities and the affectation of vain glory; and they rather pursue the amusements of this present unstable life than the arduous study of Holy Scripture. Therefore let the boys be confined and trained up in schools, to the law of sacred knowledge, that being by this means well learned, they may become in all respects useful to the Church of God. And let not the rectors be so greedy of the worldly labours of the boys as to render the House of God vile for want of spiritual advancement."

This is quoted from the same Note referred to above, and the writer goes on to point out that it indicates that boys were early put to work at trades or in the fields. In a later Canon, dated 926, the priest is directed "diligently to instruct the youth and dispose them to trades." There is rather a severe tone about the children inclining to pursue the amusements of this present unstable life, and evidently the parents were not the only ones who set them early to work.

These enactments seem to refer chiefly to boarding schools, but the monasteries took day pupils as well, the children of the villeins attending day by day; but these, in cases where they were attached to the monastic lands, would all be regarded as forming part of the "family" or household of the monastery.

We gain a curiously vivid glimpse of child life at one of these schools in *The Prioress's Tale* from Chaucer's *Canterbury Pilgrims*. This, of course, was written some centuries later; but I think we may take it that these monastic or song schools went on with but little modification from the time they were instituted till the invention of printing brought about quite other conditions. Moreover, though the Prioress places the scene of her tale in a foreign land, exactly the same story is told of the martyrdom of the eight-year-old St. Hugh of Lincoln in the year 1255. We see the little chorister trotting home beside a bigger companion, and begging to be taught the Latin chant he loved so well but was thought too little to learn, the *Alma Redemptoris*, which he had picked up and tried to sing by rote without understanding it. The elder lad explains it as well as he is able, saying, "I lerne song, I can but smal grammar." The little one masters it quickly in his zeal, and sings it twice a day as he goes to and fro the school. The way leads by the Jewry, and as he passes the wicked Jews, hearing the pious chant, seize the child and cut the little tender throat; and after he is dead, a miraculous voice continues the song.

During the time—a golden time for scholarship in England—when Bede was teaching school at Jarrow, and Aldhelm at Malmesbury, and at Canterbury the school of Theodore was flourishing, many books were written for the instruction of youth. One of the earliest that has come down to us is that composed by Aldhelm for his pupils. It was in the form of a dialogue in Latin between *Discipulos* and *Magister;* something in the style of the catechisms on common things familiar to our own youth, only that the child asks, the teacher answers, the questions. It includes riddles and puzzles in Latin hexameters; riddles being held in esteem in early days, less as a mere pastime than as a valuable sharpener of the intellect. An old riddle-book is described on its title-page as "no less useful than behoveful for any yonge man or child, to know if he be quick-witted or no."

The Exeter Book, another very ancient lesson-book, contains a father's instructions on behaviour addressed to his son. Bede also wrote handbooks for his boys besides his great work on *Ecclesiastical History*: one was on natural science, *De Natura Rerum*, another was a text-book from Donatus, whose grammar was the earliest studied. This latter used to be spoken of familiarly by the boy as "his Donet" in the same way as the child would call his horn-book "his Absey-book." The Donet, however, could hardly have been within the reach of the poorer scholars, for so late as 1447 a Donet cost a shilling, at that date a considerable sum of money. Alcuin, a little later, wrote questions and problems in arithmetic, of which a manuscript copy is in the British Museum. The problems are of much the same order as those in modern sum-books. For instance: "A swallow invited a snail to dinner: he lived just one league from the spot, and the snail travelled at the rate of an inch a day. How long would it be before he dined?" Alcuin also enumerates in a poem, among the subjects to be studied at school besides grammar, rhetoric, and poetry, "the harmony of the sky, the labour of the sun and moon, the five zones, the seven wandering planets; the laws, rising and setting of the stars, and the aerial motions of the sea ; the nature of man, cattle, birds, and wild beasts, with their various kinds and forms ; and the sacred Scriptures." In another place he wrote, " Despise not human sciences, but make of them a foundation ; so teach children grammar and the doctrines of philosophy that, ascending the steps of wisdom, they may reach the summit, which is evangelical perfection, and, while advancing in years, they may also increase the treasures of wisdom."

Besides Bede's book on natural science there were Bestiaries, in which descriptions of all the known animals were quaintly mingled with fable, as of the dragon, the griffin, and the phœnix. In the twelfth century, Anselm wrote an *Elucidarium*, or book of general information, for young children, in the form of question and answer, not unlike Brewer's *Child's Guide to Knowledge.* In those days it appears a good deal more was made of general knowledge of common things and less of the classics than obtained later ; in fact, the monks looked somewhat askance on the old mythological stories as of doubtful value for the edification of young children. But all things, whether logic, or the properties of nature, or the philosophies of the ancients, were brought into the service of religion.

It is interesting, while on the subject of school-books, to know that there exists in the British Museum a map made in the tenth century of much greater accuracy and containing fewer fabulous countries than many of later date. A Greek and Latin dictionary too, we learn from Mr. de Montmorency's *Progress of Education in England,* existed as early as the seventh century. The Saxon School in Rome supplied professors to teach the learned languages in England.

In the tenth century all this was disturbed, and in many parts utterly swept away, by the incursions of the barbarous and unlettered Danes. When Alfred re-established order in his kingdom he found ignorance prevailing throughout the land. He complains in despair, "There are no good readers in the whole kingdom!" He himself had not been taught to read until he was twelve years old, though he had not been wholly without education, for he had always listened eagerly to the songs of the minstrels, committing many to memory, and had actually learned a whole book of poems by heart in his fifth or sixth year. He had, moreover, been taken to Rome at five years old, and such a journey must have been an education in itself to an intelligent child. When he was twelve the story goes that his mother showed him a book of poems, probably illustrated, as the Saxon manuscripts often were, with fair colours that would take a youthful eye, and he coveting it, she promised it should be his when he could read it. He set manfully to work, and soon made progress with his studies, "sed proh dolor!" as he lamented, for lack of teachers; but after a while Asser, subsequently his biographer, became his tutor. By Asser's advice he kept always in his bosom a hand-book—a commonplace book, as we should call it—in which he entered everything that specially struck him in his reading.

So soon as he was firmly in his seat, and had gathered up the reins of government, he began with zeal to repair the ravages in education for all classes. At once he set up in his palace a school for the children of the nobility on the model of that which Alcuin had formed ifor Charlemagne; the germ doubtless of that education in the Court which plays so large a part in the later development of child life. For he was too wise a man not to perceive that the true aim of education is to prepare the child for his future life, so that to apply one procrustean system to all is to fit no one for anything in particular. Education, however, he wished to extend to all; elementary schools, where in consequence of the Danish invasions they had been closed, were re-opened, and a complete system of parish schools set up throughout the country. The rules promulgated by Theodulph, Bishop of Orleans, were observed in England, as well as in France. "Mass priests ought always to have at their houses a school of disciples, and if any good man desires to commit his little ones to them for instruction, they ought gladly to receive them, and kindly teach them." A Saxon Canon was enacted to the same effect. Very precise regulations were also made concerning books, that they should be free from fault, and that the boys should be restrained from tearing or injuring them.

The song school was of a higher elementary type intended more especially for choristers, where they studied the three chief branches of their education, grammar, music, and "scrivenor's craft." The children began to attend these schools at about seven years old, sometimes even earlier, for Orderic the Chronicler was put to Shrewsbury school when he was but five, and learned reading, grammar, and chanting under Siward.

There were also great episcopal schools attached to all Cathedrals and Collegiate Foundations. The important school at St. Paul's probably existed, according to Mr. de Montmorency's Note, as early as 826. The centre of education had, he says, shifted from York to London by the end of the ninth century; but Winchester, the capital of Alfred's kingdom, where St. Swithun and Bishop Ethelwold had established an important monastery school, must, I think, contest the pre-eminence—a dignity also claimed by Canterbury with its ancient foundation. It was for the use of this Winchester school that Ælfric, before the end of the tenth century, compiled a Colloquy in Latin and Anglo-Saxon. A transcript of this, made by a pupil, still exists. It is in the customary form of dialogue between master and boys. Amongst other things the subject of flogging is touched on, and the boy is made to say he would rather be flogged and taught than suffered to grow up in ignorance, which reminds the reader of the praiseworthy sentiments put into the mouths of good boys in *The Parents' Assistant.* Some of the conversations are on country things, and afford glimpses of the condition of the districts round Winchester in those far-off days. A shepherd discourses of wolves, some herdsmen of the dangers of cattle-lifters; appropriate, no doubt, when the Andredsweald and the forest of

Bere came far up the slopes of the eastern and southern downs. These dialogues on common things were very popular, and no doubt very useful. One was made in the twelfth century in Norman French by de Neckham, called *de Utensilibus*. It was not unlike the *Book of Trades* in scope and design, discoursing of building, gardening, and various kindred topics. Something of the same kind was a dictionary written in the next century by Johannes de Garlandia, containing the Latin names of things in everyday use, and scraps of curious information. It is very interesting to find mention of the Antipodes—"dwellers in the other world or hemisphere, if it be true that there be any," thus confirming the tradition of the discovery of the New World by Norsemen in the tenth century; for this book, be it remembered, was written three hundred years before the time of Columbus. Alfred in his *Orosius* included an account of the early Arctic explorer, the Finnish captain Othere, who brought a walrus tooth to the king in confirmation of his tale.

By the way, we learn from Ælfric's book of colloquies what young children in those days (1006) usually ate. In one conversation the child is asked what he eats, and replies that he does not eat meat, but eggs, fish, cheese, butter, cabbages, and beans; his drink is customarily water, but he likes ale if he can get it. This would apply to children of seven or eight and under. The diet seems to have bred up a hardy race.

What they wore may be gathered from the delightful illustrations in Strutt's *History of Costume*, all taken from ancient manuscripts. In one we see a little boy snugly clad for winter in a dark coat with long sleeves and a hood; in another a small child is muffled in a mantle brought round and clasped on the shoulder. One child wears a kind of pinafore, with the armholes deeply hollowed, and tucks his hands into the loose fronts ; and one has a long garment with capes like an "Inverness," and a little round furred cap. In warm weather, breeches with a shoulder-strap over a vest seems to have been considered sufficient. Shoes appear to have been a cheap item, for in the thirteenth century some supplied to fit out a boy for Oxford cost but two-pence halfpenny a pair! A century later they have risen to fourpence. These items figure in Rogers' *History of Prices*.

The ancient practice of children taking part in the Miracle Plays, and the still more curious ceremonies of the Boy-Bishop, were probably observed in these Saxon schools, as in the thirteenth century they are spoken of as customs of venerable antiquity. Regulations for their due observance were drawn up by Roger de Mortival, Bishop of Salisbury, in the early part of the fourteenth century, but these were evidently to regulate a pre-existing custom, not to inaugurate a new one. The children's season lasted from St. Nicholas Day to Childermass, the Holy Innocents. On December 5, the eve of St. Nicholas, the most deserving scholar or chorister was appointed Bishop. The child-bishop had to preach the sermon before High Mass, and wore full episcopal vestments, his comrades being

DRESS OF CHILDREN IN THE THIRTEENTH CENTURY

arrayed in copes. The usual order of procession was reversed, the choristers and their Bishop coming last and sitting in the high stalls, preceded by the Canons residentiary, the Minor Canons acting as taper-bearers. Besides preaching, the child chanted such portions of the Liturgy as could be sung by Cantors; but did not, of course, read the Canon of the Mass; that was taken for him by a priest. After Mass he with his child companions perambulated the town collecting money, and every one gave him a penny. The customs lasted up to the Reformation, as they are referred to by Dean Colet in his regulations for his new school. The ceremony was abolished soon after by Henry VIII., was re-introduced by Queen Mary, but again done away by her successor. It was doubtless instituted to keep in memory the lesson of our Lord, when "He took a little child, and set him in the midst."

There is a record of a Miracle Play performed at Dunstable school in the days of the Conquest, for which the children were dressed in copes borrowed for the occasion from the Abbey of St. Albans. Undoubtedly these children must have learned music of a lighter kind than church music, and also dancing, for in their Christmas games and mysteries performances rather of the ballet order were introduced. Strutt gives two pictures from old manuscripts, one in his *History of Costume*, the other in his *Sports and Pastimes*, bearing out this. Some minstrel children are represented, one clad in a scarlet tunic deeply slashed, another in white, holding a bassoon, with a little scarlet pocket at his side, and a crown of leaves on his curly hair. The other illustration shows a child haranguing a group of small boys in comic heads, asses, pigs, apes, goats, stags, etc.

As to discipline," authorities differ. Mrs. Field gathers that the rod was not so active in the hands of the monks as it became when education was secularized, for in early pictures of monastic schools the teacher is never represented with the insignia of the birch, or four apple-twigs, which the later pedagogue invariably wields. Mr. de Montmorency takes the opposite view, and quotes from a rather obscure passage in an eleventh-century manuscript dealing with the severity of schoolmasters. "It is," he says, "a story told by Henry Bradshaw in his *Life and History of St. Wedburga* (Chetham Society, vol. xv.), first printed in 1521, of a schoolmaster punished with lameness for his cruelty to his children, but miraculously cured by their prayers at the tomb of St. Ermenyede. This poem of Bradshaw's is an English translation of a lost Latin original—a *Passionary* in the library of Chester Monastery of about the eleventh century." The children are described as "dredynge theyr mayster for fear of correccyon." To my own mind the very importance given to this incident, and that the cruelty was visited with miraculous punishment, conveys the idea of its being exceptional, for it is always the exceptional which finds mention and comes down to us. The rod was, of course, from the days of Solomon regarded as a necessary means of education; it finds mention in the *Colloquies* of Ælfric, and in many educational treatises, but its use was rather for moral discipline than instruction, and mention of its abuse to the point of cruelty is rare before the sixteenth century.   In the hands of a harsh-natured man it was always liable to misuse, but if such had been the normal condition, it would hardly have been so punished.   Pleasant mention, too, survives here and there of little rewards for diligence and well-said lessons in the shape of raisins, figs, nuts, almonds, pears, or money.   And there is a charming old proverb of Hendynge's, which runs, " Seely childe is soon y'lered."

The delightful story of Ingulphus, in which he relates his own childhood in the reign of Edward the Confessor, is unhappily declared by the learned to be a forgery, or rather, one should say, a fiction, of the fourteenth century.   It is, however, hardly less valuable for the light it throws on child life and nurture, as the writer would scarcely put into the mouth of his hero anything antecedently improbable, and in his mention of Queen Edith most likely drew on tradition.   " I was born," Ingulphus is supposed to say, " in the beautiful city of London, and educated in my tender years at Westminster."   He goes on to relate the kindness of the queen.   " Frequently have I seen her, when in my boyhood I used to go and visit my father, who was employed about the Court; and often, when I met her, as I was coming from school, did she question me about my studies and my verses; and most readily passing from the solidity of grammar to the brighter

studies of logic, in which she was particularly skilful,
she would catch me with the subtle threads of her
argument. She would always present me with three
or four pieces of money, which were counted out to
me by her handmaiden, and then send me to the royal
buttery to refresh myself." This personal experience
of the benefit of encouragement above chastisement
was not lost upon Ingulphus, for when he became
Abbot of Croyland he took the greatest interest in the
school, which he visited daily, noting the progress of
the scholars, and rewarding the diligent with such little
presents as children love, resorting to the rod only when
exhortation failed.

This charming queen was the daughter of Earl
Godwin. Learned and gentle, as well as beautiful, it
was said of her, " Sicut spina rosam, genuit Godwinus
Egitham " ("As the thorn bears the rose, so Godwin
Edith"). Her knowledge of Latin and logic was no
rarity for a woman in those days, though her proficiency
may have been unusual. The girls went to school as
well as the boys, as a matter of course, to be taught
reading and writing, Latin and music, while for them
was added instruction in needlework, in which the nuns
excelled. In the Canon of Cloves-Hoo already quoted,
the abbesses as well as the abbots are exhorted to apply
themselves to educational work. Frequently the nuns
taught day-schools of " mixed infants."

The Conquest brought inevitable changes, though
the Normans did not, like the Danes, sweep away the
schools; on the contrary, Norman William was almost

as zealous in the cause of education as his great predecessor Alfred, he himself having been able to construe
Cæsar's Commentaries at nine years old ; but the principal change was one which for a century and more bore
very hardly on the children.   Like most conquerors, he
was bent on imposing his own language on his new
subjects, and ordained that instruction in all schools
was to be given in French.   This, of course, greatly
discouraged school attendance amongst the poorer sort,
for the language of the people remained Saxon for
many generations, so that the unlucky child had not
only to master his Latin lesson, but first to master the
strange tongue in which it was given.   So late as 1327,
Higden, in his *Polychronicon*, complains that children
had to construe their lessons in French, so that while
the child of the Norman noble who had spoken French
from his cradle, found things easy, the little peasant
was at a great disadvantage.

Then came the terrible year of the Black Death.
Many little children were carried off; many, many
more were left in desolate homes " to the mothering of
the east wind," as the graphic old phrase runs.   But
one indirect benefit came about—the monks of the old
order who had remained foreign had been swept away
in great numbers, and the new men who filled their
chairs had learned to speak the new tongue that was
growing up, welded together of that of the conquerors
and the conquered.

By way of warning—not example—I must close
this chapter with the school experience of a small boy

in a monastery school in the fourteenth century. So little does child nature change that I almost think it might find a parallel to-day. Not without a twinkle of unholy glee does Master John Lydgate recall those bygone pranks of his. He played truant, he says, he came late to school, he talked to the other boys at lesson time, he told lies, he mocked the masters, he climbed into other people's orchards and stole apples, he counted cherry-stones in church! Yet this ne'er-do-weel, as they doubtless thought him, has come down to posterity as a writer of some repute, while the names of the blameless boys who did none of these things have, alas! been writ in water.

CHAPTER IV

TALES OF WONDER

I N early days, when all reproduction of books was
done by the labour of the penman, and the scrip-
toria of monasteries were the sole publishing
houses, it may well be understood that no books were
written for the amusement of children. Books of
instruction there were in plenty, grammars and dic-
tionaries, *Vulgaria*, *Bestiaries*, and such, from quite
early Saxon times, as we have seen in the last chapter;
but to write stories of the doings of little boys and girls
for the entertainment of little boys and girls hardly
occurred to any one before the middle of the seventeenth century. Comparing the tales on which the
imaginations of our infant forefathers in early days were
fed with the improving stories set before them by those
worthy divines, Thomas White and James Janeway, at
a later period we shall hardly think the bookless
children to be pitied.

For their sense of wonder and mystery was not
starved—far from it. Were there not glee-men travelling up and down the land, firing their souls with the
deeds of their ancestors, or rejoicing their hearts with
the well-beloved tales we all in turn have listened to of
Jack the Giant-killer or him of the Bean-stalk; of *Robin*

Goodfellow or that marvellous hero, *Tom Thumb;* stories which were never penned for children, but grew up, no one can tell exactly how or when, to amuse the childhood of the race. I believe it is a mistake to fancy that children prefer stories written for themselves or about themselves. Give an average child, one whose mental digestion has not been impaired, free choice between *Robinson Crusoe* and the little gilded blue and red books written for school prizes, and I think the desert island will carry the day. I know a child who, at seven, distinctly preferred *Romeo and Juliet*, or even *King Lear*, to *Rosamund and the Purple Jar*, for it is the nature of the child to reach onward.

Let us try to picture the scene in some baronial hall, either before or after the Conquest; for our purpose it makes little difference. The master of the house and his retainers have come in from a day's hunting, possibly from some border foray, and have supped heavily and well. He and his lady with their guests sit at the high table on the daïs. In the broad space below, the trestle tables at which the men-at-arms and serving-men have eaten are being cleared away to make room for the glee-men, while the dogs are gnawing the bones that have been thrown down amongst the rushes with which the floor is strewn. The minstrels come in; one, perhaps, has a harp, with which he accompanies his tale or ballad. It must not be supposed that this is sung to a definite melody with an accompaniment, like a ballad of to-day; it is rather a monotoned chant, very loud and rhythmic, with probably some running of the hand over the strings, either between the verses, like the "selah" of the Hebrew Psalms, or as an undertone to them in the manner of some modern reciters.

Against the Baron's knee leans his eldest boy, the hope of his house. To excite in this boy the love of heroic deeds, and to practise him in manly exercises are the chief ends of education in the father's eyes. Perhaps another child sits on the mother's lap, or a little damsel or two play with a small dog at their feet. Not so very unlike what some of us can remember in the days when dinners used to be over before the children's bedtime, and instead of the little people appearing at tea, they were brought down to dessert, making their curtsey at the door, and sitting on the paternal knee were regaled not only with almonds and raisins, but also with tales of the return of Ulysses and the death of the faithful dog Argus, or of the cave of Polyphemus with that terrible eye in the middle of his forehead, of which one used to dream afterwards.

How round the children's eyes would grow as they listened to the gestes of King Arthur and his noble knights, or the doughty deeds of Guy of Warwick ; or perchance, if it were a noble house to which they belonged, their ambition would be fired by the recital of the achievements of their own ancestors. Surely a wholesomer training, and one that bore better fruit than the incessant contemplation of the infinitely small affairs of the nursery, of the storms in teacups, the morbid misunderstandings in nutshells, which occupy the small minds of to-day. Still more to be preferred to the careers of those terribly priggish infants in Janeway's *Token for Children*, but of these more anon. Their time is not yet.

Sometimes the amusement would be varied by the performance of juggling tricks, as is done to this day in a variety entertainment, with which, no doubt, the young folk were as much delighted as their elders. In Strutt's *Sports and Pastimes* there is a fascinating picture, taken from some very old manuscripts, of one of these jongleurs throwing up and catching three balls and three knives, while his fellow plays on the crowd or crouth, a kind of primitive fiddle. We can fancy how the little boy would clap his hands, and try to emulate the trick afterwards for the edification of his sisters. Let us hope that the nurse—a treasure which all houses of any pretension possessed in the earliest days—insisted on its being done with balls alone, and kept the knives in safe custody.

Great men usually kept some of these professional entertainers in their regular employ, either a harper or a company of glee-men, invariably a jester. And there were always numbers of them roaming the countryside getting a hearing—now in some homely grange, now in the wayside inn, or at one of the great fairs ; and always, we may be sure, the children crowded round them. It is delightful to think how many of the tales which rejoiced our own hearts in nursery days have come down to us from those far-off times, and were the joy of little people like ourselves, perhaps even in the

days of King Alfred ; it is like reaching a hand across
the centuries. For no man can say for certain when
these stories began ; they seem already old when we
first catch sight of them. *The Red Bull of Norroway*,
clearly the earliest form of our well-beloved *Beauty and
the Beast*, most probably came over with the Saxon
invaders, and is as old, if not older, than the early
Christian legends planted with the British Church.

There is a vividness about this tale that gives it
a singular charm. The heroine is, of course, the
youngest and fairest of three sisters, and when the two
proud elders boast of the mighty kings they would
marry, she laughingly says she cares not if she wed
the Red Bull of Norroway. How the little hearts of
the small listeners, especially of the little maidens, must
have thrilled when, with weird, boding chords upon his
harp, the minstrel related the coming next night of the
monster to the castle gate with awful bellowings to
demand the fulfilment of her rash words ! In vain the
King and Queen offered the noblest and fairest maidens
of their Court, only to be tossed contemptuously away
by the terrible bull, till at last there was no help for it,
the favourite child must be given up to allay his fury.
And then he gallops away with her, like Jupiter with
Europa, and she is looked upon as lost. Relief does
not come so quickly as in the case of *Beauty and the
Beast*. The Princess finds a pin sticking in the Bull's
rough hide, but when she pulls it out, the Duke of
Norroway, who appears, straightway vanishes, instead
of taking her to his heart. Far from wishing to return

to her home, she seeks her bridegroom high and low, and at length finds—according to the Scottish version of the tale—a witch-wife, who gives her three hazel-nuts, which she is not to break until her own heart is breaking. She seeks him still, and when she sees him at last riding with the fair lady who is to be his bride, her heart is indeed like to break, and she cracks the nut. Out from the kernel comes a tiny wonder—a wee wifie carding wool. She carries it to the palace and shows it to the bride-elect, who, like the Princess in Hans Andersen's story of the Swineherd, is so en-amoured of it that she bargains to put off her wedding for a day and let the stranger see the Duke in exchange for the possession of the toy. But the Duke is sleeping, and though his true wife sits by him singing the live-long night, he never wakes. With a heavy heart she breaks the second nut, and with the wee wifie spinning who emerges, she induces the lady to let her have a second chance ; but alack ! the result is the same. Now, indeed, her heart is breaking, and she sacrifices the third nut, which contains a wee wifie weaving, with which the lady is so fascinated that she amuses herself with it till morning, when the Duke awakes, recognizes the fair maid; whom he had carried off, and, released from his second enchantment, marries her. The latter portion of this tale seems as though it might be a later development, and, indeed, it is the quality of these folk-tales to grow and grow with successive generations, though the kernel may remain unchanged. In the Scottish version, quoted by Mr. Halliwell Phillips in

his *Popular Rhymes and Nursery Tales*, the Beast is
called the Black, not the Red Bull. He says the form
in which he gives it was from a story current in Scotland in 1548, and then regarded as quite old. The
internal evidence points, I think, to its having come
over with our Norse ancestors.

Several of our oldest tales point by similar witness
to early Saxon times, when England was split up into
many independent kingdoms. Such are *The Princess
of Canterbury*, Kent having been for long one of the
foremost kingdoms of the Heptarchy, and the earliest
to be Christianized. In *The Three Heads in the Well*
we find mention of three Kings of Colchester; and
in *The Three Questions* the fool of the family comes
from Cumberland, or, as it used to be called, Strath-
clyde, and successfully answering the posing questions
put by the daughter of the King of the East Angles,
wins her to wife. *Guy of Warwick* and *Sir Bevis of
Southampton* both belong to later Saxon times. Our
old favourite *Jack the Giant-Killer* goes further back
still, belonging to the cycle of the Arthurian legends,
as do also *Childe Roland* and *Tom Thumb*, though Sir
Walter Scott suggests that these also came over with
the Saxons. They were, however, deep-rooted in
Cornwall, which formed West Wales in Saxon times,
and very slowly submitted to Saxon influence. These
stories were probably current among the minstrels, and
listened to by generations of eager children and childlike men and women in simple times, long before either
Geoffrey of Monmouth or Walter de Mapes had written

them down in courtly language. No man can tell, indeed, how old is the rhyme about King Arthur's Queen and the bag-pudding. It is difficult, through the traditions which have grown up since, to see Queen Guinevere occupied in such homely tasks, but doubtless to the listening children, the "great lumps of fat, as big as my two thumbs," must have appeared intensely humorous.

To the stormy and troubled times immediately following the Conquest the story of *Thomas Hickathrift* probably belongs, for legend connects him with some obscure rising in the Fens against Norman rule, similar to that of Hereward the Wake, with which Charles Kingsley has made us familiar. Like Hereward, young Hickathrift, or Hiccafric, was gifted with colossal strength, and though his feats must have been conspicuously above those of his fellows to give him such undying fame, doubtless they lost nothing in the telling as they were handed down by word of mouth, and his figure loomed ever bigger and bigger through the mists of time.

Besides these ancestral tales, some glimmerings of old Greek mythology had filtered down, more or less Christianized in their course. The tale of Orpheus and Eurydice is found very early in a manuscript version, according to Carew Hazlitt, and though Christianity modified, it did not banish the fairy lore of either our Celtic or Norse ancestors. *The Story of True Thomas* exists in five early manuscripts, the first of which is, by some authorities, supposed to have been written in the

reign of Edward II. This Hazlitt considers to be
disproved by the mention of "Black Agnes," the
Countess of Dunbar, who foretold the great battle on
the Border in the next reign ; but this may have been
a later addition, as it comes near the end. Moreover,
these tales existed and were handed down by word of
mouth for years—nay, centuries—before they were
written down.

The hero of this story is Thomas of Ercildoune, the
supposed author of Sir Tristram, who uttered many
prophecies similar to those of Merlin. In the first
" Fytte," as the divisions were called, he describes how
he rode on a merry morning in May, the woods ringing
round about him with song of throstle, mavis, and jay,
and how he met the Fairy Queen, "a comely sight,"
riding on her dapple-grey, with jewelled saddle and
bridle, and how, when she alighted and sat upon the
bank, he lay with his head on her knee and yielded to
her enchantment. There is a curious touch when she
offers him his choice of "harpe or carpe"—the latter
probably an instrument of the lute or cithern order,
plucked by the fingers. He responds, "'Harpynge,'
said he, 'kepe I none, for tong is chief of minstrelsie.'"
And then she shows him "ferlies three," of which the
last is the road to fair Elfland, whither she bears him
for seven long years. In the later version, current in
Scotland, his reluctance to accept the boon of a tongue
that cannot lie comes out quaintly—

> "'My tongue is my ain !' True Thomas said,
> ' A gudely gift ye wad gie to me !

I neither docht to buy nor sell,
  At fair or tryste where I might be.

  " ' I docht neither speak to prince or peer,
    Nor ask of grace from fair ladye ! '
  ' Now hauld thy peace ! ' the lady said,
    ' For as I say, so it must be.' "

This version ends with his return at the seven years
end in a coat of " even cloth " and shoon of the velvet
green ; but the earlier one goes on with his prophecies
and an account of the great fight on the Border.

The traditions of Robin Goodfellow cannot be traced
back to their beginnings, but the earliest printed version
is in a black-letter tract of 1628, relating " his mad
Prankes and mery Jestes, full of honest Mirth, fit
Medicine for Melancholy." Stories of the Lubber-fiend,
as he was also called, are alluded to by both Shakspeare
and Milton. In all versions alike he comes at night to
sweep or bake or thresh the corn for those who set a
dish of cream and leave a warm hearth for him to lie
and bask at. In one of *Gammer Gurton's Pleasant
Tales* it is related how he went in the guise of a fiddler
to a wedding with his croud under his arm, and was
"a very welcome man," for his fiddling got into the
heels of the dancers, and kept them prancing merrily
till dawn. The same hero appears in *A Midsummer
Night's Dream* as Puck, and his doings were chronicled
in a book called *Merry Puck*, published early in the
seventeenth century by Bishop Corbet, who seems to
have had a wholesome love for the fairies, and wrote a
lamentation for their departure, for already people were
ceasing to believe in the wee Good Folk, and the

Puritans were inveighing against filling the children's minds with lies.

From Norman days come the entrancing stories of Robin Hood and his merry men, and the outlaw life in the greenwood, and the ballad of the *Nut-brown Maid*. If the moral of the outlaw life was shaky, the wholesome note of good fellowship, of comrades always true to each other, of generosity to the poor and feeble—only the greedy rich being regarded as lawful prey—kept the young folk scathless, and the love of the greenwood and of the free open-air life sank deep.

A little later we get what we may call the civic romance, when the cities became of importance, and the merchants began to bulk larger in the public eye. To these town tales belong *Dick Whittington and his Cat*, the story of Gilbert à Becket and his Saracen maid, and the tale of *The Cobbler and the King*. This last is reckoned comparatively late because of its reference to Henry VIII., but, I cannot help thinking, may, like so many traditional tales, have been transferred to a new hero, and made to fit Harry Tudor, having originally belonged to that other Harry, madcap Harry Bolingbroke, of whom it would have been still more characteristic. However, this story would probably please the grown-up folk better than the children, who, like the children of to-day, we may be sure cared little for humour, but loved romance and mystery. I dare say, unwholesome though it was, they took a shuddering delight in the weird tale of Mr. Fox, referred to by Shakspeare, the heroine of which, though, unlike

Fatima, she was not already wed, had an experience not very different from that of the last of Blue-Beard's wives. Briefly, thus the story runs—

Mr. Fox was paying his addresses to a certain Lady Mary, and invited her to come and see his house, so one day she resolved to do so alone and unannounced. When she got to the door and knocked, no one answered, so she opened it and went in. Over the portal and over the stairs, at the entrance to the gallery, and over a chamber door, ran the legend, " Be bold, be bold, but not too bold," followed over the last by the ominous words, " Lest that your heart's blood should run cold ! " Nevertheless she opened the door, and her heart's blood did run cold when she saw the floor covered with bones and gore. As she fled downstairs, she saw from a window Mr. Fox coming back, dragging a struggling maiden by the hair of her head. Lady Mary had just time to hide herself under the stairs before he reached the foot of them with his victim. The unhappy girl clung to the stair rail, and the villain chopped off her hand, which, with a rich bracelet that she wore, fell into the lap of the horrified spectator, who contrived to escape unseen. Next night Mr. Fox came to a banquet at the house of Lady Mary's brothers, and after the feast, when stories were being told, she related her experience as though it had been a dream, interrupted by him at every pause with, " It is not so, and was not so, and God forbid it should be so." But at the end of her tale she answered, " But it is so, and it was so, and here's the hand I have to show ! " producing

THE GOBLIN STORY

AFTER HAMILTON

the gruesome trophy.   The brothers slay the villain
and the lady is saved.

This is an even more blood-curdling story than the
ballad of "the Lady all skin and bone," who went to
church to pray, and there saw a dead man on an open
bier, "And from his nose unto his chin, the worms
crawled out, the worms crawled in."   And the Parson,
lest she might miss the application, assured her, " Thus
will you be when you are dead."   This pleasant tale
used, within living memory, to be included in volumes
of Nursery Tales.

After supping on such horrors, one can picture the
frightened rush of the little ones to bed, and one hopes
there was an elder boy valiant enough to protect his
little sisters with his wooden sword along the ill-lit,
vaulted passages between the great hall and the women's
quarters where the children slept.   The custom of
sleeping two or three in a bed, which obtained till well
on into the eighteenth century, must have been a
comfort on these occasions.   Nowadays we keep our
infants from contact with such ugly realities, and we
do well ; yet, after all, with all their rudeness, there
was a bracing quality in these old tales on which the
children throve, for their horizon was not bounded by
the nursery, as that of the modern child too often is.
Childhood was made of little account, therefore the
children themselves did not think their small affairs of
so much consequence, but reached forward with eager
hands into the great world where there were great
doings.   They learned in their childish games, first, to

mimic, then to emulate the heroic deeds the minstrels sung. The hobby-horse represented the great charger on whose broad back a good-natured squire would sometimes hold little master when his short, fat legs had not yet learned to grip the saddle.

It is difficult to make a guess as to when children first had *Cinderella* and *Red-Ridinghood, Riquet with the Tuft, The Sleeping Beauty, Blue Beard,* and the well-beloved *Puss in Boots.* We only know that they were old in 1696, when, having been for long handed down orally, as the *Stories of Mother Goose,* they were first collected and written down. They may have been current in France for long ; if so, the Normans probably brought them over. Very likely some filtered from the East with returning crusaders or merchants; but in that year they were published at the Hague as *Contes du Temps passés avec des Moralités—Contes de ma Mère l'Oie.* They were quickly translated into English by a certain unknown R. S. Besides those already enumerated, they contained the story of Little Thumb of well-known antiquity, and the tale of the two sisters, out of the mouth of one of whom fell pearls and diamonds whenever she spoke, and out of the other—for her sins—frogs and toads. To a little boy belongs the distinction of writing this first story-book for children, for Perrault states in his preface that he had been in the habit for years of narrating these old tales to his little boy, and when the child was between ten and eleven, he wrote them down, and the father, much pleased at the way they were done, got them printed.

Other like collections were current, as the *Tales of Mother Bunch*, to which belongs *The White Cat*, and *Gammer Gurton's Pleasant Tales*, containing *Patient Grizzel* and *The Babes in the Wood*.

It was not until some time later, not, indeed, till printing was getting cheaper, that the chapman, or "paultrie pedlar," whose rounds were such an event in the life of the countryside, began to add broad-sheets containing ballads old and new, and queer little chap-books illustrated with most amazing woodcuts, sometime gaily coloured, to his wares. We, whose children's bookshelves are so well laden that they rarely condescend to look at the same book twice, can hardly realize the excitement of these visits, nor the joy of becoming the possessor of *That Noble Piece of Antiquity, the King and the Cobbler*, to read again and yet again ; or *The Children in the Wood*, with most moving pictures, or perhaps Scripture stories, such as those printed by Wynkyn de Worde—Joseph and his Brethren in skirted coats and hoods, and the Ishmaelites in cocked hats, though leading camels, the sun and moon of Joseph's dream being represented with broad, smiling faces. *Sir Richard Whittington* was a very favourite subject in these chap-books, so too was *Dr. Faustus*, who succeeded in popularity as a magician to Friar Bacon. This was illustrated by an appalling wood-cut of a black devil with horns and hooves and a tail, very unlike the gentlemanly, sneering Mephistopheles of Goethe's version.

Nor was it on fiction alone that the imaginations of

the little boys of old were fed : very early chap-books contain the travels of Sir John Mandeville and stories from Hakluyt. Long, long before, as we have already seen, King Alfred was telling the tale of the Polar expeditions of the old Finnish sea captain Othere, and his account of the midnight sun which so amazed the king. Earlier still, Beowulf told of his voyage to Heort by the " Swan-path," and these travellers' tales must have been welcomed with as keen delight by the boys of old as are the adventures of Nansen or of Scott in our own day.

So their outlook into the great world was wide ; so too into the world which lay beyond, the world of mystery peopled with spiritual beings, good and bad, angels or demons, fairies or genii of strange powers. There was no unwholesome, namby-pamby sentiment about these old tales ; but they all, whether fairy-tales or gests of men of renown, inculcated a high morality, a love of country, chivalry towards the weak, an adventurous spirit, a brave heart, a joyous delight in outdoor life, in the song of birds in the wood, in May mornings in the fields. Their maxims ring true, and though, according to recognized convention, virtue was always rewarded and vice met its deserts, as does not always happen in this present evil world, yet their truth to the broad fact of human nature is unquestionable.

CHAPTER V

TOYS AND GAMES

PLAYTHINGS of some kind, we may be sure, are as old as the race. No record survives of their introduction, nor should we expect it any more than of the first making of tables and chairs. The simple requirements of humanity are fulfilled by in-stinct; a child would find itself a toy as naturally as a bird builds itself a nest. A hedge-stake with a crooked head for a hobby horse, a ball to toss, a doll to cuddle, something to rattle or dangle before the baby's eyes, answered to an instinctive craving.

I do not know if there is definite mention of a ball before that legendary game played by the little St. Hugh of Lincoln, in 1255, when—

> " He tossed his ball so high, so high ;
> He tossed his ball so low.
> He tossed his ball in the Jews' garden,
> And the Jews were all below."

But I think we may be tolerably certain that the British children, as well as those of the Roman settlers and their Saxon successors, played at ball. Balls are depicted on some Anglo-Saxon manuscripts of the ninth century, though I do not know that any of these represent children playing with them ; they are mostly of the conjuring tricks performed by the jongleurs or glee-men. However, balls there were, and that being so, we may be very sure children threw them.

In the same way the nature of little girls proves dolls. Some antiquarians have sought to account for the name by the supposition that when Christianity was introduced the small household images, the Lares and Penates, were given to the children for playthings in mockery of their former sacredness, and the word idol was corrupted on the infant tongue to doll. I can remember my feelings in childhood being deeply wounded by being told this ; for to my intelligence an idol was something both wicked and contemptible, and it pained me to associate the beloved of my heart with anything of the kind. Mrs. Earle, in her book on *Child-Life in Colonial Days*, ascribes a very recent origin to dolls, and thinks they were merely the dressed-up figures that were used to show the fashions before the invention of the fashion-plate. These were manufactured in the Low Countries, and were known as " Flanders babies." Dressed in the latest mode, they were sent from Paris to England, or out to the Colonies, which, like modern America, rather outdid than merely followed the fashion. When out of date no doubt they were handed over to the children to play with, but that they were the origin of dolls it would be impossible to believe, even did we not know of actual dolls of an earlier date. Mrs. Earle speaks, indeed, of " Bartholomew babies," but apparently regards these as a

later attraction of the great fair. No; the doll
originated in the heart of the little girl, who cuddled
and crooned to a stick wrapped in a handkerchief if
she had nothing better, we may be sure, just as she
will now if left to herself without toys.

It is tantalizing that Strutt, who, both in his *Sports
and Pastimes* and in his *History of Costume*, gives so
many very early and most interesting pictures of
children and their games from illuminated Missals,
never once, so far as I am aware, shows a doll ; but the
scarcity of little girls is almost equally remarkable.
Perhaps the charm of the little girl not appealing to
the monkish chronicler, there were no such pictures ;
that there were no dolls would be as impossible to
believe as that there were no little girls. Given the
dolls, I think we may conclude that they were made
of wood, wax, or rag. The wooden ones could have
joints, so that they could be made to sit or lie, the rag
were the least destructible and most cuddlesome, while
to the wax could be given a most engaging life-like
look. The earliest doll to have her portrait painted
seems to have been of wax, and was the property of
Lady Arabella Stuart, when three years old, in the
reign of Queen Elizabeth. She may, however, have
been of wood, with a composition face. She wears a
red dress with the sloping cut of the gowns then worn,
and sleeves puffed and slashed ; she is, moreover,
adorned with a ruff and an Elizabethan head-dress.
The picture belongs to the Duke of Devonshire, who
kindly permitted a photograph of it to appear in *Home*

*Life under the Stuarts.** In the next century dolls were evidently quite a matter of course, and little Mrs. Lucy Apsley rather prided herself on despising them, and teased the poor little girls who came to visit her, and whom she was expected to entertain, by "pulling their babies to pieces," as she relates of herself.

Pictures of dolls in the eighteenth century are very frequent, and to judge by them the dolls were quite as natural and well-finished as the ordinary ones of our own day. There is a fascinating large one, in a picture by Singleton, which two little girls are nearly pulling in two in their strife over it; it looks as if of wood. The oldest doll of my personal acquaintance was one of ninety years ago, and was presented to a relative of mine by the then Duchess of Buckingham, at Avington, in the year of the battle of Waterloo. It was very large, almost as large as a real baby. Its limbs were of wax, beautifully modelled, sewn on to a stuffed body, and it had a complete suit of baby-clothes "to take off and on"—always the prime desire of the little owner. When I knew it, its waxen complexion had suffered much by time, and had turned a tallowy yellow. I never was allowed to play with it, but it was displayed to me in my infancy as a great treasure. A doll's house of much the same date belonged to the same old lady, and was full of beautifully made wooden furniture, fourpost beds, etc. Very similar things may

---

* Two "babies," *i.e.* dolls, costing 13*s.* 4*d.*, for the Lady Elizabeth to play with, figure in the account of Lord Harrington's disbursements, quoted in *Lives of the Princesses of England* by Mrs. Everett Green.

be seen at Kensington Palace among the toys of the late Queen. Though these highly finished toys were probably not manufactured till civilization had made some strides, knowing the propensity of children to make houses of boxes, or cards, or anything they can find, we may be sure the dolls early had homes of some sort, and for the furniture, a brother with a jack-knife, if he was good-natured to his little sisters, could soon fit them up with all that was needed.

Children of to-day, living—even the well-to-do ones—in comparatively small houses, with everything supplied from shops, can hardly realize what wealth of possibility in the way of playthings was afforded by a country house in the olden time, with its blacksmith's forge on the premises, its carpenter's shop, full of delightful chips of all sorts and sizes, and great pots of paint with fat brushes, as well as the inestimable glue-pot, and hard by the harness-maker's shed with all its clippings of leather. Little master, and little miss, too, would be sure to haunt these, and get innumerable toys made for them in days when toyshops were few or none, as well as being allowed to imperil their own fingers and pinafores in making for themselves.

Talking of toyshops we must not forget the fair. There were great fairs in London, of which the most noted was Bartholomew's, established in 1133. At these all manner of merchandise was sold, but amongst the more important goods were always stalls for toys and sweets for the little people. Dolls, as mentioned above, used to be called Bartholomew babies, but the old cry of "Tiddy, diddy, doll," which used to be heard in fair or street, did not, as one would suppose, denote a doll but gingerbread—possibly the "gingerbread husband" we used to hear of as having been sold at fairs a century ago. Not for London children alone were the joys of the fair, but one was held in most country towns of any importance, or in the centre of a group of villages. Tan Hill Fair still lingers, and has been immortalized by Hardy, and Maun Hill Fair in Hampshire was held within my recollection, though now brought down to small dimensions in Winchester Broadway. From very early days there would be drums and hobby-horses, popguns and kites; probably also the "young lambs, two a penny," that used to be hawked in the streets of London, and are thus described by Andrew Tuer. "The fleece," he says, "was made of white wool spangled with gold, the head was of composition, with cheeks painted bright red (!) and black spots for eyes; it had horns and legs of tin, and a finishing touch was given by a piece of pink tape round the neck." These with the gilt gingerbread, which is known to have been manufactured as early as the fourteenth century, and peppermint drops, twenty for a penny, would be amongst the wares most eagerly sought by the children. Were the gingerbread horn-books, I wonder, as highly appreciated as the gingerbread husbands? It may have been an incentive to learning to be given a letter to eat on recognition; but, on the other hand, it may have seemed like the powder in the jam.

Drums and hobby-horses were among the traditional

PLAYING AT SOLDIERS

G. KEATING

toys in the time of Bishop Earle, writing on *The Child* in 1628. The latter were not the highly finished and realistic rocking-horse of the modern nursery; at first merely a stick with a horse's head at one end, sometimes a wheel at the other, which the little boy put between his legs, and did the galloping himself, so that, like Pat in his sedan chair with the bottom out, " but for the honour and glory of the thing, he might so well have walked." But for the child, it is just the honour and glory of the thing that matters. By 1628, though, it had really developed into something you could ride upon, with rockers, as may be seen by a rocking-horse belonging to the childhood of Charles I., and once in the old Palace at Theobald's, now preserved at the Great House, Cheshunt. It has a solid wooden body with an archaic looking head, no legs apparently, but huge rockers instead.

All military toys were highly favoured by the elders from the first, for a soldier's career was looked forward to for all but those who showed a leaning towards the cloister. Toy bows and arrows would lead the way to the use of the real thing when little arms had grown long enough to wield them. Popguns with a pellet of clay are mentioned in an old comedy of 1546, called *The Knave in Graine;* the sling to send missiles to a distance was of very early use. Pipes made of elder with the pith drawn out, and trumpets of cow's horn, as well as drums, would be used for martial music. Children played at tournaments, as may be seen in Strutt's *Sports and Pastimes*, little boys being mounted on big boys' shoulders. I have not met with any mention of toy

soldiers, but children early learned military manœuvres.
William the Norman at five years old could drill and
marshal a little regiment of children of his own age, who
went through their evolutions at the word of command.
They were doubtless armed with little wooden swords.
The Mummers with their traditional usages come down
from such very early days that they prove the ancient-
ness of toy swords and of dolls too ; for St. George and
the Paynim Knight were always armed with swords, and
Little Johnny Jack, with all his family at his back, used
to be laden with a basketful of dolls or puppets.

The mention of puppets brings us back to the fair
and its attractions. Here would be swords and popguns
in plenty, peg-tops and whips to whip them with, hoops
and hoopsticks. How early these latter made their
appearance I am unable to say, but according to
Monroe's *Text-book of Education*, mention was made of
them in a treatise belonging to the early days of the
Renaissance, in which the writer, urging the importance
of physical training, recommends the ball and the hoop
for quite young children ; and very good exercise it was
too, not only inducing them to run and keep themselves
warm in cold weather, but also to run straight and
steadily, a thing which it takes very little ones some
time and practice to do, and to use the arm at the same
time with a steady motion. I have somewhere seen it
advised, but not, I think, in this treatise, that the child
be taught to trundle his hoop first on one side and then
on the other, so as to exercise either arm indifferently.
It would be a very good thing if it were done now ;

children as a rule need very little training to become ambidextrous.

Trundling the hoop was an amusement the little girls could share ; so too was the skipping-rope, which was practised by boys in old times, though lately it has come to be looked on as quite a feminine pastime. Battledore and shuttlecock, another game in which the girls could join, is at least as old as the horn-book, for as Mr. Andrew Tuer pointed out, it was inevitable that the latter, from its convenient shape, would offer itself to toss things up, probably at first a ball, then some genius devised the winging of a round piece of cork with feathers. About a century ago a kind of battledore horn-book in coloured cardboard was found lingering in a little old toyshop in Wales, probably more as a toy than a lesson-book, though it had the alphabet with pictures printed on it; but it cannot have been very durable for either purpose. The shuttlecock is said to be derived from the practice of cock-fighting on Shrove Tuesday; certainly there was an immemorial fashion by which shuttlecocks used to appear on that day.

The game, however, may be much older, having some affinity with hand-tennis, or paume, as the Normans called it, which after a time came to be played with a racket. Boys played this hand-ball against church walls, both outside and inside, in very early days, for in the fourteenth century appeared an edict forbidding it, which was re-enacted in the time of Elizabeth. In Elford Church, near Lichfield, is an effigy of a child with one hand pressed to his head, and a ball held in the other; it is to the memory of a little grandson of Sir John Stanley, who, in 1460, was killed by a blow on the temple from a tennis-ball. Games of ball were various. There is a picture of two children, one in a hood, playing at trap-ball, in a fourteenth-century manuscript. Wind-ball was recommended as healthful play by the celebrated Buxton physician, Dr. Jones, in the reign of Elizabeth, but, as we have seen, was no new thing then. Cricket took its rise in the middle of the thirteenth century, in a game of ball with a crooked stick called a crick, in front of a three-legged stool, which the player had to ward. It was first called stool-ball.

There were ninepins, of course, but these were for grown folk as much as for children. Humming-tops and teetotums, or whirligigs, are considered to be of later introduction than peg-tops; but marbles are reckoned by Strutt among the ancient toys. Peg-tops are referred to, in 1579, in Northbooke's *Treatise against Dicing*: he advises the young to " play with the top and flee dice-playing." The Whirligig figures in *Love's Labour Lost*, act v., scene 1. Kite-flying, too, was old in 1634, and a paper windmill is represented in an old painting of five hundred years ago. Swings and see-saws, like balls and dolls, are probably primeval, and made themselves, so to speak. One can hardly doubt that a plank, accidentally lying across a felled trunk, offered itself as an obvious balance for two children, one at each end, one up, one down; while a rope chancing to hang from a tree was similarly appropriated, and, leading to a fall, suggested to the elders the propriety of fixing one firmly and strongly, with a bit of board to sit on, that would carry the little one up among the tree-tops, if not, as he fondly hoped, up to the stars.

If the children of an earlier day than ours were less rich in toys, they were far richer in the number and variety of their games, both outdoor and indoor, many of which are now almost forgotten, or only survive as curiosities. *Hunt the Fox* (or hare) is mentioned in an old play of the end of the sixteenth century, entitled *The Longer Thou Lives, the More Fool Thou Art.* A character in this, called the Idle Boy, says—

> " And also when we play at Hunt the Fox,
> I outrun all the boys in the schole."

This survives in the *Paper-chase* of to-day. *Hop-Scotch*, too, is not yet passed into the limbo of forgotten things. The same Idle Boy in another place boasts, " And I can hop a good way uppon my one legge." No one ever invented hopping any more than *Leap-frog;* they came to the children of themselves as naturally as running and jumping, and the former no doubt soon developed into a regular game, with marked squares and a system of counting.

Hide and Seek was equally suitable for the big gardens, with their pleasaunce and wilderness, mizmaze, or covert alleys, or for the long rambling corridors and priest's holes indoors. It may have been played by Queen Elizabeth in her romping days at Ewelme, where the tree she used to swing on is still shown, and we know it was a favourite game with James, Duke of York, and his sister and little brother in their captivity at St. James's Palace, and had a not unimportant bearing on his history. For indoors on winter evenings a very favourite pastime was *Blindman's Buff*, or *Hoodman Blind*, as it used to be called. It is mentioned under this name in a very old manuscript in the Bodleian, the player being blinded by a hood pulled over the face instead of a kerchief. This is too simple and familiar to need description. Others, perhaps a little later, are *Puss in the Corner* and *Post ;* the last charmingly recalling the old days when news was carried by post-horses, with a fresh relay at each stage. *Hunt the Slipper* was probably evolved by the children's instinctive habit of sitting on anything they wish to hide. *Honey-pots*, where the small child clasped its hands beneath its knees, and was lifted and swung by two bigger children, developed into an organized game of *The Forty Thieves*, but this must have been later than the arrival in England of the stories of *The Thousand and One Nights*.

A more curious study is to be found in the artificial games which survived so many social changes, and are only now dying out. Century after century they were handed down through generations of children, with their rigid laws, their traditional customs, their unchangeable wording. No one taught them to the children ; the elder ones handed them on to the little ones, and no child so bold that he would venture to introduce fresh customs or words of his own into what had always been played just so. Among the best known of these are *Here we go Round the Mulberry Bush*, with its quaint imitations of various crafts, and *Oranges and Lemons;* the former belonging more to the country children, and the latter to those who lived within sound of Bow bells. *Thread the Tailor's Needle* appears in many forms: the essence of it is that a train of children, holding to each other's skirts, run under the joined hands and raised arms of two, who clap down upon one and make him prisoner. In *Cat and Mouse,* which is not very dissimilar, there is a circle, hand in hand, in and out of which the cat chases the mouse, the sudden lowering of the arms either hindering the pursuit or preventing the escape of the mouse. Another country game referred to by Sir Philip Sidney in his *Arcadia,* by Herrick in *Hesperides,* and also in Suckling's *Poems,* is *Barley Brake,* a kind of *Prisoner's Base,* played among the barley mows, one of them being " home," another " hell," or " prison." In one of Massinger's plays, *The Tragedy of Hoffman,* written in 1632, occurs the line " I'll run a little course at Barley Brake."

Mr. Halliwell Phillips has made an immense collection of these traditional games. A very popular one was *My Daughter Jane.* A player, representing the mother, has a flock of girls behind her; to them come two players, singing—

> " Here come two dukes all out of Spain,
> A-courting to your daughter Jane."

To which she replies—

> " My daughter Jane, she is too young;
> She can't abide your flattering tongue."

Her daughters keep circling round behind her, so as

to present a defended front to the unwelcome wooers ;
but at last one of the latter catch the hindmost, singing—

> "Through the kitchen and through the hall
> I'll take the fairest of them all."

When the lot are pretty well divided, the wooer and the
mother pull, with their respective trains pulling behind
them, as in *Oranges and Lemons*. *The Town Lovers* is
something of the same kind, only in this case the
children stand in a ring, and a girl walking round the
inside sings a rhyme, bringing into it the name of
the one she wishes to chase her. In *Drop-cap* she
throws a cap or a handkerchief to the chosen one. A
similar game was—

> "Queen Anne, Queen Anne, she sits in the sun,
> As fair as a lily, as white as a swan."

This looks more like James's golden-haired Queen from
Denmark than her of the eighteenth century. Here
again a handkerchief knotted into a ball was thrown.

A very funny game, and one which cultivated
activity, was *Now we dance Looby, Looby*, in which one
player set the movement which all had to follow,
beginning with, "Shake your right hand a little, and
turn you round about." When all have got their right
hand in motion, the leader adds the left hand, then one
foot (if the players are seated, both feet), and lastly
heads are set nodding, the chorus of "Looby, Looby"
going on all the while till the children are exhausted
with laughter at each other's antics. No one who has
not tried to play it can have any idea how difficult it is.
A game of much the same character was—

"Buff says buff to all his men,
And I say buff to you again."

"Buff" nods, winks, and makes faces, but neither laughs
nor smiles, and the child who is betrayed into a grin or
chuckle has to pay a forfeit.

A very curious old game called *Questions and
Commands* is mentioned in Mr. Halliwell Phillips's
book, and I have a dim recollection of having played
it; it was a form of forfeits or *Hot Cockles*. One child
is set on a high seat, and says, "A king am I." Another
replies, "I am your man." The king then asks, "What
service will you do?" And the subject responds, "The
best and worst, and all I can." The king then sets each
one in turn some task, such as the traditional practical
joke, "Bite half an inch off the poker," or perhaps the
time-honoured "Bow to the prettiest, kneel to the
wittiest, and kiss the one you love the best." Similar
tasks are devised in *Hot Cockles* by a child with his eyes
hidden in some one's lap while the forfeit is held above
his head. A curious attempt was made in an article in
the *Gentleman's Magazine* for 1738 to date the game of
Questions and Commands at the time of the Commonwealth, supposing it to contain an implied scoff at
kingly power; but I must say this seems to me far-
fetched and improbable, for children do not understand
nor care for satire. It is, however, not unlikely that an
existing game may have been made use of by grown-up
people for mockery.

An old game, belonging to the days of bear-baiting,
is depicted in more than one eighteenth-century print,

in which a little boy plays "bear," going on all fours, and being baited by slaps from the knotted pocket-handkerchiefs of the other players. Before leaving these kind of games I must quote a few of the curious old traditional rhymes used for starting them, or for selecting the leader, such as *Hoodman Blind*, or the *Wooer*, or *Queen Anne*. This was one form of choice—

> "Onery, twoery, Ziccary zan;
> Hollow-bone, crack a bone, ninery ten.
> Spittery spot, it must be done!
> Twiddleum, twaddleum, twenty-one.
> Hink, spink, the puddings stink;
>   The fat begins to fry.
> Nobody at home but Jumping Joan,
>   Father, Mother, and I.
> Stick, stock, stone dead. Blind man can't see,
> Every knave will have a slave, you or I must be he."

"Ring me, ring me rary," was another form of counting out. For starting a race they had—

> "One to make ready, two to prepare,
> God bless the rider. Away goes the mare!"

Or—

> "Good horses, bad horses. What's the time of day?
> Three o'clock, four o'clock. Fare ye away!"

To hurry a child who was slow in taking up his turn, the children clapping their hands would cry—

> "Jack be nimble, Jack be quick,
> Jack, jump over the candlestick!"

Little teasing rhymes were current in the nursery for many generations. "Liar, liar lickspit!" is of great antiquity; so too is—

> "Tell-tale-tit, your tongue shall be slit,
> Every dog in the town shall have a little bit."

PLAYING "BEAR"

BARTOLOZZI

"Cry, baby, cry" is probably as old, for little people would soon learn to point at each other's little sins.

We hardly know whether to marvel more at the long tradition which handed these games down intact from child to child for so many centuries, or at their swift disappearance in the course of a generation or two. They are preserved in antiquarian literature; perhaps a few who are now fathers and mothers know them—at any rate the grandmothers may; but what child of to-day can play them without being taught? Possibly a few still know *Blindman's Buff* or *Puss in the Corner*, but I fear that *Queen Anne* and *My Daughter Jane* are on their way to join the horn-books of the past. Even the conservativeness of childhood seems passing away, and children are swayed by fashion as much as their elders. Dancing parties, even for quite little children, are the thing nowadays, and though sometimes a conjuror or a Christmas-tree may be added, a party which relied on games for its attraction would be reckoned very slow and old-fashioned.

The one characteristic these old games and toys had in common was imaginativeness; they all, especially the toys, required a certain amount of make-believe. A materialistic age has brought in realistic toys, trains or motors that really run, and model steam-engines that really work; these may be more instructive, but a child brought up on them will not so readily find toys for himself when left to his own devices, nor will he prove himself so resourceful in later life.

CHAPTER VI

NURTURE IN KINGS' COURTS

I N feudal times, when not only the king but all
noblemen and people of position kept great
households of followers and dependants, it was the
custom to send well-born children, so soon as they were
old enough to leave the nursery, either to the Court or
to the family of some noble kinsman to act as pages
or bower-maidens, and to be bred up in all the
traditional rules and customs of courtesy and knighthood.
This would seem to have been practised more in
England than in other countries, for it is alluded to in
An Italian Relation of England, describing the customs
of this country in the reign of Henry VII., the writer
commenting rather severely on the absence of affection
between English parents and their children which it
seemed to him to imply. We meet with it, however, in
France: quite a bevy of little girls learned and played
with the young French princesses when the little
Dauphiness, Mary Queen of Scots, was among them,
being brought up by her mother-in-law, Catherine de
Medici. In Germany, too, we find the sons of the Counts
Palatine frequently sent abroad to learn manners at
foreign Courts.

In the palace of King Alfred we gather there were

a goodly number of the sons of the nobility being instructed in all the learning of the day, in which the king was himself so proficient. Where there was a young prince, he, of course, needed playfellows; and, moreover, could be led along the thorny path of lessons more easily with the stimulus of other children to learn with and try to rival. The institution of "whipping-boys" for the prince was less commendable, and could not always have been made practical use of, since the guardian of young Henry VI. was greatly exercised how to chastise that monarch when he grew big and rebellious. The office was, however, in existence up to the childhood of Charles I. We do not hear of its being resorted to in his nursery, and it certainly was never brought in again at the Restoration: probably it had long become a sinecure. One may well believe that with a generous boy the sight of an innocent comrade taking the punishment due for his own fault may have had a deterrent effect; but with one of an evil nature it would seriously foster pride and contempt for inferiors, and was well suffered to fall into disuse.

At the Court of Edward IV. were six "enfauntes" of whom one was Thomas Howard, eldest son of that Sir John Howard who afterwards became Duke of Norfolk, and fell at Bosworth Field—the "Jockey of Norfolk" of the familiar rhyme. Strict rules were laid down for the behaviour of these children, and tutors and governesses appointed for their instruction. It really was an admirable up-bringing, calculated to fit them for the station they were expected to fill. Left at home to the "cockering and apish indulgence of mothers and nurses," so much deprecated by Mr. Peacham in his *Compleat Gentleman*, they would most likely grow up rude and boorish. In many cases their homes would be in some feudal castle in the depths of the country, the father much away in Court or camp, while the Wars of the Roses were continually breaking out afresh, or in earlier days, gone perchance to the crusades. Manly exercises they might have learned from the seneschal left in charge, and Latin from the nearest chantry priest, but of the manners of the great world they would have grown up in ignorance, and those things are the hardest to learn when early youth is past. Our forefathers had a good grip of the true end of education, a wider one than many theorists of to-day ; they had not come to regard it as solely a matter of books nor synonymous with scholarship ; their idea was to fit the child for his probable future career : scholarship for the clerk, handicraft for the peasant, manners (in the fullest sense) for the courtier, discipline for all, and Latin for all ; for it was the universal tongue of the educated, and with Latin a man could make himself understood in any part of the civilized world where his lot might be cast, and wherever the Church was planted would find himself at home.

It is needful that we realize that manners meant not merely courtesy but serviceableness ; it included for these children knowledge how to carve and wait at table, how to serve their lord both at the board and in his chamber ; the pouring of water for his hands, the handing of napkins, and how all these things should be done with urbanity and grace. Then the boys must learn skill in riding, in jousting, and to wear their harness becomingly—not easy at first for little limbs that had till now been clad in petticoats, for they were often sent as early as seven years old, and had not long been breeched. Then for accomplishments they must master sundry languages besides Latin: French, when it had become once more a foreign tongue, Italian, or sometimes Spanish, much spoken in days of Spanish alliances; also instrumental music, harp, pipe, or lute; to sing, which meant reading prick-song at sight in parts, and to dance galliards, pavanes, or whatever figure was the mode. Moreover, a knowledge of poetry, of ballads, of early chronicles or romances was expected, as in the afternoons and evenings these young people were in attendance in their lord's chamber or in the bower of the lady, to make music, dance, or relate tales to entertain the company. Occasionally a knowledge of drawing was added to the curriculum, and in late days Greek, but this was not made of quite so much account at Court. Truly no narrow nor easy education.

And all this with "temperate behaviour and patience." Proper demeanour at table was much insisted on, and "how mannerly" the little pages should eat and drink. Chastisement was by no means so severe as it was, or afterwards became in schools, but they were corrected, we learn, in their own chambers, presumably with the rod. Their religious observances were also carefully regulated, "with remembrance daily of God's service accustomed."

As early as the old ballad of King Horn this kind of training was customary, for Aymar the King, putting his adopted son into the charge of his steward, enjoins him—

> "Stiwarde, tak mi here
> Mi fundlynge for to lere
> Of the mesterye
> Of wude and of rivere.
> And teche hym to harpe
> With his nayles scharpe;
> Before mi to kerue
> And of the cup serue."

We find the same insistence on courtesy in other old ballads, and also on music, which seems to have been universally taught and practised; it was one of the indispensable subjects of the Quadrivium. The moral training was excellent; habits of obedience and service were at the very foundation of knighthood.

Sometimes if the boy showed greater aptitude for Latin than for field sports or chivalric exercises, he would go from the Court to Oxford to be made a scholar of, and certain bishops took in scholars to board and train for the priesthood. Thomas Bromley, at Hyde, near Winchester, had, in 1540, eight *gentiles pueri* boarding in his house; his predecessor, Thomas Langton, seems to have done much the same thing, for Richard Pace speaks of the keen interest the Bishop took in the progress of his pupils both in music and literature, rewarding a well-learned lesson with praise and little presents.

Little girls were sent out in the same way: the *Paston Letters* and other family correspondence make frequent mention of the practice. Anne Boleyn and her sister were placed in the care of Margaret of Savoy when Anne was about eight years old. She was then transferred to Mary, sister of Henry VIII. and wife of Louis XII. of France, and afterwards served Princess Claude.

Besides these children, who were sent out by their parents as pages or bower-maidens, there were the Wards of the Court—little heirs and heiresses who would in these days be made Wards in Chancery. In those fighting times early orphanhood was sadly frequent, and the Crown always laid its clutch upon any orphan of importance, as the matches of these young folks might be of considerable importance, binding adherents by alliances ; and, moreover, there soon grew up around the whole business an unblushing system of jobbery, which made wardships very lucrative, and helped to fill the royal coffers. This was at the root of those early marriages which are so astonishing to our modern notions, but were customary, not only amongst royal personages, but in all families of consequence. We read of children being married at five years old— quite frequently at nine—while girls of twelve or thirteen were considered on the verge of womanhood. Little Moll Villiers, the Duke of Buckingham's little girl, was not merely a wife but a widow at nine, and we read of her romping in the garden and climbing cherry trees in her widow's veil. The Earl of Cork did, indeed, protest against the marriage of his sixteen-year-old lad, urging a betrothal rather. " He is but a silken thread," he writes to the future mother-in-law, " to be wrought into what pattern you please, either flower or weed." Sir Edmund Verney, one of the best men of his time, on the other hand, did not scruple to bid for the wardship of the little heiress, Mary Blacknall, nor to wed her at twelve years old to his son Ralph at sixteen sending the young bridegroom to complete his studies at Oxford afterwards.

The astonishing thing is that these child marriages should so often have turned out well; perhaps because the young people were brought up together with a view to adapting themselves to one another. Certainly never was happier wedlock than that of Ralph and Mary. Matrimonial disaster quite as often, if not oftener, followed hasty love-matches where suitability was set at defiance. But to return to the training of these children at Court. The girls shared in the instructions of the tutor, and so far as regarded languages, music, and dancing, were taught much the same things as the boys; but the time which the pages had to devote to fencing and *manège* was spent by the little maidens over the sampler or in the still-room; for all women were expected to be proficient with the needle, and even queens were taught to understand household management. Sometimes there was a governess for the girls—one is mentioned as early as the reign of King Stephen in a letter of Osbert de Clare—but more often they were instructed by a tutor. There is a curious treatise in Norman-French, written by one Walter de Biblesworth, who was tutor to a little Kentish heiress, Diane de Montchesney, for her instruction. It conducts the infant from its birth through all its experiences and small duties, describing what it wore, even to its bib. It was penned in the year 1300, and still exists in a worn parchment roll in the British Museum. In spite of glosses in the margin in red ink, it is very hard to decipher, since the English is so old as to be quite as difficult to make out as the French. It is full of quaintly simple precepts, such as that the child must tie its shoes, cover its head, do up all its buttons. "My gentle child," it says, a little further on, "learn well to speak French, and listen well to those who talk to you." The little pupil was to go to Mass, and, when there, not to look about her, and she must willingly give gifts to the poor ; she must have care for others, and love those about her. After supper she was to be coiffed, and work in thread or silk, in which her "tutresse" would instruct her. One maxim was that she was not to cry on a *jour de fête* but be merry. It is quite a long roll, and probably the child for whose behoof it was written did not persevere to the end, for the latter part looks so much fresher and less rubbed at the edges by little dog's-earing fingers.

Nearly two centuries later Palsgrave, tutor to the Lady Mary, younger daughter of Henry VII., wrote *Lesclaircissement de la Langue Française* for his pupil, and another work, *On the French Tong*, was dedicated to her by Giles de Guez. Doubtless, as she was to marry the French king, a knowledge of the language was considered indispensable for her.

In 1475 *The Babee's Boke* was written for the instruction of the "six enfauntes" at the Court of Edward IV., described as "a little report of how young people should behave." It is among the Harleian manuscripts, and has been printed for the Early English Text Society, edited with notes by Dr. Furnivall. It is addressed to children of blood royal or noble, who are spoken of as the Bele Babees or Fair Children. They are exhorted in the beginning if they meet a word they do not know to ask the meaning of it ; very necessary, as some of these little ones were not more than seven years old.

The instructions open with manners at meals ; and this does not mean primarily their own meal, but at the table of the master whom they served. First, when they came into their lord's presence, they were to salute the company and say "God speed." They must come in steadily, hold up the head, and kneel on one knee. They must pay attention when spoken to, not chatter nor stare about, nor yet look sulky, but have "a blythe visage and a spirit diligent." The maxims are very quaint and practical, such as, " Answer shortly and pertinently ; stand until you are told to sit ; bow to your lord when you answer him ; give place to your betters, and turn your back on no man ; keep silence while your lord drinks." There was to be no whispering, laughing, nor joking in his presence, and no naughty stories whispered to each other. When told to sit, the little page must do so at once ; but if praised, he is to

stand up to express his thanks "with demeanour meek
but cheerful." When the lord and lady talk together,
he is not to interfere, but be on the watch and ready to
hand the cup, hold the taper, or to do whatever service
may be required of him. If the lord offer his own cup,
the child must take it in both hands and drink, but
offer it to none else. Meat being ended, he is to bring
water for his lord to wash his hands, to hold the
napkin, and to remain in attendance until grace is
said.

The instructions for behaviour at the children's own
meal are very precise. Each boy must keep his knife
clean and sharp, which shows that every one in those
days ate with his own pocket-knife. A tradition of this
custom lingered long in some schools, where the boys
were expected to bring each his own knife and spoon.
The bread, it is insisted on, was to be cut, not broken,
and the child was to lay a clean trencher before him.
The trencher was, of course, of wood; plates were quite
unknown, and broth served in a bowl. These wooden
trenchers were used up to the middle of the last century
at Winchester College, and the boys had a clever dodge
of building a wall of bread round the meat to keep the
gravy in. The precepts for eating were very particular:
"Eat broth with a spoon, do not sup it, and do not leave
the spoon in the dish; do not fill your mouth too full,
and wipe it when you have drunk; do not dip your
meat in the salt-cellar, nor put your knife in your
mouth; taste of every dish, but when your plate is
taken away do not ask for it again; do not hack your

meat like a labourer; have a clean knife and trencher for cheese; share with strangers of the best. When the meal is over, clean your knives and put them away; keep your seat till you have washed, then go to the high table and stand until Grace is said."

Even these high-born Bele Babees had some naughty habits, as may be gathered from the need for such exhortations as not to pick their little noses, nor poke their little ears; not to scratch themselves, nor lean against a post; to keep head, hands, and feet still, and not to handle things while being spoken to. Not to lean over the table, stoop over the dish, drink with the mouth full, dirty the cloth, pick nails or teeth at table. A somewhat similar manual of good breeding adds the advice, "Burnish no bones with your teeth, for that is unseemly," and further suggests that the pocket-handkerchief be used to blow the nose in preference to the table-napkin! But this was in 1577, after the introduction of pocket-handkerchiefs. Previously the method was similar to that practised in America for clearing the throat, and even in England amongst vulgar people to this day; very careful instructions were given as to the doing of it with propriety.

The general advice was excellent: "Be not too loving, nor too angry; too bold, nor over-busy; be not cruel nor cowardly, yet not officiously courteous. Do not drink too often; be not too haughty, nor too anxious to please; too fierce, nor too familiar, but of friendly cheer. Not too fond of meddling in other men's matters, nor of joking. Hate oaths and flattery.

Be not too much given to gadding, nor yet churlish, but
keep a safe middle course."

Truly a very complete scheme of good breeding,
and doubly remarkable if we consider when it was
written—in an interval of the Wars of the Roses,—times
we are apt to look back upon as almost barbarous.
This little treatise and similar ones, of which there were
very many, were often recommended as reading-books
or primers for children at school.   In these days we
smile at the notion of using books of etiquette for such
a purpose, but truly I am not sure that to study a code
of manners was not of quite as much practical utility as
easy readings in popular science or moral tales.

About two generations later, in the reign of Henry
VIII., appeared *Stans Puer ad Mensam*, "The Boy
Standing at the Table," containing precise instructions
for carving, handing meat and drink, and all the service
of the table, duties which were in those days always
performed by well-born children, little pages, or young
esquires.   The breeding of the Squire described by
Chaucer in the Prologue to *The Canterbury Tales* was
no exceptional thing—

> "Curteys he was, lowly and servisable,
> And carf biforn his fader at the table."

The rules as to nice habits and proper behaviour
among the pages are much like those in the foregoing,
and it adds thereto an exhortation to children not to be
quarrelsome and revengeful.   "The wrath of children,"
says the writer, "is soon provoked and soon appeased
with a bit of apple ; " a little touch which shows the book

was meant for quite young children. Their quarrels, he adds, are first play, then crying. He would have them well disciplined, and endorses the ancient maxim, " Spare the rod, and spoil the child."

This old treatise is preserved amongst the Lambeth manuscripts, and in the same collection is another of the same date, called *The ABC of Aristotle*, consisting of a series of rules of manners arranged for committing to memory on the principle of *A Apple-pie*. Many of the rules in the end of the *Babee's Boke* are incorporated in this. A, not too Amorous, nor to Argue too much ; B, neither Bold nor too Busy ; C, Courteous and not Cruel ; D, not Dull, and so forth. J, forbids Jangling and also Japes.

For a couple of centuries there was a regular succession of these Books of Urbanity, as they were called. In 1577 Sir Hugh Rhodes, Master of the Children of the Chapel Royal, put forth for their instruction *The Boke of Nurture; or, Schoole of Good Manners*. This book begins with exhortations to parents to bring up their children in virtue, good manners, and Godly learning. Idle talk and the habit of stammering should be noticed and put a stop to at once, as well as uncomely gestures in going or standing. The duties of children, whether at Court or at home, as here set forth, give a very good notion of a child's daily life. He was to rise at six, and say his prayers, then make his bed, sponge or brush his clothes, clean his shoes, wash his hands and face, button or lace his clothes, and tie his points, and, lastly, blow his nose

before leaving his chamber. Then he was to wish his
mates "good morning," and hasten to pay his respects
to his parents, doing them reverence whenever they
appear. At church he must not talk, stare, nor sleep.
With his comrades he must be gentle in speech, not
crossing them, and in relating anything he must not
point his tale with his finger.

To much about the same date belong the articles
drawn up by Sir Nicholas Bacon for the bringing up of
wards in the Court of Elizabeth, and these regulations
show the order of daily life in the Court. Divine service
was at six; there was no breakfast, that was a comparatively modern luxury. The children studied Latin
till eleven, then dined; the music-master gave his
instructions from twelve till two, then came an hour of
French. From three to five Latin and Greek lessons
were given. At five came evening prayers, then supper.
Pastimes were allowed until eight, then more music,
and to bed at nine. These rules were framed for the
young people under sixteen, but probably the very
little ones had shorter lesson hours and an earlier
bedtime.

Even the great Erasmus did not disdain to draw up
A Little Book of Good Manners for Children. Some of
his instructions are very quaint. He gives elaborate
directions how to carry the head, brow, and eyes; not to
wink nor blink, not to roll the eyes, bend the brows, or
make any unbecoming grimaces. He thinks it necessary
to enter into minute particulars : "Let not thy nose-
thrills be full of snivel like a sluttish person. . . . To

dry it on the cape of thy coat or on thine elbow is the propriety of a fishmonger. It is good manners to dry it with thy handkercher, and that with thy head turned somewhat aside if more honest persons be present." Needless to explain that honest in this connection implies more worthy of respect. Sneezing in company was to be avoided if possible, but "if it may not be, to stop it were to prefer manners to health." If quite inevitable, the sufferer was to thank those who blessed him, and not to forget to bless others in like case. The writer treats also of blushing and gaping; in the latter case he says, "Close thy mouth with thy handkercher or the palm of thy hand." He enlarges on how to bear the body upright, with shoulders straight and arms carried easily. Neatness and niceness of apparel in the fashion of the day is enjoined, and good manners at table, much the same as those prescribed in the previous Books of Nurture, *Stans Puer* and the rest. Behaviour in church is also touched on ; no talking or walking about in church is to be allowed, so it would seem that the custom of Paul's Walk had not grown to such an abuse as it became a century later. The Blessed Sacrament was to be saluted with reverence, not only in church, but whenever met, carried in procession, and the Holy Cross also.

In company the child must learn not to shake his head, wriggle his shoulders, pick his ears, nor scratch his head ; a child sitting among his elders should never speak till spoken to. Greediness is rebuked, not only in the form of eating too much, but in daintiness and

BOY WITH A HAWK
NICHOLAS MAES

grumbling. "To find fault with any meat," says the mentor, "is against good manners." In the bedchamber manners are also to be observed, such as to keep silence, not to tumble nor vex the bedfellow with pulling the clothes off him. Both before sleeping and on waking, to make the sign of the Cross on forehead and breast.

Perhaps these little books have been enlarged upon somewhat unduly, but not only are they very curious and interesting in themselves, but they throw a light not otherwise obtainable upon the doings and ways of children, upon their habits bad and good, and on the course of their daily life in times when individual children were very rarely described.

Wherever the children brought up in this manner do come before us in drama or in history, we find them much what this kind of breeding would be likely to make them : self-possessed, quick on an errand, ready of tongue—too ready sometimes with a sharp-witted answer,—serviceable, obedient, and with sense beyond their years. Well trained in all accomplishments, able to entertain the company with lute or harp, with song or story, or perhaps with riddles and quaint conceits. Able, also, to converse with foreign visitors, or to hold their own if sent abroad. Proficient in dancing in the graceful manner of the day. Ready-witted, avoiding quarrels by their urbanity, but quickly ready to defend their honour at the sword's point if needful ; given somewhat early to amorous badinage, less with the little maidens of their own age with whom they had been brought up, than with the ladies in waiting or maids of honour, who amused themselves with their precocious gallantries, and taught them the lore of the courts of love.   Punctual in the performance of their religious duties, and with a high sense of honour and of the maxim " Noblesse oblige."

CHAPTER VII

CHILDREN IN SHAKSPEARE'S PLAYS

A S the manners of our own day, its domestic ways, its types of character down to its children, are found reflected in our novels, so those of an earlier day must be sought in the dramatists—supremely in Shakspeare; for where Lyly, Greene, Peele, Kyd, and the rest set before us the conventional page or princeling of the Elizabethan era, Shakspeare gives us the living child; such a child as we might find to-day, given the same breeding and surroundings. For human nature, specially child nature, endures with much the same characteristics at bottom in the twentieth century as in the sixteenth or in the ninth. Nearest to Shakspeare stands Marlowe; truly his little prince smiles at us across the centuries, a veritable child. In years to come perchance the antiquaries will gather what our children were like, less from Blue-Books and Educational Reports than from the frivolous pages of the children's books, from Mrs. Ewing or Kenneth Grahame; or from the novels written for their elders in which they figure, from Jane Austen down to Rhoda Broughton or Mary Cholmondeley, and they will not be far wrong. Our stage has become too conventional to show any convincing child, but in old days it was the drama, not the novel, that reflected the life of the times; and he who could so well "hold the mirror up to nature" with men and women, did, we may be sure, depict child nature as he saw it.

The books of nurture and urbanity which we have been considering certainly tended to develop a distinct type of page which lent itself to conventional treatment on the stage. With good material it wrought courtesy, self-possession, obedience, and serviceableness, with quick wit and a ready tongue; with bad, pertness, precocious knowledge of the seamy side of Court life, wit to deceive, sauciness to flout, such a type, in short, as is shown in the malicious little Lorenzo in Kyd's *Spanish Tragedy*. With Lyly, as with most of the earlier dramatists, the saucy page is used as a somewhat conventional figure, whose quips and jests serve to lighten serious situations and provoke a laugh. But if conventional we may be sure they were true to the prevailing type, for it must be remembered, though they might be given classic names and placed in classic surroundings, it was not the boys of old Greece or Rome the writer had in his eye, but the boys of London as he knew them in the days of Elizabeth.

Shakspeare's pages have the same general characteristics, but with the individual touch that makes them live, each apart from all the others. Who would confuse Robin and Moth, Lucius and Bartholomew? Robin is a little masterpiece; slim scrap of a child as he is, "an upright rabbit," Bardolph calls him, he follows the fat knight, Sir John Falstaff, sailing "like a pinnace" in the wake of a great galleon. He has more wit than presence, he is swift to serve, and loyal to his master, yet not without a twinkle in his bright eye, and lends himself willingly to the befooling of Sir John in *The Merry Wives of Windsor*. Mrs. Ford and Mrs. Page both make much of him, and he enters very heartily into the joke of the buck-basket. He knows how to turn a compliment like the "little gallant" that Mrs. Page dubs him. "Oh, you are a flattering boy : now I see you'll be a courtier," says she to him.

His virtue is not proof against being bought over by bribes. Prince Hal gives him a pourboire, the jesting dames a new waistcoat to decoy his master into their nets, yet in any serious matter we feel he would have been loyal to the death, and he makes a very noble end in France after Falstaff's decease. It is a fine touch, pointed out by Herr Tetzlaff in his very illuminating Dissertation upon this subject, that even one of Falstaff's degraded followers, Poins, who was not lost to all good feeling, exclaims—

"O, that this good blossom
Could be kept free from cankers!"

On quite different lines is little Moth, one of the most fascinating of the many fascinating figures of the too rarely seen comedy of *Love's Labour's Lost*. He, too, is little—little and pretty—and his quickness at repartee is as the flash of summer lightning, swifter than rapier thrust. His master is the fantastic Spanish gentleman, Armado, who is greatly given to an extravagant euphuism in his speech ; a trick the boy has

caught, half unconsciously, half of malice prepense to
jest at it. He and his master are excellent friends, and
Armado addresses him as "dear imp," and "tender
juvenal." "Pretty and apt," says Armado to one of
his saucy speeches.

> "*Moth.* How mean you, sir? I pretty, and my saying apt? or I apt,
> and my saying pretty?
> *Arm.* Thou pretty, because little.
> *Moth.* Little pretty, because little. Wherefore apt?
> *Arm.* And therefore apt because quick.
> *Moth.* Speak you this in my praise, master?
> *Arm.* In thy condign praise."

Occasionally Armado wearies on this swift word-play,
and answers, " I love not to be crossed ; " more often it
amuses him, and he flatters and pets the child. The
small elf can quote instances, as Hercules and Samson,
of strong men in love, and can give the date of the
ballad of *The King and the Beggar*—Cophetua and the
Beggar-maid, to guess by the context, and he is ready
with riddles and old rhymes, such as—

> "The fox, the ape, and the bumble-bee,
> Were still at odds, being but three."

He is, as his master avers, "a well-educated infant."
He can sing, too, and has a nice perception of the
sentiment appropriate to a love-ditty. When Armado
calls upon him—

> "Warble, child ; make passionate my sense of hearing,"

he responds with a song, of which the words are no
more than Concolinel, and presently adds to it a
dissertation on the art of the love-song—

> "No, my complete master : but to jig off a tune at the tongue's

end, to canary to it with your feet, humour it with turning up your eyelids, sigh a note and sing a note, sometimes through the throat, as if you swallowed love with singing love, sometimes through the nose, as if you snuffed up love by smelling love ; with your hat penthouse-like o'er the shop of your eyes ; with your arms crossed on your thin-belly doublet, like a rabbit on a spit; or your hands in your pockets, like a man after the old painting ; and keep not too long in one tune, but a snip and away. These are compliments, these are humours ; these betray nice wenches, that would be betrayed without these ; and make them men of note—do you note me ?—that most are affected to these."

Singing and lute playing were indispensable accomplishments for these young pages. The Duke, in *Twelfth Night*, calls upon his boy—

"That strain again : it had a dying fall."

And

"If music be the food of love, play on."

The two pages who make a brief appearance in the last act of *As You Like It*, sing, and also make merry over the excuses of those called upon for a song—

"Shall we clap into't roundly, without hawking or spitting or saying we are hoarse, which are only prologues to a bad voice ? "

And they sing, *It was a Lover and his Lass*, but win no compliments on their performance from Touchstone.

Singing seems to have been one of the chief duties of Lucius, the page of Brutus, in *Julius Cæsar*. This boy is one of the most winning figures in the portrait gallery of Shakspeare's children ; so devoted to his master, so ready in service, so anxious to do his best, even when he cannot understand what is required of him, as in the scene with Portia, his master's wife, when, distracted with apprehension, she bids him run to the town and hasten back to her—"stay not to answer me, but get thee gone"—and yet never tells him what errand she would have him do there. The little scene in which he makes his first appearance, lighting the taper, finding a sealed letter lying on the window-sill, and fetching the calendar to look out whether it be the Ides of March, and all without inquisitiveness as to the strange things he must have been conscious of about him, all show his sweet and serviceable nature. And then his readiness to make music for his overwrought master, when dropping with childish drowsiness, is very engaging. He was very mindful, too; he knew quite well that the letter had not been in the window when he went to bed, and he was quite certain he had not mislaid the book his master lost—

> "*Brut.* Look, Lucius, here's the book I sought for so :
> I put it in the pocket of my gown.
> *Luc.* I was sure your lordship did not give it me.
> *Brut.* Bear with me, good boy, I am much forgetful.
> Canst thou hold up thy heavy eyes awhile,
> And touch thy instrument a strain or two?
> *Luc.* Aye, my lord, an't please you.
> *Brut.*   It does, my boy :
> I trouble thee too much, but thou art willing.
> *Luc.* It is my duty, sir.
> *Brut.* I should not urge thy duty past thy might ;
> I know young bloods look for a time of rest.
> *Luc.* I have slept, my lord, already.
> ♪ *Brut.* It was well done ; and thou shalt sleep again ;
> I will not hold thee long : if I do live,
> I will be good to thee."

The boy plays until he drops asleep, and his master gently takes the instrument from him.

Bartholomew in *The Taming of the Shrew* can hardly be reckoned among the children; he must have been a lad of elder years to play the *rôle* assigned him, so we will pass him by.

The little princes whom Shakspeare takes from the pages of history must really be reckoned to him as his own creation, for though he may borrow the bare facts from Holinshed or other old chroniclers, he clothes them with flesh and blood; in truth, he made Arthur a child for the story's sake; the real Arthur of history was almost a man grown at the time of his death. Little Rutland, "the white rosebud," as Tetzlaff calls him, appears but to die; a tender and timid little fellow, clinging first to his tutor, and when torn away from his protection, to the cruel Clifford himself, who was about to put him to death, childlike, so convinced that he could win pardon, as he had often done in his little life for childish faults, by his tears and piteous cries, hardly able to believe he would not be heard. There is but little room for characterization here; yet the few strokes tell.

Far different is it with the young King Edward V. and his little brother, Richard, Duke of York. With consummate skill the characters of the two children are contrasted, the gentle gravity and dignity of the elder boy, newly conscious of his high calling, and weighed down a little under the sense of it; and the forward, saucy tongue of the little one. A very loving child nevertheless is little Richard, both to his brother and to the uncle he had not learned to doubt. How natural is the talk of his having overtaken his brother in his growth, and his quoting his uncle Gloucester, who told him, "Small herbs have grace, great weeds do grow apace." So since then, he says, he does not want to grow too fast. He is thoroughly childish even in his precocity, sharp in repartee as a much-noticed boy will be, and something saucy. His mother says to him—

"A parlous boy : go to, you are too shrewd."

And on a later occasion his uncle—

"O, 'tis a parlous boy ;
Bold, quick, ingenious, forward, capable :
He's all the mother's from the top to toe."

The whole short scene of the arrival in London of the young king, and his meeting with his brother, is touched in with a marvellous naturalness. Edward is weary with his journey, disappointed at not being greeted by his favourite uncles, his mother's brothers, a little fretful and perplexed. Gloucester greets him with—

"The weary way hath made you melancholy.
Ed. No, uncle ; but our crosses on the way
Have made it tedious, wearisome, and heavy:
I want more uncles here to welcome me."

He will not admit for a moment that they were false friends to him, as his other uncle would have him believe. He wants his mother and his brother with a childlike impatience—

"Fie ! what a slug is Hastings, that he comes not
To tell us whether they will come or no ! "

And when the messenger appears, how eagerly he asks—

> "What, will our mother come?"

When at length the little Duke of York is brought, how like a child is his at once going back to the saying about the ill weeds that had so struck his fancy—

> "O, my Lord,
> You said that idle weeds are fast in growth :
> The prince, my brother hath outgrown me far."

Then with boyish inconsequence he begs for his uncle's dagger, like a little spoilt prince that has but to ask and have. The elder gently rebukes him—

> "*Prince Ed.* A beggar, brother?
> *D. of York.* Of my kind uncle that I know will give ;
> And being but a toy, which is no grief to give."

After a little more badinage Edward again interposes with an apology for the little one—

> "My Lord of York will still be cross in talk :
> Uncle, your grace knows how to bear with him."

The younger child was evidently considered forward for his years, for Buckingham says—

> "With what a sharp provided wit he reasons !
> .   .   .   .   .   .
> So cunning and so young is wonderful."

And when the children are gone, they wonder whether "this little prating York" has been prompted by his mother.

The shrinking repugnance with which the two children go to the Tower foreshadows their doom. Yet for all his gentleness the elder shows the most courage, a spirit truly kingly. We are spared the sight of their murder; but the very murderers themselves wept to tell how they found the two little boys asleep, clasped in each other's arms—

> "Their lips were four red roses on a stalk,
> Which in their summer beauty kiss'd each other.
> A book of prayers upon their pillow lay."

Like in cruel circumstance, yet quite distinct in portraiture, is the little Arthur in *The Life and Death of King John*. As gentle as Edward, but with less dignity; with such a clinging need of love that he spends a wealth of affection upon his harsh gaoler, and almost succeeds in softening that rough nurse—

> "I would to heaven I were your son,
> So you would love me, Hubert."

And then—

> "Are you sick, Hubert? you look pale to-day :
> In soothe I would you were a little sick,
> That I might sit all night and watch with you :
> I warrant I love you more than you do me."

How purely a child's argument it is when he says—

> "Have you the heart? When your head did but ache
> I knit my handkercher about your brows,
> The best I had, a princess wrought it me,
> And I did never ask it you again."

And again his promise to be good, like a child in the dentist's chair—

> "Alas, what need you be so boisterous-rough?
> I will not struggle, I will stand stone-still.
> For heaven's sake, Hubert, let me not be bound
> Nay, hear me, Hubert, drive these men away,
> And I will sit as quiet as a lamb ;

> I will not stir, nor wince, nor speak a word,
> Nor look upon the iron angerly."

He has no ambition to wear a crown; his only longing is for freedom and simple country pleasures—

> "So I were out of prison and kept sheep,
> I should be merry as the day is long."

He is full of tender consideration for his mother, and could wish himself out of the way for her sake—

> "Good my mother, peace!
> I would that I were low laid in my grave:
> I am not worth this coil that's made for me."

It has been objected by some German critics, notably Kreyssig, that some of Arthur's speeches, the simile and hyperbole he here and there makes use of, are out of place in the mouth of a child; but the same kind of objection would urge that people in real life do not speak blank verse: of course they do not: but then poetry is the essential condition under which the tragic drama is written; that, of course, is a convention, but granted this, the whole scene conveys an effect most tender, childlike, and natural. If there is a jarring touch it is in the rhymed couplet with which he makes his exit, falling from the castle walls in the endeavour to make his escape.

Such a portrait makes us regret the more that Shakspeare should have taken the opposite poet's licence with the wife of Richard II., and made her a woman grown instead of the little girl of twelve years old, which she really was at the time of his deposition. From such a hand what a picture might we not have had of the child drawn into such a web of tragedy, taking sad leave of the young husband who must have been more like an elder brother to her! The story is prettily told in a child's book of historical ballads by Miss Smedley. I do not think that Shakspeare gives us any little girl except Margaret, the child of Clarence, in *Richard III.*, who, with her little brother, gives occasion for some of the grandmother's bitter speeches, but has no very distinct existence of her own. These two children, had they stood alone, might have lent force to the criticism made by some that Shakspeare's children are not childish. Much such an unchildlike boy is found in *Macbeth* in the little son of Macduff; he is a man in miniature. Probably in these instances Shakspeare was merely following the chronicles on which he built his story, and had not thrown them into the crucible of his own imagination.

No such objection can be brought against the brief and brilliant portraits of two schoolboys and a little spoilt child. Mamillius, in *A Winter's Tale*, is quite a little fellow, still in petticoats, as we gather by Leontes' reference to himself at that age, unbreeched, in a green velvet coat; the word in those days always denoting petticoat. His almost babyhood may be seen too in the baby talk his father addresses to him—

> "I' fecks!
> Why that's my bawcock. What, hast smutched thy nose?
> They say it is a copy out of mine. Come, Captain,
> We must be neat ; not neat, but cleanly, Captain."

The worst of it is that no child small enough to

represent Mamillius has wit enough to act the part, so
on the stage he usually seems too old. A very exquisite
scene is the one where the child is teasing his mother,
and she bids her ladies take him. He is petted, and
has his likes and dislikes. To the one who offers to be
his playfellow he says—

> " *Mamillius.* No, I'll none of you.
> *First Lady.* Why, my sweet lord?
> *Mamillius.* You'll kiss me hard, and speak to me as if
> I were a baby still. I love you better."

His little personal remarks are thoroughly childish ; so
too is his beginning to tell a tale and his mother coaxing
him—

> " *Hermione.* Come on, sit down: come on and do your best
> To fright me with your sprites ; you're powerful at it.
> *Mamillius.* There was a man—
> *Hermione.*   Nay, come, sit down ; then on.
> *Mamillius.* Dwelt by a churchyard : I will tell it softly ;
> Yond cricket shall not hear it."

How one thinks to hear the little lisping voice! This
is the child's last appearance ; the terrible coil of
suspicion unrolls itself and robs him of his mother.
A tender little soul, made for sunshine, he pines away
and dies.

Another small masterpiece is William Page, in *The
Merry Wives of Windsor*, being examined at his
mother's request by the Welsh schoolmaster, Sir Hugh
Evans. William is evidently smarting under a sense
of injury in that, school being closed and a playing day
announced, he should be thus caught and caged and
unfairly called upon to answer questions in his accidence.

He answers pretty well but sullenly, and his gravity, after the manner of childhood, appears quite unmoved by the malaprop interpositions of Mrs. Quickly. We see him unwillingly coming forward, chidden by his mother, and told to hold up his head and answer his master. The book out of which he was questioned was probably Lilly, the grammar in general use in Shakspeare's day. After answering patiently for some time, on being demanded the declensions of the pronouns, he rebels with, "Forsooth, I have forgot," and is released and bidden to go and play. He recalls the schoolboy from the Seven Ages in *As You Like It*—

> "The whining schoolboy, with his satchel
> And shining morning face, creeping like a snail
> Unwillingly to school."

More than one critic has suggested that Shakspeare was not improbably drawing on his own recollections of his school days at Stratford-on-Avon. Not in vain, says Professor Elze, was this boy named William.

The figure of the little Lucius with his school-books brings a pathetic and tender charm into the lurid horror of *Titus Andronicus*. He cannot understand the grief and gloom that are round him, and tries to cheer his grandfather and aunt in his childish way—

> "Good grandsire, leave these bitter deep laments:
> Make my aunt merry with some pleasing tale."

Evidently he was himself a lover of old tales, and, as his father says, had often been sung to sleep by his grandfather, who tells him tales "meet and agreeing with thine infancy." As he comes from school laden with his books, his aunt, crazed with the injuries that have been done her, pursues him. Terrified, he cries on his grandfather and uncle for protection. But it is evident there is method in her madness, for the poor creature, who has lost hands as well as tongue, searches with her stumps among his books that he has thrown down, and with his help finds Ovid's *Metamorphoses*, a very favourite reading-book in English schools in the reign of Elizabeth, and one with which Shakspeare would be familiar, and turns up in it the tragic tale of Philomel and the rape of Tereus. From this scene we gather that the boy was well acquainted with poetry, with Tully's *Orations* also, which, in happier days, his aunt used to read to him, and with the *Tale of Troy*.

One more picture completes Shakspeare's gallery of child-portraits—the sketch of a boy at play, a perfect drawing in a few strokes. It is in *Coriolanus :* the wife and mother of the censor sit at their sewing, and to them comes Valeria to call upon them. The whole scene is so natural—I had almost said so modern—the greetings between the ladies and the compliments of the visitor on their industry might have been spoken to-day. Then she inquires for the child—

> " How doth your little son ?
> *Vir.* I thank your ladyship ; well, good madam."

And the grandmother puts in—

> " He had rather see swords and hear the drum than look upon his schoolmaster."

And the visitor responds—

> " O' my word the father's son : I'll swear 'tis a very pretty boy.

O' my troth, I looked upon him o' Wednesday half an hour together ; he has such a confirmed countenance. I saw him run after a gilded butterfly ; and when he caught it, he let it go again ; and after it again ; and over and over he comes and up again ; catched, it again ; or whether his fall enraged him, or how 'twas, he did so set his teeth and tear it ; O, I warrant how he mammocked it."

Here is a thorough child, a child at play. If some of these children seem in their apt and pretty answers at times too precocious, is it not because the children of that age were precocious and were brought up to be so ? The nursery was then not an end, only a means. The aim of the parent was not to preserve babyhood as long as might be, but to have quickly a capable and quick-witted son. The heroes of the nursery on whose deeds these little minds were fed were not little Tommies and Frankies, but Arthur and Roland, Guy of Warwick, and gay Robin Hood ; the children learned in Courts to be self-possessed and ready with repartee. Doubtless the great master of human nature drew children as he saw them.

CHAPTER VIII

SOME ROYAL CHILDREN

A MONG State Papers and such ancient documents,
here and there in the midst of chronicles of wars
or records of important political changes, comes
a little bit about the children: some letter showing a
trait of childish character, some note of expense incurred,
or arrangement for upbringing, things which if recorded
of other children are for the most part lost in domestic
correspondence, buried under piles of weightier matter.
We have seen William the Conqueror at five years old
playing at soldiers, and construing Cæsar's *Commentaries*
at nine. A curious little tale comes down to us of his
own boys, less creditable, but no less characteristic.
We can picture the three: Robert, high-spirited,
arrogant, jealous of his younger brothers, whom he
fancied his father loved better than himself; the
red-haired William, always ill-disposed and quarrelsome; Henry, devoted to his books, the good boy of
the family, winning for himself the title of Beauclerc,
and not impossibly irritating to his elders. These two,
provoked perhaps by some assertion of authority on
their elder brother's part, or in mere boyish mischief,
poured a pail of water from an upper window on
Robert's head. He was by that time of an age to wear

a sword, and drew it on them, and had their father not been at hand, serious mischief might have been done. In bitter resentment the elder lad left the Court not long after, and this childish quarrel was the seed of an estrangement between the brothers that lasted their lives long. In what old chronicle this story lurks I am unable to say; no modern historian gives it so far as I am aware. I find it in a little book of historical stories for children, published in 1846. No reference is given to the authority from which it is quoted, but if the evidence for it is shaky, it is so credible that one may say of it, *Si non è vero, è ben trovato.*

The boyhood of Edward III., on whose young shoulders such an early weight of responsibility rested, is painted vividly in Marlowe's *Tragedy of King Edward II.*, wherein the writer follows closely the chronicles of Holinshed and Stow, taking also some few details from Fabyan. This is a very gallant boyish figure; the keynote of modesty and courage is struck in his answer to his father, who would send him on an embassy to France:—

> " *King Ed.* Boy, see you bear you bravely to the King,
> And do your message with a majesty.
> *Prince Ed.* Commit not to my youth things of more weight
> Than fits a prince so young as I to bear,
> And fear not, lord and father, heaven's great beams
> On Atlas' shoulder shall not lie more safe
> Than shall your charge committed to my trust."

The boy is in a hard position between father and mother, as may be seen in his attempt to persuade the Queen to return—"Madam, return to England, and

please my father well." He is so pathetically sure he
can make reconciliation between them—

> "I warrant you, I'll win his highness quickly;
> He loves me better than a thousand Spencers."

He clings to his mother too. When Sir John Hainault
offers an asylum to the prince and the queen, his
answer is—

> "So pleaseth the queen my mother, me it likes:
> The King of England, nor the Court of France,
> Shall have me from my gracious mother's side."

The fear of this boy's heart being turned against him
barbs the sharpest arrow in the afflictions of the king—

> "Ah, nothing grieves me, but my little boy
> Is thus misled to countenance their ills."

When Edward is deposed, and Isabel seeks to make her
son king in his father's room, the boy answers, pointing
to his uncle, the Earl of Kent—

> "Mother, persuade me not to wear the crown:
> Let him be king—I am too young to reign."

He deeply distrusts Mortimer, and when his mother
will have him accompany her and her lover—"Come,
son, go with this gentle lord and me"—he answers,
"With you I will, but not with Mortimer," and cries
piteously on his uncle for help when they will carry
him away by force. The murder of the Earl of Kent at
last opens his eyes to the iniquity of his mother, and
the hand she had in that of his father. It is a stern
young judge who says to her—

> "If you be guilty, though I be your son,
> Think not to find me slack or pitiful."

The conclusion of the story, however, hardly belongs to Edward's childish years.

Glimpses are found in memoranda of royal disbursements of the babyhood of Henry V. (Madcap Harry), who was born at Monmouth, first Prince of Wales. He was but a sickly infant, and was put out to nurse with a Welshwoman, Johanna Waring, at Cornfield, about six or seven miles from Monmouth, where his cradle used to be shown. The Wardrobe Accounts note payments "for a long gown for the Lord Henry," and later on eightpence for harp-strings for him, and four shillings for seven books of grammar. Most likely Johanna spoilt him, and not improbably her "fond cockering" had much to answer for in his wild ungovernable youth ; still, later he did valiantly, and the seeds of good may have been sown in early days. He was extremely well-read in his Bible, we are told, and doubtless his first Scripture lessons were conned at Johanna's knee.

His son was king in his cradle, and at eight months old presided at the Council, sitting on his mother's lap. He spent his childhood at Windsor, and at six years old was placed under the tutelage of the Earl of Warwick. Mr. de Montmorency has noted a very curious and interesting entry in the records of the Privy Council (II. Hen. VI., vol. iii. p. 132) concerning the education of the young king. The Earl of Warwick submits his difficulty to the Council thus—

" That consideryng howe, blessed be God, the kyng is grown in years, in stature of his persone, and also in conceyte and knowleche of his hiegh and royale auctoritie and estate, the which naturally

causen hym, and from day to day as he groweth shal causen hym
more and more to grucche with chastysing and to lothe it." The
guardian, fearing lest the king should bear malice and visit it on
him later, asks the Council "trewely to assisten hym in the exercise
of the charge and occupacyon that he hath about the kyng's
persone, namely in chastysing of hym for his defaults, and support
the said Earle therein."

No whipping-boy here evidently, to stand between
the young king and the rod. The Note from which I
quote goes on: "It was a delightful position. The
theory of education demanded that the king should be
thrashed early and often, while the bloodiness of the
age rendered it probable that the king, as soon as he
came of age, would have his wretched guardian murdered
for doing his duty. The Privy Council were asked
therefore not only to sanction, but to order the use of
the rod in the upbringing of the royal boy. It was
not the first time the Council had had to interfere.
Before the year 1428 it had ordered—

"That the kyng be chastysed for his defaultes or trespas, that
for awe thereof he forbeare the more to do amys and intende the
more besily to vertue and lernynge."

In the same year the Council thus defined the course of
his schooling—

"Et faire estre apris des bons moeurs, literature, langages,
norture, et courtoisie, et autre enseignments tiel come a si grand
prince come loez en soit."

"It was," adds Mr. de Montmorency, "a fine ideal,
and, seconded by regular flogging, produced that unhappy person, King Henry VI. of England."

In quaint contrast to this is the comment of Timbs on the same extract in his *Schooldays of Eminent Men*: "It made him an accomplished scholar as well as truest Christian gentleman that ever sat upon a throne." So much for the verdicts of posterity at various periods, viewing events from differing standpoints. Both true in their measure. Unhappy Henry certainly was; scholar and gentleman also; but statesman, in days when capable statesmanship was needed, by no means, though whether in spite of or because of the floggings, who shall say? Like a later king who fell, he failed utterly to estimate the forces against him, or to understand the character of the times he lived in, and for this his education may have been to blame. That he was a usurper cannot be laid to his charge, since he was born one in the third generation, and did not grasp at a throne that was not rightly his.

Of the little Yorkist king, Edward V., whose sovereignty was so brief, we get our most vivid notion from Shakspeare's play quoted in the last chapter; but there is an interesting record of the regulations drawn up for the ordering of his little Court at Ludlow Castle, for his morning attendance at Mass, for his schooltime, his playtime, his meals. At the hour of meat "noble stories, as behoveth a prince to understand," were to be read to him; stories of "virtue, honour, cunning, wisdom, and deeds of worship."

Brief mention occurs of Richard III. having for his governess a lady of rank; and we also learn that in his childhood he was very fond of ball and taw. One little

EDWARD VI IN INFANCY
HOLBEIN

glimpse we get of Henry VIII. as a child, receiving Erasmus at Greenwich, who describes him as a well-bred, well-grown boy of nine, standing between his two sisters, Margaret, almost a woman at twelve years old, and soon to be the bride of the King of Scots, and the lovely little Mary, a chubby creature of four.

His only son, Edward VI., was a very delicate child and losing his mother at his birth, was placed in the charge of the Sidney family. Sir Henry Sidney as a child was appointed his companion and playfellow, and writes—

"I was by that most famous King Henry VIII. put to his sweet son, Prince Edward, my most dear master, prince, and sovereign, my near kinswoman being his only nurse, my father his Chamberlain, my mother his governess, my aunt in such place as among meaner personages is called a dry-nurse."

So soon as he could read, a precocious course of study began ; he learned philosophy and divinity with Sir Anthony Cooke, Greek and Latin with that learned crank, Sir John Cheke, while, under the instructions of Cranmer, he kept a journal of all his lessons in five different columns. He seems to have been a generous, well-disposed child from the little stories related of him. On his fifth birthday he received the gift of a silver service, probably with miniature cups and plates such as small children love, and several little friends were invited to spend the day with him. At the end of the feast he presented a piece to each child, keeping nothing for himself. He was brought up in great reverence for the Bible, and on one occasion, seeing one of his playfellows step on a big Bible to reach a toy he wanted, the little prince reproved him, and would not play with him any more.

Three little princesses, all of the same name, in successive generations, claim our attention. Elizabeth, daughter of Henry VIII. and Anne Boleyn, had a childhood of great vicissitudes. Born, as her father had been, in the palace at Greenwich, which had been the property of her grandmother, Elizabeth of York, after whom she was named, her advent, though she was not the longed-for son, was hailed by her father as most propitious, and her baptism was celebrated with great splendour, while her half-sister Mary, degraded from her position as Princess Royal, was commanded to attend upon her as lady-in-waiting. Magnificent robes were provided for the infant who, pending the arrival of a brother, was for a short while looked upon as future Queen of England. Ere she was three, however, all this brilliance was overclouded ; her mother was disgraced, discarded, beheaded, and but for the kindness of that mother's supplanter, Jane Seymour, the poor little girl would have found but a harsh fate. As it was, she seems to have been much neglected. She was sent down to Hunsdon in the charge of Lady Bryan, her governess, a relative of her mother, and among the State Papers of that date are found piteous appeals on her behalf for necessaries which it seemed no one's business to supply. Lady Bryan writes—

"She hath neither gown, nor kirtle, nor peticoat, nor no maner of linen, nor fore-smocks (pinafores), nor kerchiefs, nor rails, nor body stitchets (corsets), nor handkerchiefs, nor sleeves, nor mufflers, nor biggens (gaiters?)."

In another letter—

"God knoweth my Lady hath great pain with her great teeth, and they come very slowly forth, which causeth me to suffer Her Grace to have her will more than I would. I trust to God, an her teeth were well graft, to have Her Grace after another fashion than she is yet, so as I trust the King's Grace shall have great comfort in Her Grace. For she is as toward a child, and as gentle of conditions as I ever knew any in my life."

Her sister Mary, who was seventeen years older, writes to her father from Hunsdon in the same year, "My sister Elizabeth is in good health and a toward child." The next year saw the birth of the longed-for heir, and the two dispossessed sisters were at the christening. Mary held him at the font, and in the procession led her little four-year-old sister by the hand.

Lord Chancellor Wriothesley, seeing the little princess at six years old, professed himself charmed with her manners and her sprightly forwardness. She was a clever child and very well taught according to the custom of the day. She studied Latin and Greek with that learned man and gentle tutor, Roger Ascham, spoke and wrote French fluently, and had professors for dancing, (she was extremely vain in her achievements in this line,) and for music, playing the lute and virginalls. She excelled with her needle also, to judge by the specimen shown at Penshurst—an embroidered card-table top, and also the very handsome book cover which is figured in Green's *Short History*.

She seems to have been a warm-hearted little girl, for a great affection existed between her and her small brother and supplanter, and very loving little letters passed between the pair. She was a high-spirited child, and must have been pretty, to judge by her portraits as a young woman, which always represent her with straight, small features and the fair bright colouring and ruddy golden hair of the Tudors. Her younger aunt, Mary, for a short while Queen of France, and afterwards Duchess of Suffolk, had this complexion and very beautiful pale golden hair, less red in tint than that of Henry. Doubts of her legitimacy and devotion to the cause of her lovely cousin, Mary Queen of Scots, seem to blind a good many people to Elizabeth's unquestionable good looks in her youth; and, moreover, we have a tendency to forget that she was not always old, and it was when age was creeping on that her vanity increased, and she demanded compliments which it was not always easy to pay with sincerity.

She was fortunate in the article of step-mothers. With the two who so quickly followed on the death of Jane, and passed off the stage, she had little or nothing to do; but Katharine Parr was very kind to both her step-daughters, and between her and Elizabeth there was warm affection. After the death of the King the younger princess, now reinstated in the succession after her brother and sister, was placed in the guardianship of the Dowager Queen and her new husband, Sir Thomas Seymour. An old manor house in the village of Ewelme, near Wallingford, used to be shown as the

home in which some of Elizabeth's childish days were
passed, and in the garden a tree is pointed out as the
one in which she used to swing. I have not been able
to ascertain whether this belonged to the time which
she spent in the custody of the Seymours, or to her
earlier days, when she was bandied about from pillar
to post. We can well imagine her swinging or climbing
trees, for she was something of a hoyden, and her romps
with her guardian rather exceeded the bounds of propriety, and were, indeed, the cause of her removal; for
Queen Katharine found that freedoms were permitted
unbecoming the young lady's age, and had to speak
severely, and though there was no quarrel, she was
removed to other care.

With her later life we have here no concern, but
pass on to the youth of her god-daughter and namesake, James I.'s only daughter, who at six years old
was brought from her home at Holyrood, when her
father succeeded to the English crown. No question
was ever raised as to the beauty of this little lady, who
was early dubbed the Queen of Hearts, though perhaps
she owed the title as much to her gracious, loving
nature, which endeared her to all with whom she came
in contact, and the charm she inherited from her
fascinating Scottish grandmother, as to her fair skin,
brilliant dark eyes, and straight nose. She was not
quite so fair as her mother, Queen Anne of Denmark,
and had a darker shade of the Tudor russet in her locks
than had her godmother.

On her first arrival in England she was placed in

the care of the Countess of Kildare, who was a Howard, daughter of the Lord High Admiral. But her father found time in the midst of taking up the government of his new country to interest himself in the progress of his little girl, and as soon as she could manage her pen encouraged her to write letters, both to himself and to her brother Prince Henry, who was a few years her senior, and to whom she looked up with sisterly devotion, mingled with the admiration of a small girl for a big boy. In his replies he teases her just as a schoolboy of to-day might tease a little sister. When she was seven years old, the King, who is seldom allowed credit for the good sense he not infrequently displayed, decided to remove her from the distractions of the Court, and place her in the household of Sir John Harrington, at Combe Abbey, in Warwickshire. Here the child grew up in wholesome surroundings, with an immense park to ramble and play in, with guardians of quiet taste and excellent sense, and with admirable examples in their two children, John, in his sixteenth year, the bosom friend of her brother Prince Henry, and Lucia, just blossoming into womanhood, celebrated by both Ben Jonson and Daniell for the graces of her mind and person, and for her accomplishments, which a younger girl would be likely to emulate with eagerness. Elizabeth certainly did copy her model in many things, for Lucia had a great taste for gardening and for architecture, two hobbies which distinguished the Princess's later years. She had other playfellows, too, nearer her own age, and with Anne Dudley, Sir John's niece, formed a lasting friendship, Anne following her to the Palatinate on her marriage, and remaining through the troubled years that ensued, her most devoted friend and adherent. The only cloud on the happy country life was the separation from her brother, to whom she wrote—

"MY DEAR AND WORTHY BROTHER,

"I most kindly salute you, desiring to hear of your health; from whom, though I am now removed far away, none shall never be nearer in affection than your most loving sister,

"ELIZABETH."

This was written in her eighth year.

The quiet and order of the household must have been an excellent discipline for the child, who was of an eager and pleasure-loving disposition, and no doubt helped to form in her that constancy and firmness in troubles that stood her in such good stead in after life. "The habits of Combe Abbey," says her biographer, Miss Benger, "were as regular as those of a religious community." Her hours for lessons, in which she was very proficient, for play, for gardening, or attending to her pets, of which she had good store and always loved, were carefully apportioned; also the duties of her household, both of her playfellows and those who waited on her, over whom she was taught to rule as a little princess, being allowed to dispense favours and presents, a great pleasure to her, for she was always a most generous child. Her guardian wrote of her, "With God's assistance, we hope to do our Lady Elizabeth such service as is due to her princely endowments and

natural abilities, both which appear the sweet dawning
of future comfort to her royal father."

An amusing account is quoted in Miss Benger's
book of the state visit of the Princess Royal to Coventry.
The description is taken from the Corporation Annals—

"On Tuesday, the 13th of April, 1604, the Princess, Lady
Elizabeth, the King's eldest daughter, came from Combe Abbey,
nobly accompanied. Though scarcely eight years old, she was
sufficiently expert in horsemanship to have headed an equestrian
train in the old manner of the maiden Queen ; but the fashionable
usage of carriages attested the degeneracy of public taste, and
instead of this graceful exhibition was instituted a procession of
coaches, in one of which sate the Princess. . . . The city poured
forth men, women, and children to greet the royal child, whilst the
mayor and aldermen in scarlet robes, followed by the burgesses
attired in gowns and hoods, all well mounted, proceeded to Jabet's
Ash. . . . In this manner they proceeded to St. Michael's Church,
all the burghers standing at arms. The master of the Free School
preached a sermon, to which the little Princess had been taught
to listen with profound attention. She was then conducted to St.
Mary's Hall, where she dined, sitting for the first time in a chair
of state, of which the novelty might perhaps in part atone for the
uneasiness ; but on being presented with a silver gilt cup, she was
constrained to accept Lord Harrington's aid to sustain the weight
when she took it in her hand and received the civic pledge. From
St. Mary's Hall she went to the Free School and Library, and
thus made her progress through the streets, till she once more
found herself at Jabet's Ash, where the mayor and aldermen,
hitherto her constant satellites, with the usual ceremonies, took
their leave."

To loyal Coventry the little Princess was conveyed
during the alarms of the Gunpowder Plot, since it was
feared lest the conspirators might endeavour to get her
into their hands. She wrote a very solemn little letter

to her brother on the occasion, winding up with the words, " If God be for us, who can be against us ? "

She had been very religiously brought up by the Harrington family, who were of somewhat Puritan tendencies ; indeed, she was, perhaps, rather overdone with theology, after the fashion of the day. Her little brother Charles was competent to sustain a theological disquisition at ten years old ; and her small betrothed, the young Elector Palatine, who was about her own age, used to express himself in the most serious Calvinistic strain. She had been contracted to him in her cradle, and was married at an age which, in these days, would be considered childhood, being in her sixteenth year. But her marriage, and the history of her children, belong to another story.

Let us now turn to another Elizabeth, one of the third generation, niece and namesake to the last. This gentle little soul was of very different fibre to the two high-spirited Elizabeths who preceded her, and if ever child died of a broken heart, this little maiden surely did. Born towards the close of what Clarendon describes as "the halcyon time," before the coming storm, life smiled upon her opening years. Charles and Henrietta Maria were fond parents, and there was no oppressive regal state about the simple nursery life. Little glimpses are to be found of it in the private correspondence of Endymion Porter, Gentleman of the Bedchamber, who, like his master, loved children ; and also in the Memoir of the Queen, lately published, by Miss Taylor. It is amusing to read of Prince Charles, like

any other child, strongly objecting to take physic;
insomuch that the first letter his mother wrote him was
an exhortation to be a good boy and take it, else she
should be obliged to come herself and make him. In
a little letter of his own, written in a round text hand,
to his tutor, the Earl of Newcastle, the same subject is
touched on ; it evidently rankled—

"MY LORD,
    "I would not have you take too much physicke, for it
doth alwaies make me worse, and I think it will do the like with
you. I ride every day, and am ready to follow any directions from
you. Make haste back to him that loves you.
                                                "CHARLES P."

The stately King himself was not averse to romps
with the children. In the Porter letters we see him at
play with the little Villiers, of whom he was very fond,
especially of "pretty, sweet Moll," as he used to call
the eldest girl ; and to his own little girls he was a
very tender father. We can fancy the merry little
party at play in the great nurseries ; riding, perhaps, on
the old rocking-horse, which had belonged to their
father, already described in the fifth chapter, and seem
to know the children all by sight, so vividly are they
portrayed in the several groups by Vandyck in the
Royal collections and elsewhere. In one of these the
little Elizabeth appears ; a round-faced, chubby, con-
tented-looking little mortal, in a close cap, and long
frock down to her toes. She seems to be trying to
amuse and keep quiet the next child, Baby Anne.
The first sorrow that clouded the little life was the

death of this baby sister, very touchingly related in
Miss Taylor's book. In her last illness, this baby of
three, "being minded by those about her to call upon
God, even when the pangs of death were upon her, 'I
am not able,' saith she, 'to say my long prayer' (meaning the Lord's Prayer), 'but I will say my short one—
Lighten mine eyes, O Lord, lest I sleep the sleep of
death.' This done, the little lamb gave up the ghost."
The story is told by Fuller, on the authority of one of
the Princess's rockers.

The little one was taken from the evil to come;
Elizabeth was but a mite when sorrow and separation
came. From the time of the outbreak of the trouble in
Scotland there was but little peace for the royal nursery,
which was shifted from pillar to post. The mother took
her eldest girl to Holland, to hasten on her marriage
with the Prince of Orange, and London soon became so
disturbed, the children were hardly safe there. On the
hurried journey to Oxford, several of them had to sleep
in the same room with their father and mother—an
inconvenience which Mr. Porter, separated from his
"sweet Tom," envied his master. All too soon another
separation came as the war swept on its ruthless way.
The Queen fled to France, leaving her new baby in the
charge of the Countess of Morton, and the three middle
children fell into the hands of the Parliament, and were
placed in the custody of the Earl of Northumberland
at Sion House, where they seem to have been treated
with all kindness and respect. James must have
been about twelve years old, his little sister perhaps

nine or ten, and the Duke of Gloucester not above five.

When their father was brought as a prisoner from Holmby House to Hampton Court, they were allowed, on his earnest petition, to meet and dine with him at Maidenhead. Great must have been the joy of the little Elizabeth, grave beyond her years, and very loving, at seeing her father again, after so long and sad a separation. There could hardly have been any merry play, unless with the little Harry; for the King's mind was too full of the serious charges he had to give them. He impressed upon Elizabeth that she must not consent to any proposal of marriage without the sanction of her mother and eldest brother. Even the little one was gravely bidden to be loyal to his brother, obedient to his mother, and true to his religion; he showed later that he was not too young to understand. While Charles remained at Hampton Court he was allowed, from time to time, to "refresh himself with the company" of the children, and no doubt often played with them in the big and beautiful gardens there.

After his attempted escape, when he was immured in Carisbrooke Castle, the three children were brought to St. James's Palace, in the grounds of which was played that historic game of Hide and Seek, by means of which James got away, and was spirited over to the Hague to his sister. After this, the Earl of Northumberland refused to have the responsibility of the other two any longer, and it was thought desirable they should be in the country, where they would be less

likely to be made a centre for disaffection; so they
were sent to the Earl's sister, the Countess of Leicester,
at Penshurst. This was a happy change for the little
Princess. The Countess treated them with the tenderness
of a mother, and the respect due to the children of
her sovereign, while her eldest daughter, the young
widow, Lady Sunderland, became the object of Elizabeth's enthusiastic devotion. No doubt the little girl
enjoyed playing with Dorothy's babies ; " Poppet " and
Penelope and the baby Harry, born since his father's
death. Here she and her brother had a tutor, Mr.
Lovel, with whom they learned Latin and French ;
and we may suppose Lady Sunderland would instruct
the Princess in needlework, and very likely in lute-
playing, in which she was herself very proficient.

At the time of their father's execution they must have
been at Leicester House in London, as they were taken
to receive his last blessing and farewell, he being lodged
at St. James's the night before. Elizabeth was then of
an age to understand the terrible sorrow, and she wept
most bitterly, her little brother crying too to see her cry.
The King took them both on his knee, and admonished
them of their duty and loyal observance to the Queen,
their mother, and to their eldest brother. They commanded their tears, and gave him, says Sir Thomas
Herbert, an eye-witness, " such pretty and pertinent
answers as drew tears of love and joy from his eyes;
and then, praying God Almighty to bless them, he
turned about, expressing a tender and fatherly affection.
Most sorrowful was this parting, the young Princess

shedding tears and crying most lamentably, so as moved others to pity, that formerly were hard-hearted ; and at opening the bed-chamber door, the King returned hastily from the window and kissed 'em and blessed 'em ; so parted."

Poor little maid ! no doubt Lady Leicester and her daughter did their best to comfort her, but she drooped, and, indeed, their kindness was her undoing, for rumour coming to the Parliament that Charles Stuart's children were treated with too much respect, Mr. Speaker Lenthall went down to Penshurst to investigate, and finding them served at a table apart, their removal to their father's former prison at Carisbrooke was ordered ; and there one Sunday, not long after, in one of those gloomy rooms, the little Princess, who had been suffering from a feverish attack, was found dead, her cheek resting on her open Bible.

CHAPTER IX

CONCERNING PEDAGOGUES

GRADUALLY as the centuries went on changes came about in education, both in its ideals and in its methods. With the new enthusiasm for learning which from the dawn of the fifteenth century was spreading through the whole continent of Europe, issuing in the invention of printing, which in its turn quickened and developed it, came a new conception which still holds its ground, and sees in education less a training of the child for his future life than a method for the manufacture of scholars. Along with this went the gradual secularization of life. Not only was the monk less of a power with the layman, but he was himself less devoted to religious ideals. Very many embraced the monastic life purely from love of learning, some from less praiseworthy motives. Religion ceased to dominate as it had done, though still until some time after the Reformation it was the basis of education. For a long time yet churchmen were the chief instructors, but with the Renaissance the lay schoolmaster begins to appear.

The new ideas of learning had considerable influence on schools. One change which bore hardly on the children was the much increased harshness of discipline the rod for failure to understand, for stupidity as well as for idleness, for slowness as much as for naughtiness. In all pictures of schools the pedagogue now always appears armed with the birch. And the lessons were so much harder ; the revival of classical learning brought in a taste for a purer latinity than that of the schoolmen, and this meant an increased devotion to grammar, of all studies the least suited to a young child. The *Catechism on Common Things*, the *Vulgaria*, the *Bestiaries*, were more and more giving place to Lilly, whose grammar was, in the reign of Henry VIII., even ordained by Act of Parliament. The children wept and were beaten, yet not without protest, for every writer on education—and there were many—deprecates the abuse of the rod. The parents themselves were as stern as the schoolmasters. Agnes Paston in the fifteenth century, sending her little son to school, sends with him a request that the master will "well belashe him !" And this, not from cruelty or an unnatural aversion to her child, but simply as a mother of to-day might write begging that the boy should be regularly physicked. A story is told of Sir Peter Carew's little boy that he was such a stubborn little truant that his father led him back to a school in a leash like a hound, and no doubt thrashed him like a hound too.

One cause tending to excessive severity in schools, which I think is often overlooked, is that when the Renaissance had kindled in many young men an enthusiastic zeal for learning, they frequently became teachers in order to earn money to pursue their own studies. It is easy to understand the impatience of such a youth with childish idleness or stupidity, and his utter lack of comprehension of the average childish capacity. Under provocation he might resort to that more cruel punishment, depicted in Mercier's picture of a schoolmaster, of lifting up the unlucky boy by the ears.

In the reign of Elizabeth the children took the matter into their own hands and made themselves heard. Quite a number of boys ran away from Eton, where the head master, Nicholas Udall, was noted for his addiction to the four apple-twigs, and the event was taken notice of by no less a person than the Secretary of State. The matter was discussed at a dinner party at his rooms at Windsor, where were present several of the Privy Council, Sir Henry Wotton, afterwards Provost of Eton, and Mr. Ascham, who had been tutor to the Queen. Sir William Cecil expressed strong disapproval of Udall's severity, saying that to beat a child for faults in his lesson was to drive him from his book. After dinner Sir Richard Sackville drew Mr. Ascham aside into a window, and talked of the matter further, being very anxious that his own little grandson Robert should not suffer as he himself had suffered as a child. Under Sir Richard's persuasions Ascham, gentle and retiring as he was, put forth his book called *The Schoolmaster*, earnestly advocating the methods of love rather than of fear in tuition. An oft-quoted example was that of Lady Jane Grey, who having had severe parents and a gentle tutor, so loved her book that at thirteen she was well read in Greek as well as in Latin, and preferred studying Plato to a hawking party in the park. Locke, writing a century later, pleads against the rod being used to quicken tardy scholars, and would have it reserved for moral faults, and those of the worst, lying or obstinate rebellion and stubbornness.

Ascham's book, by the order in which he would have a child study, shows the hold which grammar had already gained—that is, grammar in the narrower sense in which the word is now used ; anciently it included the whole art of reading, writing, and speaking. When the boy had mastered the eight parts of speech, and learned to join substantive with adjective, noun with verb, he is to construe a simple sentence ; unlike the earlier method by which the child first learned the Latin names of common things, and to put little sentences together, and then went on to "his Donet." A little grammar for young children, more elementary than Lilly, was Holt's *Mylke for Chyldrene*, in which, by way of making them remember the different cases, there was a print of the human hand with the five principal cases printed on the five fingers, the sixth on the ball of the thumb. This was probably the origin of the expression hand-book, an earlier thing, it would appear, than the horn-book. These latter were used in school as well as in the nursery for small beginners ; the first pages of Coote's *Schoolmaster* were to be obtained in this form, for, as he observed, parents would grudge to buy books for a little young child who would soon tear them.

This book was evidently intended for the ABC or

First Grade school, and we can fancy the little country lads conning it, and learning to distinguish "A fowl flying over a foul way," or "A mill a mile from the town;" perhaps reading a very moral little tale of fetching a nag from pasture. It is wonderful how many little hints and touches of schoolboy life are to be gleaned from the pages of these ancient lesson-books. One of the most fascinating in this respect is *The School Colloquies of Corderius*, edited by Hoole, to teach boys to speak Latin. For in the Grammar Schools of that day the boys were expected to talk together in Latin, as girls in modern schools were required to do in French.

There is a quaint presentment of the little new boy, just come to school; he is taught to be very polite, greets his schoolfellow, and is greeted by him with a Salve. He soon gets into trouble, for he proposes to play in schooltime, and is promptly snubbed by a rather self-righteous elder. Those who imagine that the schooldays of old invariably consisted of tyranny on the part of the master and fear on that of the boy, should read a very charming little dialogue between the pedagogue and a small child who was evidently rather a pet. After the customary "Salve, Preceptor," the Master begins: "Whence come you so very early?" "From our chamber." "When got you up?" "A little before six, Master." "You are up early: who waked you?" "My brother." "Did you say your prayers?" "As soon as my brother had combed me I said them." "How?" "Kneeling upon my knees and holding up my hands together, I said the Lord's

Prayer with a thanksgiving." "In what tongue?" "In the English tongue." "Who sent you to me?" "Nobody." "What, then?" "I came of my own accord." "My little sweetheart, what a fine thing it is to have a good wit! Is it not breakfast time?" "I am not hungry yet." "What would you do then?" "I would repeat the nouns we use to say every day, if you please to hear me." Then follows a simple Latin lesson, after which the Master says, "Go now and ask the maid for your breakfast." "I had rather have it of you, Master, if it may be no trouble to you." "Oh, how I love you for that saying! Come, follow me: I will give you something that is good because you have done your business well. What is this?" "White bread and dried figs." "Count them." "Oh, pretty little boy! Now get your breakfast at your own leisure."

One boy brings his breakfast to school, another says his mother gave him some before he started, so he will ply his book while his comrade eats. The hours for dinner seem divergent. One boy dines as early as half-past eight in the morning, and says his family usually do in summer. Another does not dine till half-past ten, when his father, who is an Alderman, returns from the Common Council; he is therefore excused from the singing of Psalms in Hall. Some are boarded out, and while one pays six farthings or doits for his dinner, his friend pays four sols or stivers. A little boy forgets his books and has to run home for them, being sharply chidden by an upper boy, probably prefect or monitor. The monitors seem more severe than the master: "If

the monitor catch us talking," says one little fellow,
"he will say we are prating." There is a curious bit
about pens; a boy comes with a handful of goose-
quills, plucked from his mother's geese, and bargains
with his schoolfellows for payment in money or kind—
sealing-wax, blotting-paper, and so forth. One little
boy, not eight years old, is chidden for being unwilling
to lend his pen. The lead pencil, it would seem, was
unknown, and each boy brought his own ink-horn
filled with home-made ink—sometimes very bad. The
price of writing-paper, we gather, was three halfpence
a quire, with a piece of blotting-paper thrown in. A
German penknife, bought of a pedlar in the market
place for twopence, figures in one Colloquy.

We get some notion of the books a boy was
expected to be provided with in the seventeenth
century: *The Grounds of Grammar*, *School Colloquies*,
Terence, *Tully*, with a French translation, *Cato*—a very
popular school-book for a long time; not to know your
Cato was to be unlettered indeed—a Dictionary, and
a paper book for dictation lessons. A *Virgil* is
mentioned which was lent and pawned by the un-
principled borrower for threepence! A very praiseworthy scholar saves up his money and buys a *Terence*,
well bound and gilt for tenpence. A notion may be
gathered by the way of the forwardness of children in
that day by the incidental mention of a little brother of
five years old, not yet big enough for school, who talks
Latin fluently, and this does not seem to have been an
exceptional accomplishment.

A pretty little dialogue sets forth how the master takes a deserving pupil for a country walk, bidding him change his clothes, lest he should "bedusty" his new ones, and take his "bonegrace" (umbrella) for the sun.

Similar little personal details are to be gleaned from Seager's *School of Vertue*, published about the middle of the sixteenth century; it is somewhat of the same order as the *Babee's Boke*, but intended rather for school boys than little pages. The boy is bidden to rise early and make his bed, to dress carefully, to get his satchel and be off to school, and be sure not to forget pens, ink, and paper. Good manners are inculcated; in the street he is bidden to put off his cap to those he meets, to call for his schoolfellows by the way; on arriving in school to salute the masters and the other boys, and go straight to his place and at once begin his lessons. On the way home the boys should walk two and two orderly, not running in heaps like a swarm of bees. On reaching home he salutes his parents and waits at table. For, as the little pages waited on their lord, in middle-class houses the children served. One section is headed "How to order thyself in church;" the directions are to pray kneeling or standing, to behave comely, and not to chatter.

A useful little bit gives precise instruction how to take a message: first the child was to be sure he understood the sense of it—those who have any experience of an eager child will understand the importance of this. He was to make humble obeisance to the person to whom sent, and deliver his message "in words well-pleasing," returning straight with the answer as exact as possible. These little trivialities seem to set the boy for whose behoof they were composed before us in his habit as he lived. It adds to the interest to know that these maxims were written in the reign of Queen Mary.

A somewhat similar little book, Symon's *Lesson of Wysedom for all manner Chyldren*, would seem specially suited for those in elementary schools in the country, for it is the hood, not the cap, the child is bidden to doff, and the hood was the wear of the little peasant. Also where the grammar-school boy says "*Salve*" he is to say "God-speed." Moreover, there is not so much about behaviour in the street, but the boy is forbidden to throw stones at dogs or pigs, to climb walls after fruit or birds' nests, or break windows ; neither must he play in church. He is to get home by daylight, and 'ware fire and water, brooks and wells. At school he must take care not to lose book, cap, or gloves, else he'll be whipped. (Book in the singular seems to imply horn-book.) The concluding advice that he should learn fast that he may come to be a bishop some day points to the road that led through these chantry schools to the highest offices in Church or State, and was the surest way to preferment for the villager's son.

A very sensible little book on the training of quite young children was written by Richard Mulcaster, Master of Merchant Taylors' school in the days of Elizabeth ; this was addressed to parents, and dealt with "the verie infante from his first entry till he be thought fit to pass to the grammar school." The writer takes it that the father and mother will be themselves the first teachers, and says that "since everything while it be pretie and yonge draws liking" there will be more risk of "dalying and too fond cokkering" than of over-severity. He begins with the feeding, and adds a caution against cramming and over-loading, especially of giving meat to young children. The clothing, too, should be warm and light, and the little body not burdened with heavy dress. It was a pity more heed was not paid to this excellent advice ; but to judge by the portraits of infants of this and two or three succeeding generations, the little ones, even boys, were impeded with long, full petticoats, cramped with stiff stomachers, and weighed down with brocades. Mrs. Earle records a pair of stays, preserved in an old colonial family, which, tradition says, were actually worn by a little boy of five years old ! And some portraits of American children show them in skirted coats and long, embroidered waistcoats. In England, however, the boys, once they were breeched, were better off in their little doublets and trunk-hose.

In those days the child was usually taught to read so soon as he could speak, and Mulcaster, like John Locke nearly two centuries later, rather leans to teaching him to read Latin first, as being easier in spelling and pronunciation, while his own tongue he naturally picks up from those about him. Also in these young years he is to learn much by rote, especially what will lay the foundations of religion and obedience. Writing

BOYS PLAYING PEGTOP

PAYE

will follow, and when some strength of hand is gained, drawing, "cozen-germain to faire writing;" colouring may be added rather by way of amusement. Music, both singing and instrumental, is to be taught early; it is healthy for children to sing ; Nature makes them cry and shout to open their lungs. "Music," he adds, "is a medicine from heaven for our sorrows on earth; princess of delites, and delite of princes." Dancing also he specially recommends as well as all other bodily exercises, for directly a child is made to sit still for a time at lessons, he needs the more exercise in play-time. Playing at ball, or whip-top, "the whirligig of the ancients," are suggested, and it is urged that with the latter the child should have plenty of room to avoid stooping, and should be encouraged to whip with both hands as well as to drive his hoop with either. These are all best in the open air, but in bad weather can be played in a gallery ; only let the child make as much noise as he likes. Tops, says the author, are in season in Lent, and adds sententiously, if these games make children quarrelsome, the parties must bear the blame, not the play. Swimming he enjoins in summer time, showing that our ancestors were not quite so much afraid of cold water as some would have us believe. He, like Mr. Peacham in the next century, complained that school hours in England were far too long ; six to eleven and one to six were those usual in grammar schools in his day, and he considered seven to ten and two to five would be quite sufficient. It certainly would, as children began to attend at seven years old.

Such were the ideals set before middle-class and country children and those who had the breeding of them; for the young courtier Ascham adds many bodily accomplishments to those of scholarship, which included the fluent speaking of Latin and French, as well as the study of grammar he held so needful. "Therefore," he says, "to ride comely, to run fair at the tilt of ring, to play at all weapons, to shoot fair in bow or surely in gun, to vault lustily, to run, to leap, to wrestle, to swim; to dance comely, to sing and play on an instrument cunningly; to hawk, to hunt, to play at tennis and all pastimes generally which be joined with labour, used in open place and by the daylight, containing either some fit exercise for war, or some pleasant pastime for peace,—be not only comely and decent, but also very necessary for a courtly gentleman to use."

So much for the boys. If little has yet been said about the girls, it was not because their education was neglected, but that it was so much a matter of course it hardly called for separate discussion; it was implied with that of their brothers. As we have seen already in the Canon quoted by Mr. de Montmorency, the education of the girls as well as the boys was provided for, and the Statute of Richard II., in answer to the petition concerning the children of the labouring class, mentioned by the same authority, provides that either son or daughter may be sent to school. The elementary teaching was practically the same; the little girls studied their horn-book side by side with their brothers, and learned Latin and singing. It was not till the time

of the Puritan ascendancy that we meet with the first
question whether they should learn Latin or no. Their
education was not carried quite so far as that of the
boys, as they did not go to grammar school, and those
of the upper classes were often educated at home by
governess or tutor. Governesses are referred to as early
as the reign of King Stephen, but on the whole we
gather that, except in convent schools, the girls studied
chiefly with a tutor, and the lady was rather a "governess for manners," acting as chaperon and instructing
in needlework and domestic duties. Royal princesses
usually had tutors. Vives was tutor to Princess, afterwards Queen, Mary, and compiled a Latin primer for
her use, and she was also taught by Andrew Borde,
who wrote a very curious book on geography, containing descriptions of the various races of men inhabiting
the then known portions of the globe, illustrated with
quaint wood-cuts, coarsely executed, but clever. In
plan it was not unlike a book of fifty years back, called
Far off and Near Home.

Boarding schools for girls, except in convents, seem
hardly to be found before the seventeenth century,
when we read of one set up at Putney by Mrs. Bathsua
Makyns; but no doubt the boarding of girls in Court
or in great houses as bower-maidens fulfilled much the
same end, especially when many girls were thus brought
up together, a governess being kept for manners, and
the tutor to the pages giving instruction in Latin and
French, music and dancing.

On convent schools for girls Mr. de Montmorency

has an interesting note : The earliest reference to girls'
schools after the Council of Cloves-Hoo deals with the
famous Carow Nunnery near Norwich. This, he says,
seems from its foundation in 1146 to have taken as
boarders and educated the daughters of the best families
in the diocese of Norwich. A still more famous girls'
school was at Dartford Nunnery in Kent, founded
about 1355. Bridget, fourth daughter of Edward IV.,
was a nun in this house. According to an enactment
by Archbishop Greenfield of York (who died in 1513),
"young gentlewomen who come to the nunneries either
for piety or breeding, should wear white veils to distinguish them from the professed who wore black ones."
This shows the ancient custom to have been identical
with that of the nunnery schools of our own day. The
same writer gives an interesting list of the pupils who
were at St. Mary's Nunnery in Winchester when it was
suppressed in 1539: Bryget Plantagenet, Mary Pole,
Bryget Coppeley, Elizabeth Phyllpot, Margery Tyrell,
Johñne Barnabe, Amy Dyngley, Elizabeth Dyngley,
Jane Dyngley, Susan Tycheborne, Elizabeth Tycheborne, Mary Justyce, Agnes Aylmer, Emme Bastne,
Myldred Clarke, Anne Lacy, Isolde Apulgate, Elizabeth
Legh, Mary Legh, Alienor Merth, Johñne Sturgys,
Johñne Ffyldes, Johñne Ffrancs—many of them Hamp-
shire names, and most of them distinguished.

Mulcaster, in his *Positions*, quoted above, says that
girls should learn to read and write, sing and play, and
study both the learned and the spoken languages ; for
the last he considered women had a special aptitude.

They were also to be taught religion and "civil and domestic duties." They might attend the infant school at the same age as boys, though he remarks that girls are more forward and prattle sooner. The amount of learning bestowed ought to be in accordance with the position in life. He thus sums up the matter for the upper-class child : " A young gentlewoman is thoroughly furnished which can read plainly and distinctly, write fair and swiftly, sing clear and sweetly, play well and finely, understand and speak the learned languages, and those tongues also which the time most embraceth, with some logical help to chop, and some rhetorick to brave." His view was that the girl was to be trained "in respect of marriage," and he frankly says that the training of boys is of more importance.

In Holinshed's *Chronicles* there is a passage describing the accomplishments of the ladies of Elizabeth's Court which fairly corresponds to this. They were, he says, skilful in Latin, Greek, and modern languages, in spinning, needlework, and music, while the elder ladies excelled in surgery and herbalist lore.

Another interesting question, much debated in later times, Mulcaster touches on, namely, whether all should be equally educated. His decision is that all should be taught to read and write ; but since there may be too many learned men for the good of the State, too many "gaping for preferment," he would not encourage all to pursue the higher walks of scholarship ; but his choice would not be between rich and poor, but according to capacity. He would cull out from all classes boys of ability, and also those who " in tender age show themselves obedient to school orders, will not lightly offend ; but if they do, will take their punishment gently, not wrangling or quarrelling with their fellows, but ever ready to put-to a helping hand." These boys he would select for special training, unlike the system of our own day, by which the stupid and those unlikely to profit are kept longest at school, while the clever, quick boys pass through and leave at an earlier age, to forget in a year or two all that might have been of value to them in after life. Truly it would be well if we were not too proud to profit by the wisdom of our forefathers.

CHAPTER X

PLEASANT PASTIMES

ENGLISH life in the olden time was full of colour
and variety. Until the Puritan ascendancy
Religion did not place amusement in the hostile
camp and turn her back upon it, but rather adopted
and controlled it. The Church had her holidays, her
plays, her games, as well as her discipline, and in all
the children had their share. Life in the Middle Ages
was often hard and rough for the little ones, but at
least it was merry. In all the great religious functions
they bore their part, as singing boys or taper-bearers,
and the little maidens walked in procession, as they do
still in Catholic countries, on the Jours de Marie or
Corpus Christi, in their little white veils and wreaths
scattering flowers. Any one who knows much of
children knows how they love a pageant, trebly if they
take part in it themselves.

Many quaint customs of the various seasons, old
already when Christianity came, were found deep-
rooted in the memories of the people ; some of Saxon
origin, some possibly coming down from the Druids
some, it may be, left by the Roman provincials. The
Church did not stamp these out, but adapted them to

her own ends. Such were the Rogation processions, the May-day games, the Midsummer fires on the Eve of St. John Baptist, the Hock-cart, the Katterning, the Wassail bowl, the Yule log, and the Christmas Mummers. To these the Church added stories from the Bible, and legends of the saints, represented as Mysteries or Miracle Plays, or acted parables, called Moralities. Little troops of children to sing or dance were an essential part of all these, and some of them required child actors. Of all these amusements only a wan tradition of the Maypole and the Mummers has survived to our own day.

In some places, notably in Ashby-de-la-Zouche and in certain parts of Hampshire, the old Mumming Play is still acted, having been handed down, in most by word of mouth alone, though I believe in one or two it has been committed to the safe keeping of a book. A little story by Miss Yonge, written about the middle of the last century, called *The Christmas Mummers*, preserves the tradition as it used to be followed in Otterbourne, and this corresponds exactly, even to its corruptions, with what my nurse recollected as used in her childhood at Purbrook, a village on the landward side of Portsdown Hill. In both cases—I am told also in Ashby-de-la-Zouche—St. George has become hopelessly mixed with King George, the reigns of four successive Electors of Hanover of that name having confused the rural mind; but in the Middle Ages the recollection of the prowess of St. George in slaying the Dragon was fresher in remembrance. In Hampshire,

too, the Turkish Knight was invariably apostrophized,
"Get up, get up, you *curly* dog!"

The mummers used to go the round of the parish,
calling at every house of importance, and were usually
admitted to the hall or house-place, where they began
their performance with this chorus—

> "I wish you a Merry Christmas,
> And a Happy New Year,
> A pantry-full of good roast beef,
> And barrels full of beer."

Then Father Christmas comes to the front—

> " Room, room, brave gallants, room,
> I've just come to show you some merry sport and game ;
> To help pass away
> This cold winter day.

> " Old activity, new activity,
> Such activity as never was seen before,
> And belike will never be seen no more."

> " Here comes I, Old Father Christmas, Christmas, Christmas !
> Welcome or welcome not,
> I hope Old Father Christmas
> Will never be forgot.

> " All in this room there shall be shown,
> The dreadfullest battle that ever was known ;
> So walk in St. George, with thy free heart,
> And see whether thou canst claim peace for thine own part."

St. George then steps forth with—

> " In comes I, St. George, St. George, the man of courage bold,
> With my broad sword and spear, I won ten crowns of gold.

> " I fought that fiery dragon,
> And drove him to the slaughter ;
> And by that deed I won
> The King of Egypt's daughter.

> " Therefore if any man dare enter this door,
>   I'll hack him small as dust ;
>   And after send him to the cook-shop,
>   To be made into mince-pie crust."

The Turkish Knight thereupon arrives, and says—

> " Here comes I, the Turkish Knight,
>   Just come from Turkey land to fight ;
>   I'll fight thee, St. George, St. George,
>   Thou man of courage bold ;
>   If thy blood be too hot,
>   I'll quickly fetch it cold."

After a good deal of dialogue, they fight with wooden swords, and much clatter, but when the Turkish Knight falls, St. George exclaims with dismay—

> " Oh, only behold, and see what I have been and done,
>   Cut and slain my brother, just like the evening sun ! "

The Prince of Morocco, father of the fallen knight, now appears upon the scene, and with him the doctor, armed with an immense bottle of " elecampane." The last of the characters is Little Johnny Jack, carrying all his family, a numerous one, on his back, in the shape of all the dolls the actors have been able to collect from their sisters, and he carries round the hat.

The version quoted by Mr. Halliwell Phillips, in his *Popular Rhymes*, differs considerably from this; his is probably the older and more authentic. He has Prince Paradine instead of the Prince of Morocco, and Little Devil Doubt in place of Little Johnny Jack; his lines also run more smoothly, as though less corrupted by the local tongue. There used also to be an old Mumming Play for Easter, connected with the ceremony of the

Peace or Pasch Egg. The tradition of this lingered
late in Yorkshire, as readers of Mrs. Ewing's charming
stories will remember.

There were many other Christmas customs ; that of
the Boy Bishop, reigning from Santa Claus to Childermass, has already been described. The Yule-log was
brought in with ceremonies of singing and dancing, in
which the children bore their part ; then there were the
Twelfth Night festivities, with the Lord of Misrule,
sometimes a child, chosen by drawing a bean, hence
called sometimes King of the Bean. This enshrines
curious memories of the Three Kings in its rhymes of
Lavender's blue, and *I saw Three Ships*. To some old
Pagan rite, probably given a meaning connected with
Purgatory, belongs the rather dangerous game of Snap-
dragon, snatching plums from a bowl of flaming spirit.
The German Christmas tree, so far as I can gather,
seems to have had no place in England till comparatively
recent times.

Little children singing probably formed part of the
old Rogation processions for blessing the fields, which
survived the Reformation in the shape of " beating the
bounds ; " less pleasant for the children, as it became
the custom to flog a few boys in order to impress the
parish boundaries on their memories! May Games
were chiefly for older young people, but without doubt
the children helped to bring in the green boughs and
deck the May-pole with garlands, or build Robin Hood's
Bower ; and they formed part of the May Queen's
Court, dancing hand in hand round the May-pole,

perhaps with those pretty twining ribbons, which have
been introduced of late from some old custom. Children,
with their love of apples, would highly appreciate the
ceremonies of St. Katharine and St. Clement, whose
days fall near together, when the apples are stored.
The young folk used to go to every well-to-do house in
the parish, collecting apples and beer for a feast, with
these lines—

> " Katharine and Clement be here, be here ;
> Some of your apples, and some of your beer :
> Some for Peter, and some for Paul,
> And some for Him Who made us all ;
> Clement was a good man ;
> For his sake give us some,
> Not of the worst, but some of the best ;
> And God will send your soul to rest."

This custom survived long in Worcester, and in the last
century the Cathedral Chapter kept up the practice of
preparing a spiced bowl of wine on that day, called the
Kattern bowl.

The Mysteries and Moralities gradually made way
for Masques and Interludes of a more secular character,
and in descriptions of these there is very often mention
of children, sometimes dressed as fairies, reciting compli-
mentary lines, sometimes as little imps, wearing comic
heads, such as those in the old illumination mentioned
in an earlier chapter, where a little boy appears to be
preaching to a company of stags, hares, asses, pigs, apes,
goats, etc. In the masques got up for the entertainment of Queen Elizabeth, or of James I. and Queen
Anne, we often read of the Children of the Chapel
Royal being employed.

THE TRAVELLING SHOWMAN
JOHN HOPPNER

PLEASANT PASTIMES 157

School Plays were frequently given, especially about the time of the Renaissance, when Greek Plays were so much in fashion. The Westminster Play survives to this day. A few years ago the *Athenæum* published some very curious old accounts of expenses in connection with the production of this entertainment in 1564 and 1606. They were quoted in *Social Life under the Stuarts;* they contain such quaint entries as— " Bestowed upon three gentlewomen that did attyre ye children iiid.—For sugar candee for ye children iiid.— For buttered beere for ye children being horse xiid." In most schools these traditional plays were put down by Puritan influence, and never revived.

Above all, there were the amusements of the local Wakes and Fairs. In those days, when the sending of goods was slow and difficult, and attended with much risk, so that shops as a rule did not attempt to supply foreign goods, the Fair was a great institution. I have already touched on the merchandise, the toys, the gingerbread, the peppermint-drops, to be obtained—far more highly valued no doubt when they were only to be bought once a year—but little has yet been said of the entertainments, the tumblers, the peep-shows, Punch and Judy, and the puppet-show. Puppets came in with the clockwork figures and " moving Jacks " that adorned several old church clocks, coming out to strike the hour. There is record of a Puppet Play as early as the end of the fifteenth century, mentioned by Strutt in his *Sports and Pastimes*, and in the next century some are referred to in *Gammer Gurton's Needle*. They soon became a great feature at Bartholomew Fair, and at Southwark a play of the Creation of the World, followed by Noah's Flood, was performed by puppets, the entertainment being wound up by singing and dancing by a child of eight years old.

Punch and Judy did not arrive in this country till the seventeenth century, having been first introduced in Naples in the year 1600. But when it did come it came to stay. While the puppet play gave way before the pantomime, and has practically vanished from the scene, to this day you may see a little crowd of children collect at the first squawk of Punch's unmistakable voice, and the roll of his drum. While at the Fair we must not forget the merry-go-round and the flying boats. What their precise antiquity may be I could not venture to say, but I make no doubt the children of the olden time enjoyed these wild delights, and were as sick and giddy afterwards as the immortal Jackanapes and his friend Tony.

The whole repertoire of the circus and variety entertainment is as old as the nation. The Saxon glee-man was not only a minstrel, but a juggler and acrobat as well, and he was succeeded by the mountebank, who travelled from Fair to Wake, often accompanied by a dancing bear. Besides the ninth-century picture, already mentioned, of a juggler throwing up three balls and three knives, there are very early ones of acrobats tumbling or standing on head or hands. There are some very funny pictures belonging to the thirteenth century, in a manuscript in the Cotton

Library, of morrice-dancing, with its varieties of egg-dance, sword-dance, and so forth, which must have highly entertained the juvenile spectators. Leaping through hoops, as circus performers do now, feats on the trapeze, walking on stilts, and other like achievements, are represented in plates from *The Vaulting Master*, a book published in 1652.

In the days when boys learned horsemanship as a fine art, and the "*manége* of the great horse" meant something more than merely keeping your seat upon his back, equestrian feats must have been doubly interesting, and even possible to rival so soon as little legs could stretch across the saddle. Boys were encouraged to attempt all feats of strength and skill for training in chivalry, and when too little for a real horse, would play at tournaments on hobby-horses. A curious old print in Strutt shows a little fellow mounted on a headless wooden horse, dragged by two other boys, armed with a long spear, and tilting at a quintain set up upon a pole; sometimes this quintain would represent a Turk or Saracen. Little boys were allowed to play at water quintain, and lest they should spoil their clothes by a tumble into the water, are in one picture tilting stark naked. In this case a tub serves for quintain. This picture is from a Bodleian manuscript dated 1343. Another shows boys rowing in a lake, one standing up at the back of the boat with his pole; not unlike the ancient game of push-ball recently revived.

Three very curious illustrations, one of which is

dated 1344, show boys' games. In one, two boys, foot to foot, one on a stool, the other standing, are trying to pull each other over ; in another they are both on the floor, also foot to foot, holding a stick between them. The last shows how ancient is the time-honoured hoax, popular as a method of receiving a new boy at school. Three (apparent) seats were placed in a row, covered with a rug, the middle one being a pail of water, and two boys with great ceremony invite the new-comer to take a seat between them ; as he does so, they rise abruptly, and he plunges into the pail to their huge delight.

A picture of a dancing bear is found as early as the tenth century in a manuscript book of prayers, and one of the thirteenth shows a bear standing on his head, and in another he has a monkey riding on his back—a jackanapes, as he used to be called.   In the same century there were performing horses, doing just the same tricks as they do in the circus of to-day ; and in the year 1334 there is a picture of some dancing dogs. The clown, with his painted cheeks and his venerable jests, can no doubt claim a like antiquity.

The Wild Beast Show was an early form of entertainment. No doubt children who visited London would be taken to see "those roaring boys, the lions," as Mr. Peacham calls them, when enumerating the London sights that were to be seen for a penny. These were kept at the Tower, and there was a bear-pit at Southwark, but the bears were rather for baiting than as a mere show. I do not know how early the

elephants and giraffes, lions and tigers, at the Exeter
Change in the Strand, were to be seen, but it was one of
the most popular sights in the eighteenth century. The
travelling showman carried these wonders into the
country, and they were probably among the attractions
of the Fair.

Illuminations are mentioned by Stow, writing in the
reign of Elizabeth, and in all probability are of ancient
origin, as it is such an instinctive method of testifying
joy. Fireworks, equally a delight to children, were a
newer thing then, but became quite common in the
next reign ; even made and played with by children,
as may be seen in the anecdote of Marmaduke Rawdon
already referred to, when he met with an accident, and
got so badly burnt. A fire-drake and a fiery kite are
described by John Bates in 1634, and in *The Mysteries
of Art and Nature* there is an instruction "for composing
all manner of fireworks for triumph and recreation."
An earlier work still, published in 1628 by Robert
Norton, enumerates rockets, coloured fires, serpents,
and wheels. Set-pieces most likely came a little later,
and were among the fascinations of the Spring Gardens,
which preceded Ranelagh and Vauxhall in public favour.
These were, of course, primarily places for grown-up
entertainment, but we may gather from pictures of the
seventeenth and eighteenth centuries that it was very
much the custom for people to take their children there,
even quite late in the evening, that the little ones might
be amazed with the fireworks and the lighting-up of the
trees with coloured lights. The grottoes, too, would

enchant the children, and there were panoramas to be seen as well as puppet-shows.

So we see the long train of laughing children pass— Saxon, Norman, Tudor. Truly, the children of long ago seem to have had a merry time of it.

FAMILY OF THE DUKE OF BUCKINGHAM

GERARD HONTHORST

CHAPTER XI

THE GOLDEN AGE

AFTER the distracted years of the Wars of the Roses, when the succession was established, and when the violent mutations in religion had subsided into a modified acceptance of the reformed doctrines by the English National Church, came nearly a century of peace ; a golden time, when the sword was sheathed within the realm, when men had leisure to settle down, to improve their estates, to build homes rather than fortified castles, to plant trees, to lay out fair gardens ; and last, not least, to become acquainted with their children and interest themselves in their education. It was a great time for theories of education—but of that more anon ; our concern just now is with the home and family life. Through all the memoirs and domestic correspondence of the day the little children flit in brief but often pregnant notice ; petted and made much of like the children of to-day ; their little sayings recorded in family letters, sometimes even their toys, their horn-books, their small garments preserved and handed down ; their beauty and quaintness made permanent on many a canvas by Holbein, Vandyck, Milani, or Miereveldt.

These children seem to have led happy lives for

the most part. The rod, it is true, was more prominent than it is now, not only in schools, but also in the nursery amongst quite little ones. Protest was, however, being raised against it in many quarters, and its use was more and more mitigated until the prevalence of Calvinistic views, when the children were regarded as little imps of darkness, and well whipped accordingly. In these tenderer days it is, perhaps, wise to remember that, used judiciously in the hands of a responsible person, whether parent or pedagogue, it is in reality far more wholesome and far less cruel than many methods of punishment which found favour later, such as the lengthy detention in a close schoolroom of a wearied and half-stupefied child while his fellows are let out to play, with a long imposition which, of course, has a tendency to set the boy against books altogether, or the bitter penalty of bed on a hot summer afternoon. The rod, short, sharp, and not excessive, has ever been found most salutary with boys for moral faults, though we may agree with Roger Ascham and Richard Mulcaster that neither rod, ruler, nor box on the ear should ever be permitted for stupidity or slowness to comprehend; it only makes the child stubborn and more stupid than before.

When we do hear of it, it is generally by way of protest; as in a skit published in 1570, written by Thomas Ingeland, entitled *A Pretie and Merie New Interlude called the Disobedient Child*, which rather shows the disrepute into which whipping was falling than its prevalence. It sets forth how a rich man was desirous to put his son to school, and the son objecting, the father condescends to argue the point with him. The son declares—

> "When all is saide and all is done,
> Concerning all things both more and lesse,
> Yet lyke to the Schole none under the Sonne
> Bryngeth to Chyldrene so much heauinesse.
>
> .   .   .   .   .
>
> At other Boyes handes I have yt lerned,
> And that of those truelye most of all other
> Which for a certayne time remayned
> In the house and prison of a Scholemayster."

He rambles on for some time, enlarging on the gory condition to which the wrathful pedagogue reduces his victims, but the father objects—

> "For it is not to be judged that any Scholemayster
> Is of so great fiersenesse and crueltie,
> And of yonge Infantes so sore a tormentor
> That the breath should be about to leaue the bodie."

But the son brings forward the case of a boy

> "Which through manie stryppes was dead and cold."

This seemed conclusive, for in the end the argumentative son is permitted to "take a wyf" instead of going to school, which would point to the fact that he was better able to take care of himself than a "yonge Infante," and most likely it would have done this precocious young hopeful a world of good to have been put to school and "well belasshed." These extracts are given in a little article entitled "The Good Old Times," by Professor John Adams, M.A., which appeared in the *Academic Review* for March, 1903. Being written just about the time that Ascham and others were uplifting their voices against the excessive use of the cane, the little play was doubtless intended as a kind of squib.

Aubrey was surely far too sweeping in his indictment of the pedantry and severity of the days of Erasmus and later. He draws an amusing and highly coloured picture of men of thirty or forty years old obliged to stand bare-headed and mute before their fathers, while the daughters, women grown, had to stand at the cupboard-side when the mother was present, unless by a stretch of indulgence a cushion to kneel upon was brought them by the serving-man. One instance, indeed, this calls to mind : the little Elizabeth Tanfield, in the days of James I., who was brought up on the old-fashioned plan by a mother of great severity, who insisted on her always addressing her on her knees ; but even she was made much of by her father, and she grew up to be a very tender mother to her own.

By far the greater number of domestic pictures— and these not fancy ones, be it observed, but genuine contemporary records—show a very different state of things. Even in the very time of Erasmus, which Aubrey points to as characterized by a starched formality and harshness, in the home of his especial friend, Sir Thomas More at Chelsea, the children were evidently happy enough. Green draws a charming picture in a few strokes, based partly on the Letters of Erasmus, partly on the recollections of Margaret, the favourite daughter, of the clever, kindly father luring the little girls to interest in their studies by showing them

his collection of coins and curiosities in his cabinet, and
rewarding them by taking an equal interest in their
pets and games. We see him conducting grave states-
men who visited him into the big shady garden by the
river to see the rabbit-hutches and the monkey, and
perhaps to display little Meg's proficiency in Latin.
" I have given you kisses enough," he writes to one of
them, when abroad on some important business, "but
stripes hardly ever." He was an admirable musician,
and as the girls grew up they were able to take part
with their father in the home concerts in which he
delighted.

Penshurst, the beautiful home of the Sidneys in
Kent, nurtured several generations of happy children.
Philip, the Mirror of Chivalry, as he came to be called
when he grew up, Light of the Household, as his father
fondly dubbed him in his childhood, was the first Sidney
born under its sheltering roof, though the house was
already old, an ancient feudal castle, when it was
bestowed by Edward VI. upon his grandfather Sir
William. In Philip's boyhood it was much smaller than
it is now, having been enlarged and beautified by his
father Sir Henry some few years later, but the old hall
with its fireplace in the middle and its raised daïs was
just as it is now, and we can picture the quiet dreamy
boy, poring over old romances, sitting in the deep
embrasure of a window, or wandering in the pleached
alleys under the century-old yews that are still one of
its chief glories. His early childhood must have been
rather lonely, for the two next sisters, Margaret and

Ambrosine, the latter Queen Elizabeth's godchild, died almost as babies, and the little Mary who grew up to be his companion-sister and closest friend was some five years younger. He went to school at Shrewsbury at ten years old, and his kinsman and neighbour, Fulke Greville, who had been his playfellow and became his comrade at school, speaks of him as strangely manly for his years—"with such staidness of mind, lovely and familiar gravity, as carried grace and reverence above greater years." Even his very play, says this admiring schoolfellow, tended to enrich his mind : he well justified his father's proud name for him : *Lumen familæ suæ.* He was, says one of his biographers, "a clerk in Holy Orders" at ten years old; but this can hardly mean more than that he was made lay rector of Whitford in the diocese of St. Asaph, settled on him merely as a piece of property : it does not appear that the priesthood was ever in contemplation for him.

A letter from Sir Henry to "his little Philip," written while the boy was at school, is a model of fatherly counsel. It is far too long to quote entire; in those days of rare and costly post, letters were treasured, read and re-read, and of a length to be worth the sending. It opens with a serious exhortation to regular and attentive prayer, "thinking of Him to whom you pray, and of the matter for which you pray." The writer recalls to his son's mind the noble blood from which he is descended on his mother's side—she was a Dudley—reminding him that only by virtuous life and good action he will become an ornament to that illustrious family; the true essence of the principle, *Noblesse oblige.* The letter is full of wise and moderate counsels such as to "use exercise but without peril of your bones and joints;" to drink wine but seldom, yet sometimes, lest being unused he should be quickly overcome when mixing with the world; to be courteous of gesture and affable with all men, with diversity of reverence, according to the dignity of the person. He exhorts his son to be merry by his own example, for Philip, it would seem, was a little inclined to gravity. Niceness of person and of garments is insisted on, and also modesty: "rather," says the father, "be rebuked of light fellows for maiden-like shamefacedness than of your sad friends for pert boldness." How well Philip followed these precepts was shown by the singularly lovely character he developed; well fitting him to be held up as an example to his little brothers, Robin and Thomas. The letter was concluded by a postscript from his mother, winding up, "Farewell, my little Philip, and once again the Lord bless you! Your loving mother, Mary Sidney." By thirteen years of age the boy was ripe for Oxford.

Delightful must have been the holidays in that fair home, welcomed with joyful acclamation by the baby brothers and the little sister Mary, a tall golden-haired child, clever and forward for her years and eager to make herself a companion to the adored brother. We can picture the two, wandering together through the wide gardens, under the dense clipped yews or by the fragrant lime avenue, exchanging their fanciful imaginings, perhaps even making up some of that fantastic romance written many years after by Philip, but published as *The Countess of Pembroke's Arcadia;* much of it reads like boy and girl fancies, though Philip may have thought out and given deeper meanings to their dreams in later days.

There was not, however, too much idleness in the life of these young people; to be accomplished in those days, as this brother and sister became, involved a considerable amount of study: the Renaissance had greatly quickened the taste of the age both for polite learning and for art. They had to study the classics and modern languages, French, Italian, probably also Spanish—Philip, it may be remembered, was godson to the King of Spain; but they must learn as well to sing in parts at sight, to touch the lute sweetly, to bear their part with grace in galliard or *contredanse*, or to dance a "ballet," singing the while. Dancing was not at that day considered the mere pastime—or waste-time—it afterwards became, but an important part of training to give ease and dignity to the carriage of the body. Then for the boy there would be manly exercises, the *manége* of the great horse, fencing, and all the mysteries of hawking and hunting; the girl the while being absorbed in mastering all the wonderful stitches that went to the embroidery in which the women of that day excelled, beginning with the sampler, with its tent-stitch and cross-stitch, long and short stitch, crewel and feather-stitch, leading up to "the great wrought sheet" on which were depicted roses and tiger-lilies, pinks, gilliflowers and forget-me-nots, all the sweets that ran riot in the Elizabethan garden; sometimes further adorned with birds and beasts, lambs and stags, lions and tigers, even human figures with beads for eyes and real hair skilfully worked in little curls. The great stately rooms at Penshurst, hung with ancestors or old suits of armour, the wide lofty corridors, the windows looking on the Italian garden, seem fit setting for these dignified employments.

"Whom the gods love die young." A few years pass, and not Philip, so well fitted to adorn the post, but Robin, the younger brother, reigns at Penshurst, and Robin's children fill the wide hall and passages with their mirth. He married Barbara Gamage, a Welsh heiress, and had a numerous family, and being much away from home, had constant accounts of their doings from his steward, Rowland White. In 1595 the birth is announced of "a goodly fat son," who testified his strength by crying lustily. This was Robert, the future Earl of Leicester in the reign of Charles I. He was followed by three more sons and eight daughters, of whom several died in infancy. Rowland White reports on various occasions that Mrs. Mary and Mrs. Katherine "do much profit at their books;" that Mr. William danced a galliard one evening in his doublet and hose, and that Mr. Philip can already go alone. When old Lady Fitzwilliam, the children's great-aunt, visits them at Baynard's Castle, she is greatly delighted that Mr. William can "lead a measure" with Mrs. Mary and Mrs. Kate. A little later we learn that Mrs. Mary's birthday was spent at Penshurst, where all things were finely prospering in the garden.

But the chief delight of the good old steward was little Mr. Robert, the flower of the flock, a "born courtier" at five years old. He was taken to Windsor on St. George's Day and presented to the knights assembled at table. "I brought in Mr. Robert while the knights were at dinner," writes the old man, "who played the wag so prettily and boldly that all took pleasure in him, but above the rest, my Lord Admiral, who gave him sweetmeats, and he prated with his honour beyond measure."

This Robert, in his turn, inherited Penshurst, and became the father of a large family, the eldest being Dorothy, known to fame as Sacharissa, but in her own home as "dear Doll." She was considered very like her great-uncle Philip, with the same "lovely and familiar gravity." Next to her came lively Lucy, and then another Philip, Lord de Lisle, and Algernon, always a moody, odd-looking boy, to judge by his portraits. Then there were little Mary, Betty, and Frances, sweet-natured children, and gay enough in their bright, brief youth, before consumption laid its cruel hand upon them ; and, lastly, wilful, spoilt Isabel and two more little boys, another Robin and a Henry. By the time these were added to the family the elders had left childhood behind. The young Wallers from neighbouring Groombridge were frequent visitors and playfellows ; so, too, was the rector's nephew from the Parsonage just outside the park gates, young William

Temple. The verses which the Wallers' older cousin Edmund, poet and young widower, addressed to the fair Dorothy, afford a suggestive glimpse of her and her girl-friends, grown a little too old for romps, straying through the long flowery alleys, exchanging confidences after the wont of girls, while the boys and the little ones make the old gardens re-echo with shouts as they race about at rounders or hide-and-seek, or nearly pull each other's arms out at Barley Bridge or My Daughter Jane.

A few years pass, and how changed the scene! Doll has parted in sadness and anxiety from her young husband, Lord Sunderland, and come back to her old home with her little children, Poppet, to whom the young father sends such pretty little messages in his letters from camp, and little Robert, just toddling. Baby Penelope is born during that sad time, and the youngest, Harry, in those sadder weeks just after his father's death. This little boy, "the sweet little boy, Harry Spencer," his grandfather calls him, died at the age of five at Leicester House. To the little party were added the King's two children, Elizabeth and little Harry, Duke of Gloucester, as mentioned in a previous chapter.

Another large family, of whose upbringing much may be gained by diligent search, was that of the "great Earl of Cork," as he was deservedly called, who rose from a comparatively private station to be something like a petty king in Ireland, and but for jealousies and warring ambitions might have done much to pacify that always distracted country. He certainly ruled his household and his own children well, save and except, perhaps, Mary, his youngest spoilt darling ; and the *Lismore Papers* contain, besides a mass of letters, a voluminous diary, in which he carefully entered all disbursements, and in which little bits, by the way, about the children are continually cropping up.

There were fifteen of them, and as he was very anxious they should not be weakened in mind or body by cossetting, they were all in turn put out to nurse in an Irish cabin, where, as we have seen in the chapter about cradles, they were hung up out of harm's way, in what Robert describes as a kind of "pendulous satchel," with a slit out of which the baby's head could peep. After this the girls were placed in the charge of Lady Clayton, wife of Sir Randal Clayton of St. Domenic's Abbey, Cork, a lady of good position, who was like a mother to them after the death of their own, whom they lost when the two youngest, Mary and Margaret, were but tiny toddling creatures. Little Margaret died in early childhood, and Mary, afterwards Lady Warwick, seems to have been as much spoilt by her tender guardian as she was by her fond father. The entries in his diary show him actively supervising their health and expenses. There is mention of white cambric sent to Lady Clayton to make summer frocks for the little pair, and a jewelled feather of her mother's is sent to Mary long before she can have been old enough to wear it. Not much is said of the elder girls till their father began to concern himself for their "matching" —a time which arrived very early in those days.

The eldest boy, Roger, must have been a very winning child, as much so as the little Robert, of whose pretty ways we hear so much later. At seven years old he was sent with William Supple, a ward of his father's, to his uncle John, Prebendary of Lichfield. The prebendary was a poor man with a large family of his own, and perhaps did not bestow quite sufficient care on his nephew, as a year later the child was sent on to Deptford, and boarded in the family of a kinsman, Mr. Christopher Browne of Sayes Court, who had married the boy's great-aunt, and here he attended day-school. Mr. Browne's account-book gives some notion what his clothes were like. For winter he had a baize gown faced with fur ; for high days his suit was of ash-coloured satin, doublet, hose, stockings with silk garters and roses all to match, with an embroidered girdle and a cloak of the same colour trimmed with squirrel fur. With this he had a taffeta "pickadel," or ruff, and his sword fastened with a green scarf; a gallant little figure—"My jewel, Hodge," his grandfather Fenton called him. We also learn from the same records that he wore out five pair of shoes a year, and that a book of French verbs for him cost but sixpence. At Christmas his father sent him and Will Supple an angel of gold apiece. Christmas was always kept as high festival at Lismore, and one cannot but wonder whether the child was homesick. His little letters, written in the formal and elegant style customary at that day, betray nothing if he was. At ten years old he fell sick, apparently of a chill, and though very tenderly nursed by his great-aunt, Mrs. Browne, he died, patient and resigned, with his little prayers upon his lips.

There are a considerable number of letters about the two younger boys, Francis and Robert, who were taken to Eton by their tutor or "Governor for Manners," Robert Carew, who wrote to their father full reports of their journey, their arrival and their behaviour, especially of the golden opinions they won. He writes : " They are very well beloved for their civil and transparent carriage towards all sorts, and specially my sweet Mr. Robert, who gains the love of all. Sir Harry Wotton was much taken with him for his discourse of Ireland, and of his travels, and he admired that he would observe or take notice of those things that he discoursed of." So the future scientist and Fellow of the Royal Society already showed an observing temper. Later, Carew adds, " Thanks be to God, they are very jocund, and they have a studious desire." Mr. Francis, it appears in a letter written after a few months' stay, was not so much given to his books as his little brother, " my most honoured and affectionate Mr. Robert," as Carew describes him, "who loseth no hour of his idle time without a line." He had grown "very fat and very jovial, and pleasantly merry," though he "preferred learning before all other virtues and pleasures." He took part in a little play, and though it was but a mute part, he "did bravely for the gestures of his body and the order of his pece." Truly he must have been an engaging little soul.

The letters of Mr. Endymion Porter, which appeared some few years ago in a charming volume by Mrs. Townshend, are full of delightful little touches about the children. He was away from home so much in attendance on the King that his domestic correspondence is unusually complete, and being a very fond father he is constantly asking for details about his "little partridges;" indeed, he seems to have been more tender than their mother, for Olive was a lady of quick temper, and in one letter we find him begging her not to beat George, the eldest, too much. He would have him hardy though, and he urges her to let him run about without a hat, else, says he, you will have him constantly sick; so the modern practice is not so new as some people fancy. Locke, too, writing a few years later, was all for hardening a child. Endymion asks many questions about the babies as they arrive; who they take after, whether they will be black or fair; he was himself fair and ruddy, his wife dark. A pretty picture of these children in the country is given by the pen of their fond grandmother, who had them for a time in her charge at a farmhouse; she speak of the delight of having her "little chickens" sitting one each side of her, and of the pleasure of putting them to bed and getting them up in the morning; the little one puts her so much in mind of what her son was at his age.

Another grandmother of that day, who appears in the midst of a weighty tome of correspondence, chiefly political, was the dowager Lady Clare, mother of the second Lady Wentworth, to whom her stern son-in-law, afterwards Lord Strafford, writes a very touching letter, sending his two motherless little girls to her care. She had expressed a wish that the elder, little Anne, might pay her a visit to recover after some childish malady, but he sends the two together, being loth to part them, "in regard they must be a stay to one another when by course of nature I am gone before them." Besides, he adds, "the younger gladly imitates the elder, in disposition so like her blessed mother that it pleases me very much to see her steps followed and observed by the other." He expresses a tender sorrow at parting with them, and commends them to their grandmother's "grave, wise, and tender instructions," and charging them to obey her entirely and cheerfully—"so far forth as their years and understandings may administer unto them." He gives some little account of their proficiency : "Nan, they tell me, danceth prettily, which I wish (if with convenience it might be) were not lost, more to give her a comely grace in the carriage of her body, than that I wish they should much delight or practice it when they are women. Arabella is a small practitioner that way also, and they are both very apt to learn that or anything they are taught. Nan, I think, speaks French prettily. . . . The other also speaks, but her maid being of Guernsey, her accent is not good." He resolves to part with them as they may learn better with their grandmother than they can "with their poor father, ignorant of what belongs to women." They are to travel under the escort of their writing-master, who will keep their accounts, and their father begs that all things needful for their apparel may be ordered from the tailor; no expense spared. "I shall think all happily bestowed," he adds, "so it be to your contentment and theirs."

This was a man with "two soul-sides; one to face the world with," and one for home.

A very happy home somewhat later in the seventeenth century was Kirtling (or Catlidge, as Lady North writes it), in Suffolk, near Bury St. Edmunds. Here Dudley, fourth Lord North, and his wife Anne brought up a numerous family of sons who all turned out a credit to them. Roger, one of the middle ones, who penned that delightful book, *The Lives of the Norths* edited by Dr. Jessop, thus describes their upbringing—

"Our childhood past as usual under the Mother's government. Wee were taught to reverence our father, whose care of us consisted cheifly in the Gravity and Decorum of his Comportment, Order and sobriety of Life, whereby no Indecent or Mischievous Impressions took place with us from his Example, and when he deposed his temper, and condescended to entertain the little credulous Impertinents, it was with an agreeable as well as moral Effect, tending either to instruct or encourage what was good, and to defie the contrary; which is not onely a care but a skill in Parents to doe, without Relucting the tender Minds of Children by the Austeritie of Commands and Threats. The constant reward of Blessing, which was observed as sacred, was a petit Regale in his Closet, and that allwais came as a Reward of what was encouraged, and denied when demerited; whereby it appears that great use may be made of that fondness which disposeth Parents to gratifie Children's little craving appetites by doing it with an adjunct of precept, as a reward of obedience and vertue, such as they are capable of, and at the same time being kind and tender in Gratifying them."

The custom of blessing here referred to, in which the child knelt solemnly before its father to ask his blessing, endured for some time later. These children, though enjoying occasional special indulgences, had their usual diet, he says, " plain, and rather short than plentyful," and were never pampered with " bits and curiosities ; " neither were they permitted to taste wine nor strong drink, though allowed as much small beer as they liked, a stone bottle of it being kept replenished in the children's quarters for them to help themselves.

Their mother's rule was, says the son, in general severe but tender ; she maintained her authority, yet condescended to amuse them, being a very clever woman, witty, and well read in history. In reproof she was " fluent and pungent," but when there was no occasion for displeasure she was " debonair and familiar, and very liberal of her discourse to entertain all, and ever tending to goodness and morality." The foundations of reading and religious knowledge she laid herself before they went to school, and always indulged her boys with a story on Sunday afternoons, the proviso being that it must be " a Sunday one," usually from Scripture history. She was too sensible a woman to indulge in baby-talk, and her son refers with disapproval to the foolish habit of some mothers and nurses, instead of correcting an infant's lisping attempts to speak, answering it in the same way so as to make its blunders permanent.

They all, confesses Roger, were of a stubborn spirit,

and would sometimes try conclusions with her, but she could always reduce them to order, and would force them to leave off crying and "thank the Good Rail (or rod) which she said was to break our spirits, which it did effectually." This shows that "kissing the rod" was no mere figure of speech in the nursery, but was really insisted upon in token of submission. With these high-spirited young Norths whipping may have been a very needful discipline, but to beat a baby of three for shyness, as was done in the Verney household, does seem absolute cruelty. Amongst the *Verney Letters* is one from a great-grandmother, pleading for mercy for the little Edmund, just sent from her care to his father in London. She writes—

"I hear he is disliked, he is so strange. Son, you did see he was not so, nor is not so to any where he is acquainted, and he must be won by fair means. Let me beg of you and his mother that nobody whip him but Mr. Parry; if you do go a violent way with him you will be the first that will rue it, for I verily believe he will receive injury by it . . . indeed, Raphe, he is too young to be strudgeled in any forcing way. I had intelligence your father was troubled to see him so strange. I pray tell him from me I thought he had more wit than to think a child of his age would be acquainted presently. He knows the child was fellow-good-enough at my house. I pray shew him what I have written about him, and be sure that he be not frighted by no means : he is of a gentle sweet nature, soon corrected."

Much of this letter, known to readers of the Verney Memoirs, I have already quoted in *Home Life under the Stuarts*, but it is here so pertinent I cannot omit it.

In the Appendix to *The Lives of the Norths* are

preserved some delightful letters of Anne Lady North, when she became a grandmother, and had the care of the three motherless children of her son Francis, the Lord Chief Justice. Some of these refer to the health of " Little Misse," or Nancy, as she is sometimes called, and to the arrangements made with the nursemaid as to the disposal of her clothes, which appear to have been the maid's perquisite; one gives so quaint and vivid an account of the breeching of little Frank, at six years old, I cannot refrain from quoting nearly the whole of it.

" You cannot beleeve the great concerne that was in the whole family here last Wednesday, it being the day that the taylor was to helpe to dress little Ffrank in his breeches in order to the making an everyday suit by it. Never had any bride that was to be drest upon her wedding night more hands about her, some the legs and some the arms, the taylor butt'ning, and others putting on the sword, and so many lookers on that had I not had a ffinger amongst them I could not have seen him. When he was quite drest he acted his part as well as any of them, for he desired he might goe downe to inquire for the little gentleman that was there the day before in a black coat (petticoat or tunic), and speak to the men to tell the gentleman when he came from school that here was a gallant with very fine clothes and a sword to have waited upon him and would come againe upon Sunday next. But this was not all, for there was great contrivings while he was dressing who should have the first salute, but he said if old Lane "—one edition gives it Jane—" had been here she should, but he gave it to me to quiett them all. They are very fitt, everything, and he looks taler and prettyer than in his coats. Little Charles reioyced as much as he did, for he jumpt all the while about him and took notice of everything. I went to Bury and bo't everything for another suitt, which will be finisht upon Saturday, so the coats are to be quite left off upon Sunday. I consider it is not yett

terme time, and since you could not have the pleasure of the first
sight I have resolved you should have a full relation from

"your most affecte Mother,

"A. NORTH.

"When he was drest he asked Buckle whether muffs were out
of fashion because they had not sent him one."

A letter, dated two days later, records the sensation
which little Master Frank produced in church. Next
year it appears that "the children have grown so riotous
that did not Ffrank goe every day to school this house
would be too little for them."

As the children emerge more and more into the
light, people begin to think and write more of childhood
in the abstract. Much had always been written about
them, but hitherto from the practical, utilitarian point
of view, how they should be taught and trained
physically, morally, mentally ; now at length childhood
becomes a subject for reflection and for verse. The
earliest specimen of such a contemplative view is the
little poem by the Earl of Surrey, on the happiness of
childhood and its unconsciousness of that happiness ; the
boy longing to be a man grown to escape the rod, only
to wish himself a child again. Bishop Earle, with his
unerring pencil, draws the abstract child in a few strokes,
noting his mimic sports, his lovingness to those about
him—"he kisses and loves his beater when the smart
of the rod is past ; " the engagingness with which nature
has gifted him in those helpless infant years—

"Nature and his parents alike dandle him and 'tice him on
with a bait of sugar to a draught of wormwood. . . . His hardest
labour is his tongue, as if he were loth to use so deceitful an organ,

and he is best company with it when he can but prattle. Wee laugh at his foolish sports, but his game is our earnest ; and his drummes, rattles and hobby-horses but the emblems and mockings of men's businesse. . . . The elder he growes, hee is a stayre lower from God ; and like his first father, much worse in his breeches. . . . Could hee put off his body with his little coate, he had got Eternitie without a burthen, and exchanged but one Heaven for another."

CHAPTER XII

SOME STRANGE ADVENTURES OF CHILDREN

SO many romantic stories have been written about the doings of children in the Civil War, that it is tantalizing to find how small are the genuine records of what they did and bore. The student of those times would give much to know how many of these tales are founded on real, though perhaps vague tradition, handed down in certain families, or clinging to certain localities, how many are merely the product of fancy. But that is just what we shall never know; the romance writer loves to hide himself behind a mass of imaginary documents, letters, or old journals, pretended to have been discovered in some hidden cabinet or secret drawer, but his real authority he will never or rarely give. Could he, or would he, his work would be of double value.

Such a war must have had a very far-reaching effect on the lives of the children, for it was brought into the midst of their very homes. War with a foreign power may pass and leave them almost unaware, but this cut family life in twain. Even the preliminary years of political strife were not without their disastrous effect, for it often happened that father and sons were divided in their sympathies, or that one brother fought for the Parliament, and another for the King. The children must have been habituated to strife, and to anxiety and to a clouded atmosphere. Education, too, was checked, and in many homes the pinch of poverty was felt. There was a sense of unrest everywhere, and when at length the storm broke, the children had to endure many strange experiences, sometimes of hurried flight, sometimes of siege, sometimes of the sack and burning of their homes. Often they were left in a desolate house in the care of servants ; not seldom carried into exile. Patient little souls! One wonders what they thought about it all. Probably they soon accepted war as the normal condition of things ; children so soon learn to acquiesce in strange surroundings.

Two brave little sisters have won a small niche in history, the Ladies Mary and Catherine Stanley. Daughters of the loyal Earl of Derby and his wife, Charlotte de la Tremouille, descendant of William the Silent, they inherited proud traditions on either side. While the earl was holding his ancient principality of Man for the King, the countess, being called upon to surrender Lathom House, valiantly defied the Governor of Manchester, preferring rather to undergo a siege than to purchase an ignominious safety for herself and her little children at the price of honour and loyalty.

The little girls showed themselves worthy scions of two noble houses. Day by day they went quietly about their small duties, diligently helping their mother and the women servants in the preparation of comforts for the wounded, and in the careful dealing out of stores for the household, and four times a day they knelt beside her at prayers in the chapel, inspiring the little garrison by the spectacle of their courage and obedience. " The Lady Mary and the Lady Catherine," said an eye-witness, " for piety and sweetness are truly the children of so princely a mother; and if daring in time of danger may add anything to their age and vertues, let them have this testimony, that though truly apprehensive of the enemy's malice, they were never startled by any appearance of danger." On one occasion, when they were sitting at breakfast with their mother, a shell burst in the very room where they were, and these little creatures hardly winced; they neither fled nor cried, but kept their seats, only turning a little pale. " They had," says their admiring chronicler, " stomachs to digest cannon." When at length rescue comes, we hear no more of the children; imagination paints the praise and petting they would have at the hands of their brave cousin, Prince Rupert, who had many little sisters of his own at home, and knew what might be expected of little girls.

The end of the story is sad indeed; after the fall of Lathom House, which took place after a later siege, when the countess was no longer there to inspire the defence, she and her children repaired to the Isle of Man, the earl continuing to hold it long after every stronghold in England had been lost; but, unhappily, on the faith of a safe-conduct from Fairfax, the children were despatched to England for education. The safe-conduct was broken, and the little girls seized and sent as prisoners to Liverpool, their sufferings being made use of as an engine to induce their father to comply with the demands of the Parliament. Though it must have gone to his heart, and especially to that of their mother, to hear of the continual illness of the younger one, little Amelia, who must have been a baby at the time of the siege, he was not to be moved from his loyalty, but replied, "That he was greatly afflicted at the suffering of his children, that it was not in the nature of great and noble minds to punish innocent children for the offences of their parents, that it would be a clemency in Sir Thomas Fairfax either to send them back to him or to their mother's friends in France or Holland; but if he would do neither, his children must submit to the mercy of Almighty God, but should never be released by his disloyalty."

After the battle of Worcester he fell into the hands of the enemy, and, despite of a promise of being treated with honour as a prisoner of war, was beheaded. His countess for some time held the Isle of Man, as she had held Lathom House; but, through treachery, it was taken, and the countess and her children kept prisoners until the Restoration, two of them dying of the small-pox, caught in the unhealthy dungeon in which they were incarcerated. She ended her days at Knowsley, a property of her husband's in Lancashire, Lathom House having been slighted. The two little heroines of the siege, Mary and Catherine, both lived to make good matches.

The story of the siege is most graphically told by

one who took part in the defence, Captain Edward Halsall. Two manuscript copies of this document exist, one in the Ashmolean Museum at Oxford, the other amongst the Harleian manuscripts in the British Museum. The concluding account of the lives of the actors in it is given in a note at the end of the Bohn edition of it. It differs in some respects from the most recent book on the subject, *The Life-Story of Charlotte de la Tremouille, Countess of Derby,* by Mrs. Rowsell, but that author appears to ignore the narrative of Captain Halsall; she makes no reference to it, nor does she give her reasons for the discrepancy between her account of the countess's later years and that hitherto received.

Some of the sad experiences the younger children of the King went through have been already touched on. From the royal nursery, with its luxuries, there was a gradual descent for them through temporary, makeshift quarters at Oxford, or honourable captivity at Sion House or St. James's, down to the prison in Carisbrooke. But one was destined for more exciting adventures. The two elder boys were but children when they were present at the battle of Edgehill, under the somewhat slack guardianship of the celebrated Dr. Harvey, who was Court physician, and for a time their tutor. They were high-spirited lads, James, who could not have been quite ten years old at the time, especially so; and in their eagerness to see something of the fun, were very nearly made prisoners. Both were destined for considerable adventures later on; but those of Charles do not belong to childhood. The escape of his young brother James, a few years later, owed its success to a children's game, and therefore has its due place here.

After the failure of the royal cause, when Charles I. was in captivity at Carisbrooke, and knew his three younger children, James, Elizabeth, and Harry, to be in the hands of his enemies, he became very uneasy at the use the Parliament might make of his second son, and more and more anxious to get him out of their power. He had already had forebodings on the subject while at Hampton Court, and able to see them, and had spoken seriously to James about it, making him promise loyalty to his elder brother, whatever might happen. The guard over the King's person in the Isle of Wight was not so strict as it afterwards became, and he managed to communicate his wishes in the matter to an adherent, who was ready to run any risks to serve him, a certain Colonel Bamfield, and through him to the family of Mr. Murray, once tutor in the royal household, whose wife had been governess to the Princess Elizabeth. Mr. and Mrs. Murray were both dead, but their son and daughter had inherited their devotion to the royal children, and Anne, when she had been shown the King's letter authorizing the attempt, threw herself into it with devotion. Her account of the way it was managed, which she gives in her autobiography, is most circumstantial and delightful in its quaint simplicity. Clarendon also gives the outlines of the story.

She got Colonel Bamfield to take a ribbon and bring her the measure of the boy's waist, and also the length for his skirt, that she might prepare a girl's dress as a disguise for him ; and she was much diverted by the surprise of the tailor when asked to make a gown and petticoat for a young lady of those dimensions, he declaring he had never made for a lady of that height with a waist of such bigness. The material chosen for the waistcoat and overskirt was a mixed mohair of a light colour and black, with an under-petticoat of scarlet. While Anne was busy with these preparations in her own department, Colonel Bamfield, who seems to have had no trouble in getting access to the boy, was instructing him in the part he was to play. The children, who were now at St. James's, had considerable freedom in their games, and were accustomed in the evenings to play at hide-and-seek in the grounds with their attendants.   James undertook to choose this game every night for a week or two, and to find such good hiding-places that it might often be a long time before he was found, so that those playing with him might be so accustomed to his being missing sometimes for quite a long while and always found again, that it might be some hours before they grew uneasy and gave the alarm. He thoroughly entered into the plot, and on the night agreed upon contrived to borrow from the gardener, on some pretence of repairs, the key of a little gate into the park. When presently it was his turn to hide, he slipped out of this little postern, and found Colonel Bamfield was waiting for him just outside, who hastily muffling him in a great coat and periwig, hurried him into a hackney coach and drove him down to the waterside, where they took boat and rowed down to some stairs by a bridge, and, in a private house hard by, Anne and her maid were waiting with the women's apparel that had been prepared.

Boy-nature comes out in Anne's graphic description of how the young duke raced upstairs, making noise enough for a whole troop of soldiers, and submitting impatiently to her embraces and expressions of thankfulness, cried, " Quickly, quickly, dress me!" With all speed she and her maid Miriam arrayed him, and the dress, in spite of the tailor's protests, fitted to admiration, " and his highness looked very pretty in it," as we can well believe, on the testimony of Honthorst's portrait at the Hague. This picture seems as if it might have been painted just after James's escape, in the very clothes he wore, for it shows him attired in a skirt and woman's bodice, though looking fully fourteen, about his age at the time ; and as he proceeded straight to the Hague to his married sister Mary, wife of the Prince of Orange, and Honthorst was residing there and giving drawing lessons to his cousin, the Princess Palatine Luise, it is not at all improbable that the picture was painted then as a memento of his great adventure.

There is another charming little touch of nature in the "Wood Street cake" which Anne Murray, knowing the boy to be particularly fond of this dainty, had provided for solace on the journey. Yet James was old enough to be quite alive to the seriousness of his undertaking, and difficulties from contrary winds arising, besought Colonel Bamfield to persevere, saying, " Do

anything with me rather than let me go back again!"
At length, however, they reached Gravesend in safety,
and he got on board the ship prepared for him. Thanks
to his clever management of his game, he was not
missed u₁ til it was too late for any chance of overtaking
the fugitive. There was nothing effeminate about
James, though he did look so pretty in his girl's clothes.
Another portrait of him about the same date, done by
Merian, whose drawings have recorded what Heidelberg
Castle was before the Thirty Years' War, and who had
followed the Palatinate family into exile, represents him
as a very manly looking boy with a tennis racquet in
his hand. And a few years later we find Pepys speaking of him as a singularly fearless skater.

The other child who escaped from England, Baby
Henrietta, afterwards Duchess of Orleans, and known
as "Madame," could do nothing to aid and, fortunately,
not much to hinder her own deliverance. Poor little
mite! she was but a fortnight old when her mother,
ill and despairing, resolved on making her escape to
France, leaving her baby in the charge of Lady Dal-
keith, who became Lady Morton later. When Charles
reached Exeter, having modified all his plans in order
to visit his adored wife and little new-born daughter, he
found the latter left behind, and stayed only for her
baptism, naming her Henrietta Anne, the second name
after the little girl he had lost. The baby was then
carried to Oatlands near Weybridge; but when she
was between eighteen months and two years old, her
guardian, hearing that there was an intention to remove

her, and place her with the others in Lady Northumberland's charge, resolved to smuggle her over to France
to her mother. Disguising herself as a beggar-woman
with a hump, she carried the child, dressed in rags, the
whole way to the coast, representing her to be a boy.
The little lady hotly resented both these indignities,
trying to assure every one she met that she was "not
Pierre, Princess," but being backward with her tongue,
her babblings were luckily unheeded, and she was
conveyed in safety to her mother's arms.

Harry, the youngest boy, was called on rather to
endure than to do. He was only eight at the time of
his last interview with his father ; but the charge he
then received sank deeply into his mind, and when, at
thirteen, he rejoined his mother in Paris, and she
endeavoured to win him over to her own faith, he was
found quite immovable. Schoolboy-like, he would not
talk much about religion. He could not argue as to
doctrine, but he had promised his dying father to
remain firm in the Anglican Communion, and firm he
remained, and neither persuasions nor unkindness had
power to move him.

In a curious old memoir of Lady Falkland, written
by one of her daughters, a little story is told of the
constancy and pluck of two little brothers—the two
youngest Carys, Patrick and Placid. These children
had been taken away from their mother, to whom they
were absolutely devoted, in accordance with the cruel
law which forbade Catholics in England to bring up
their own children ; but their fate was an easy one

enough, as they were placed in the care of their eldest
brother Lucius, Lord Falkland, at Great Tew, Chilling-
worth acting as their tutor.   There was nothing narrow
or harsh about either Lucius or Lettice, his gentle wife,
and the children might have been happy there, but they
fretted for their mother, and were, moreover, resolutely
bent on conforming to her faith, and being forbidden
" fasting-meats, as not good for children," as their sister
says, preferred to suffer hunger rather than not keep the
fasts of their mother's Church.   A plan was at last
contrived to get them away, during a visit of their
sister-in-law to London.   By the connivance of their
sisters, who were also at Great Tew, the two children
managed to be up at three o'clock one morning, and
were smuggled out of the grounds, having to run all
alone for a mile in the dark to meet a couple of strange
men who had been hired to carry them on horseback.
For part of the way, to avert suspicion, they were
obliged to trudge afoot without hats or cloaks, one man
riding on in front, and the other coming some way
behind, that they might appear to be alone.   In this
fashion they reached Abingdon, but only to find fresh
difficulties, for the watermen who were engaged to take
them on were hopelessly drunk ; and while they waited,
a report got about the town that they were stolen
children, and they were like to be stopped by the
constable.   The man in charge of them was able to
convince him that they were in truth his mistress's
children and being taken to her ; but delay seemed so
dangerous that they embarked at ten o'clock at night

with their tipsy rowers, who nearly upset the boat repeatedly with their reeling and nodding. Through all their difficulties the two little fellows showed resolution beyond their years, and succeeded in getting to their mother in London.

Sadder than perils and adventures was the neglect which was the lot of many children during the war. The *Verney Letters* draw a mournful picture of Claydon in those days : father and mother dead, the brothers absent, Ralph in exile, the others in the field, the girls growing up wild and untutored, the little ones—Molly and Betty and their small nephew Jack—all terribly spoilt, and allowed to do just as they pleased ; servants insufficient to keep that great house in order, and, moreover, demoralized by the continual quarterings of troops upon them, first one side then the other, for it lay in the midst of the most disturbed district. Most dismal reports were sent to Ralph of both house and children ; of the rickety legs of Jack and the ungovernable temper of Betty, as well as of all the destructions that war, moth, and rust had wrought upon the household gear. Truly children were not the least, though perhaps the most silent, sufferers in that cruel war.

CHAPTER XIII

UNDER A CLOUD

IN its earliest manifestations the Puritan spirit had
not been without salutary effects on the lives of
children; at least, that serious-mindedness and
care about religion which was often stigmatized as
Puritanism by the light and frivolous was a wholesome
influence in home life. We are often, I think, confused
in our judgments by the singular use which was made
of the word, meaning one thing in the beginning, and
quite another in the end. At first it was applied to all
who were of graver manners and stricter morals than
those of their contemporaries; who looked somewhat
askance on amusements, shunned the distractions of the
town, and preferred to live at home in their country
houses, caring for their tenantry, improving their estates,
and bringing up their children, as the son of Lady
North testifies she brought up hers, "under a government severe but tender." Many of these men were
strongly attached to the Church of England, and
assiduous in their attendance at all her services—daily
matins and evensong, as well as on the Sunday when
the law exacted it of them—and scrupulous in their
observance of all the fasts laid down in the Prayer-
book. Among such men were Sir Edmund Verney, the

King's standard-bearer, Lucius Lord Falkland and his friend Mr. Hyde, John Evelyn, the Earl of Leicester, and the young cavalier Lord Sunderland. The children of such parents learned their Catechism, read their Bible, and were as wholesomely disciplined as any of the children of the Parliamentarians.

Later, as the split in the national life widened and deepened, a new kind of Puritanism developed, greatly political, and with its growing ascendancy a fanatic spirit took hold of many, compounded of violent hatred to whatever savoured of "Popery and Prelacy," of extreme Calvinistic opinions imbibed from Dutch or German Protestants, and a distorted view of religion which bore very hardly on the little ones.

The contrast comes out in Milton's own childhood, and that of his children and the young nephews he brought up. Masson's classic life of the poet gives a pleasant picture of his childhood at the sign of the Spread Eagle in Bread Street, in the midst of a smaller and fairer London than that of to-day. His father, a well-to-do man of the middle class, pursued the calling of a scrivenor; he was a strict Puritan, but by no means untender to his children, taking great pride in his gifted little boy, as well he might, for the child showed early promise of the greatness he was to attain. It was a quiet home; of the six children only three grew up, the others dying in early childhood, so that for playfellows the little John had only one sister and a baby brother much younger than himself. But play he cared little for; all his pleasure was in books, and in walks with his

father in the fields round about the town. The elder
Milton taught his son himself at first, and then had a
tutor for him till he was old enough to go to school at
Paul's, and it was probably under that paternal influence
that he made himself familiar with the English poets as
well as with the classics.

From early boyhood he felt in himself the unfolding
of some unusual power, for he writes in *Paradise Lost*
in an evidently autobiographical vein—

> "When I was yet a child no childish play
> To me was pleasing : all my mind was set
> Serious to learn, to know, and thence to do : myself I thought
> Born to that end, born to promote all truth,
> All righteous things."

The portrait of him at ten years old by Janssen, shows
a serious little face, round, fair and rosy, with cropped
hair, quite unlike the more or less idealized pictures of
him which had a greater vogue. Strange that so loving
an upbringing should not have checked that harshness
of nature and moroseness that made him so cruel in his
own home. His poor young wife, herself hardly more
than a child when he brought her from her cheerful
home and the society of her young brothers and sisters,
pleaded in self-defence when she had gone home against
his will, that it made her miserable to hear his poor
little nephews, whom he was educating, cry when he
beat them. Her little girls, too, must have had harsh
treatment in their childhood to have made them render
their blind father such grudging and unwilling service
as they did. Possibly his own very great and precocious

gifts rendered him incapable of understanding or making any allowance for the slowness of the average child; certainly his *Tractate on Education* shows him to have been exorbitant in his expectations of what a child could do or learn.

The memoirs of John Wallington, of Sir James Whitlocke in his *Liber Famelicus*, and many another, afford glimpses of happy and well-cared-for, if strictly bred, children in Puritan homes. The bringing-up of little Mrs. Lucy Apsley, so graphically described in her memoir prefixed to that of her husband, Colonel Hutchinson, seems to have erred in a different direction. No great severity appears to have been used or needed with her; she was a quick, clever, forward child, loving her book, and only needing pressure to bring her to her needle, "which," she says, "I hated." Praise was evidently the most effectual spur to use with her. Carried to hear sermons at about four years old, and expected to repeat them on her return, she developed by her own account into an amazing little prig, preaching to her mother's maids, and treating the children who came to visit her to more severe exhortations than their mothers, while she pulled their dolls to pieces.

On a little girl of gentler nature, Lettice Morrison, who became the wife of Lord Falkland, this over-religious training had a very different effect. Her chaplain, who wrote a curious little memoir of her addressed to her mother, and prefixed to a correspondence with himself, gives an account of her early piety, her obedience, her care for the poor, her long hours of devotion, and her anxiety to miss none of the services of the Church. In her case it was Puritanism of the earlier type, and consisted with devotion to the cause of Church and King; but there would seem to have been some over-stimulating of an already sensitive conscience, some lack of the wholesome influence of childish play, for all her life long she was subject to long fits of morbid depression, during which she doubted of God's mercy and her own salvation.

This fostering of morbid influences comes out very strongly and increasingly as the years of the Puritan ascendancy went on, in the series of little books for children which now began to appear, many written expressly for them by Puritan Divines. These soon became so numerous that a few specimens culled almost at random must suffice.

One of the most popular is called *A New Book for Children*, by George Fox the younger, and purports to be written, "for the removing of the use of such books and Catechisms as are sprung forth of the corrupt tree, which is now to be burned and its fruits rejected, and people are to use the leaves of the Tree that grows by the River of the Water of Life that proceedeth from the Throne and Presence of God for Healing. So all friends, be faithful and walk in that which refreshes the plant, the Power of the Lord God." This preface is followed by the alphabet and syllables, and then come maxims to be learned by heart, somewhat tending, one would fear, to priggishness, such as "A sober child hath esteem among the wise," and so forth. The second chapter gives doctrinal instruction, but in spite of his appeal to the leaves of the mystic Tree, by which the reader would imagine the Holy Scriptures were meant, the writer ignores entirely the Biblical account of the Incarnation, omitting all reference to the Blessed Virgin, and giving the doctrine in these words—

"And this Word became Flesh, and in due time He was made manifest in the likeness of sinful Flesh in that Body which was supposed to be Joseph the Carpenter's Son, and He was called Jesus."

There is a great deal about the devil and original sin, and the little volume concludes with an exhortation to "all ye wicked children, who are of the seed of the evil-doers, and are learning of the wicked one to scoff and to scorn and to mock and to do wickedly," to amend their ways, lest they fall into the condemnation of the children who mocked Elisha, and were eaten up by bears.

The Book of Martyrs, by George Fox the elder, with its gruesome stories of persecution and torture, was one very frequently put into the hands of young children. Even in such a house as Claydon a copy of it habitually lay on the drawing-room table, and was, no doubt, well thumbed by the young folk, for children, especially boys, always delight in horrors. Even if the stories had been all true, they were not wholesome food for young minds, and most, exaggerated, distorted, and gathered from hearsay evidence, were not calculated to allay bigotry and intolerance, and may have gone far to foster the invincible and rooted enmity

THE INFANT SAMUEL
JOSHUA REYNOLDS

against Catholics which for generations continued to sway many otherwise just and fair-minded men. This book, of course, was not expressly intended for children.

Among the books written on purpose for them, those by James Janeway, an eminent Puritan Divine, had the greatest vogue, and were extolled and recommended throughout the latter part of the seventeenth century. He was something of a poet as well, and composed verses for children, but his specially characteristic works were *A Looking Glass for Children*, and *A Token for Children*. These show very plainly the light in which parents and teachers had come to regard the poor little mites : no longer the loving, innocent little creatures, of whom good Bishop Earle writes so feelingly—" The Christian's example, the old man's relapse : the one imitates his pureness, and the other falls into his simplicity "—nor the angel-infant whose soul, fresh from baptismal dew, according to the poet Vaughan, held " but a white, celestial thought." Now he appears as a little imp of darkness.

"Your child," says Janeway, in his preliminary exhortation to parents, "is never too little to go to hell ;" and he proceeds to relate an anecdote of a child terrified by this sentence from the lips of " a godly schoolmistress" in the country, " Every mother's child of you are by nature Children of Wrath," and so wrought upon as to be then and there converted. He further enjoins these parents, " Put your children upon learning their Catechism and the Scriptures, and getting to pray and weep by themselves." The Catechism

referred to would not be, of course, the Church Catechism, but the Westminster or Shorter Catechism, drawn
up by the Westminster Assembly convened by Parliament in 1643. This so-called abridgement contained
one hundred and seven questions and answers, most of
them very long and deep. American children were
brought up on it for a long time, it having been im-
ported by the Pilgrim Fathers, and many tales of early
New England days contain some reference to the
formidable catechizing in church which took place with
much solemnity on three Sundays each summer. It
was, however, found so hard that it was after a time
superseded by a really condensed one on the same lines
called *Spiritual Milk for American Babes.** English
babes were by that time taught the Church Catechism
compiled by Dean Nowell, and authoritatively added
to the Prayer-book after the Restoration. But to return
to James Janeway : when he comes to be addressing
the children themselves, though he calls them lambs,
he does not scruple to terrify them with hell fire.

" How dost thou spend thy time?" he proceeds ; "is it in play
and idleness with wicked children? . . . Do you dare to run up
and down on the Lord's Day? Or do you keep in to read your
book? Which of these two sorts are you of?"

Then, somewhat changing his threatening tone, he
exhorts "the pretty dear child" to give himself to the
Lord. In the midst of his fulminations stands a very
sweet little prayer for a young child—

* The Shorter Catechism reigned supreme in Scotland for centuries,
and its use in schools is even at the present time sanctioned by responsible
educational authorities.

"Dear Jesus, Thou didst bid that little children should be suffered to come to Thee, and, Lord, I come as well as I can, and would fain be Thy child. Take my heart, and make it humble, and meek, sensible and obedient. I give myself to Thee, dear Jesus; do what Thou wilt with me, so Thou wilt but love me, and give me Thy Grace and Glory."

Next he enjoins the child to get acquainted with godly people, and ask them good questions, and endeavour to love their talk; he bids them hear the most powerful ministers, and read the most searching books, and, says he, "get your father to buy you Mr. Joles' *Father's Blessing* and *Guide to Heaven*." And this to quite little children, from two or three years old up to eight or nine! Nothing is more amazing than the precocity of these infants, exemplified in the series of little histories he proceeds to relate as patterns for their emulation: the instance of one "eminently converted between eight and nine years old" seems quite mature in comparison with the rest. One story is entitled "Of a Child that was admirably affected with the things of God when he was between two and three years old. With a brief account of his death." For that is how most of these stories end. "Too good for this world" would be the phrase of those who wept over the little coffin, but the verdict of to-day is over-pressed in brain and sensibility, a victim to morbid conditions.

Nearly all the stories are in a similar vein. The mere titles are enough to show their drift; it would be wearisome to the reader to quote in detail. These are a few specimens: "Of a little Girl that was wrought upon when she was between four and five years old." "Of a

Notorious Wicked Child that was taken up for Begging and admirably Converted. His Holy Life and Joyful Death when he was nine years old." There are many more, and in hardly any of them does the subject live to grow up. The poor babies seem like little Mrs. Lucy Apsley, to have been "carried to sermons," of which they were expected to render a full account when they were brought home again, and wrought up to a pitch of precocious sensibility quite likely to bring on water on the brain, and everything that was most morbid and unwholesome rather encouraged than repressed.

Of two I will give a somewhat fuller account ; they are so grotesque, yet so characteristic. One is of a little boy between two and three years of age who could not bear to be put to bed without "Family Duty," as family prayers were then called ; and not satisfied with that would often be found on his knees by himself in a corner. He learned to read the Scriptures "with groans and tears and sobs"—not because of the difficulty, but because of the conviction of his own wickedness. A little further on we are told that he complained of the naughtiness of his heart, and was much troubled for the wandering of his thoughts during "Duty." When left alone on the Sabbath day he would not spend any time in idleness or play, but be busied in praying, reading the Bible, and "getting of his Catechism."

Another child, John Hervey by name, went off to school of his own accord at two and a half, and presented himself to the master with a request to be taught. On one occasion, seeing a relative of his the worse for drink, he severely rebuked him. Grown a little older, when he perceived his brother and sister much pleased with their new clothes, he would "with a great deal of Gravity reprove their Folly." When he himself received a new suit from the tailor's, adorned as the fashion then was with bunches of ribbons at the knee, he inquired of his mother if those would keep him warm, and being answered in the negative, added, "You are mistaken if you think these things please me," and begged her to have a care of gratifying the proud humours of his brother and sister. He read Baxter's works with much satisfaction.

A very similar book, but rather more cheerful, was written by Thomas White, and in 1703 was in its third edition, which came out adorned with the portrait of Queen Anne. It opens with a pictorial alphabet, not the traditional A, Apple-pie, but A was an Ape; another very pleasant version follows: "A was an Archer and shot at a frog; B was a blindman and led by a dog." Next come some very queer lines, probably intended as a lesson in punctuation, beginning "I saw a peacock with a fiery tail." This, unless read with the commas just where they would be least expected, makes the most weird nonsense worthy of *Alice in Wonderland*. These early pages are sufficiently entertaining; there is even a selection of riddles, simple little puzzles, such as—

> "I went to the wood and got it;
> I sat me down and sought it;
> I kept it still against my will,
> And so by force I brought it;"

familiar to the children of to-day.

In his serious address to the children, Thomas White begins more gently than Janeway; he speaks of their guardian angels, and does not seem to regard all children as hopelessly wicked. He is justly vehement in his denunciation of lies and false excuses, and earnestly enjoins pity for the poor. All this is well; but he goes on: "When you can read, read no ballads nor foolish books, but let your reading be in the Bible, *The Plain Man's Pathway to Heaven*, and get your father to buy you *The Practice of Piety*, Mr. Baxter's *Call to the Unconverted*, Allen's *Allarum to the Unconverted*, and Fox's *Book of Martyrs*." This to a child that had but just learned to read, and the children of that day read much sooner than ours! Some of his exhortations too are calculated to terrify a nervous child—

"Sleep not in church, for the Devil rocks the cradle. Be not proud of thy clothes nor curious in putting them on, for the Devil holds the glass. Fight not with thy playfellows, for the Devil will be thy second. Play not on the Lord's day, for the Devil will be thy playfellow. Play not at cards, they are the Devil's books. They that go to bed without praying have the Devil for their bed-fellow."

After some anecdotes of persecutions of children from ancient sources, such as Origen's account of the martyrdom of seven brothers, come some stories of exactly the same kind as Janeway's. There is the rather pathetic tale of a little boy of eight who cried because he thought he should go to hell though he did try to serve God as well as he could. On another occasion the same child wept because he could remember so little of the sermon. Once his mother asking him the

THE SLEEPING CHILD
BARTOLOZZI

reason of his tears, he replied he wept for his sins, and being pressed to confess them, owned that he had once whetted his knife upon the Lord's day; he failed to reprove one who swore in his presence ; and once, when his mother asked him if he were cold, he answered "yes" when he should have said "forsooth," for afterwards, doubting whether he really were cold or not, he feared he had told a lie. Poor little conscience! on which such things made such black stains. This child was accustomed to mark passages in books which struck him.

Another child of the same type was "Mr. John Langham," who at five and a half could repeat perfectly the Assembly's Shorter Catechism, and would frequently question a sister younger than himself whether she put her trust in God. The little volume concludes with some pattern letters from a child at school and *The Youth's Alphabet*, a series of maxims alphabetically arranged, similar to those found in the Books of Nurture of an earlier day.

It was no wonder that in such a dreary waste the children seized on *The Pilgrim's Progress* with avidity. It presented, it is true, the same narrow and distorted view of the religious life; but the children did not trouble about the divinity ; it was a story, and a story was what they wanted, and its vivid descriptions, its quaint personifications of qualities after the manner of the old Mysteries and Moralities, above all, the series of exciting adventures and hairbreadth escapes which befel Christian on his journey, were just what appealed to the imaginations of children, and when embellished with wood-cuts, however rude, it was a delight indeed ; and the crowning delight was that it was permitted on Sundays, that day, to them, of weary gloom.

Finding that the young folk so highly appreciated a book not primarily intended for them, Bunyan bethought him that he would write something really suited to their capacities, and produced his *Book for Boys and Girls*, a volume which now reposes on the dustiest and most forgotten shelves of the old book shops, and must be sought diligently by those who have a curiosity about dead and gone literature. It is indeed a dreary production : it begins with the ABC, a column or so of spelling, and a list of the more ordinary Christian names, that the reader might learn to spell his own name correctly. This is followed by the Ten Commandments in doggerel verse, with the idea that they would be the more easily committed to memory, and the Lord's Prayer rendered in the same form. The next poetical item is *The Awakened Child's Lament* beginning thus—

> "When Adam was deceived
> I was of life bereaved.
> Of late too I perceived
> I was in sin conceived."

This poem consists of twenty-nine verses in the same penitential strain. Imagine the whiny voice, the weary distaste of a child condemned to get this stuff by heart !

Next come a series of Emblems in verse ; these may have been in the taste of the day for strained and far-fetched conceits, but could hardly have taken the fancy of any natural simple-minded child. Between the boy, with his eager, alert curiosity as to the things around him, and the fair picture-book Nature was unrolling before his eyes, stands the mentor, giving to everything some painful significance. This is what he learns from the little busy bee—

> "This bee an emblem truly is of sin,
> Whose sweet unto a many death hath been."

And in a dialogue between a sinner and a spider, the one is represented as being as loathsome as the other. Some very uncomplimentary lines to a cuckoo compare her to a formalist, and a whip-top is in some way made to prefigure the folly and futility of a loyalist. The rose, of course, is only brought in for the sake of the thorns, and a tree being likened to a man planted in the Garden of God, suffers chill winds and blighting influences—

> "Its blasted blooms are motions unto good
> Which chill affections do nip in the bud."

It was no wonder that, in spite of the commendations of parents and pastors, the children quickly let this little book drop into oblivion, and returned with zest to the Delectable Mountains and the House Beautiful.

The wonder was that the popularity of this juvenile literature should have persisted as it did ; it continued to be produced all through the eighteenth century, both here and in America, and the Evangelical Revival of the early part of the nineteenth brought about a recrudescence. I have in my possession a curious little square paper-bound volume, undated, but belonging, I should imagine, to the days of Simeon and Carus Wilson, called *The Life of a Baby*. This infant was just like its precursors of the seventeenth century, severely rebuking its father for omitting to read Prayers one morning when he was much hurried, and refusing to speak to or smile on any she thought unconverted. This, while she was yet in arms, was supposed to be a kind of miraculous instinct on her part. She, I need hardly say, died early. The little book was old when we had it, and must have been presented to us by some elderly and pious relative. I fear we were distressingly unappreciative, but I remember our dear nurse, who read it aloud to us on a Sunday afternoon, thinking it very touching. I cannot but rejoice that our lines fell in more pleasant places, in the days of Hans Andersen and Aunt Judy.

This peculiar method of training, with its mingling of excessive severity and morbid sentiment, had very different effects on different temperaments : with some high-spirited children it wrought in the opposite direc- tion to what was intended, and once released from a burdensome restraint, they broke bounds and turned out wild, having learned to hate Sunday for its restric- tions, they cast all care for religion to the winds. With some it fostered that self-satisfaction and priggishness to which orderly minded boys and girls are but too prone ; while with other, tenderer souls, it took but too deep an effect. The longing so innate in an affectionate

baby to please and imitate those whom it loves worked
upon the little brain, till, over-pressed by the effort to
learn what it could not understand, the little heart
over-charged with emotions too great for it, the poor
little body gave way, like a sheath worn through by the
sharpness of the knife within, and the child sank into
an early grave.

Such a case was that of little Richard Evelyn, so
fully and pathetically narrated in John Evelyn's Diary.
The father was no Puritan in the narrower or political
sense, adhering, though inactively, to the Royalist
cause, and warmly attached to the Church of England
and her offices, even going the length of having private
celebrations of the Holy Sacrament in his house at
a time when it was perilous to do so, he yet was very
much a Puritan in his retired and religious manner of life.
He erred with James Janeway and his school in over-
pressing his gifted and precocious little son in matters
of religion, as well as in suffering him to learn far too
much for his tender age. At five years old the child
could read Latin as easily as English, and had begun
Greek ; moreover, having listened to a long sermon—
and the sermons in those days seldom lasted less than
an hour—could give his father an account of it, and
discuss the points that had struck him with all the
gravity of a divine. The poor little fellow, when he
lay dying, wanted to know if God would be offended
with him if, in praying, he folded his hands under the
bedclothes, as he had been bidden not to throw
them off.

These infant death-beds, as well as the little books we have been considering, represent an extreme phase : not all little children were thus hardly dealt with. In many a country home merry children were growing up, wholesomely disciplined, no doubt, like the little Norths or Carys, taught to hate lying and to shun quarrels, whipped if they were naughty, and most likely obliged to listen to long sermons and say their Catechism on Sunday, but allowed plenty of healthy play, and spending their pennies on the gaily coloured chap-books that came out of the pedlar's maund, containing tales of Arthur and his knights, or the ballad of Chevy Chace, and many another old favourite. Did Perrault's *Tales of Mother Goose* yet penetrate to English nurseries ? Whether they did or no, the little Puritans were not allowed to look into them, for these good people had not learned to distinguish fiction from lies, so all works of imagination were taboo.

CHAPTER XIV

EDUCATIONAL THEORIES

F ROM the earliest times, when the Christian
Missions set up schools for little ones, writers
on the true method of training children had
never been lacking. The principle of evolution should
make us look for a gradual growth in wisdom, each
successive age expanding the good and discarding the
worthless or temporary elements of the preceding ; but
alas! matters do not proceed in this orderly fashion ;
some of the earliest theories are the broadest and
soundest, while later days have seen not a few crazes.
The oldest view of the aims of education put first the
formation of character, based on Christianity, and
second the study of books, combining with both training in manners proper to the station. This, for the
worker, was supplemented by apprenticeship to some
trade or handicraft, putting the means of subsistence
into the hands of all.

We have seen what methods were followed or
advocated by the monastic teachers, and by the writers
of the series of Books of Nurture or Demeanour, Schools
of Vertue and Urbanity, which followed each other so
rapidly from the fourteenth century on, and became
common in the fifteenth. In the sixteenth a new view

215

of the matter was coming to the front, and through this and the following century writers on the subject of how to train up a child in the way he should go were legion.

The Renaissance, with its immense quickening of interest in the things of the intellect, developed in the newer school of teachers a tendency to regard education primarily, if not solely, from the scholar's point of view, and the Age of the Grammarians set in with severity. This brought with it almost of necessity the rule of the rod. For when the enthusiasm of the Renaissance scholars for the purity of the ancient tongues led them to devise a system by which little children were to be taught Latin by means of grammar, instead of learning to speak it at the same time as their own tongue, by getting by degrees the names of common things, and they had first to master the declensions of nouns and pronouns, the comparison and gender of adjectives, verbs, regular and irregular, and the definitions of all the parts of speech—things which must of necessity seem absolutely unmeaning to a young child—it became inevitable that Latin must be whipped into the boy, there was no way else, so the power of the rod grew and grew.

This harsh method did not prevail without protest, and many writers, scattered up and down from the reign of Henry VIII. to that of Charles II., uplifted their voices for the protection of the little ones. The early years of the sixteenth century saw a great quickening of interest in education, and though the Reformation did much to destroy it, especially as regarded the poorer classes, the very necessity for the refounding and reconstitution of many schools stimulated theory on the subject, where perhaps things had gone on for long in a traditional and perfunctory way. The group of early reformers who distinguished the opening years of the reign of Henry VIII., whose work was to a great extent swamped by the schism which followed, Colet, More, Erasmus, Linacre, concerned themselves much with the training of children, and their prevailing tone was one of gentleness. We have seen what More was amongst his own ; and Dean Colet, the famous founder of St. Paul's, was no less tender towards his little scholars. The school of his founding, which grew for some time side by side with the old cathedral school, was placed under the special protection of the Holy Child, and established on a definitely religious basis. Its constitutions were drawn up by the good dean, no doubt in consultation with his two friends, Erasmus and Sir Thomas More. The requirements set before parents who brought their children for admission show what at this time was expected of a child of seven or eight years old : " If your child can read and write Latin and English sufficiently so that he be able to read and write his own lesson, then shall he be admitted to the school for a scholar." The entrance examination for Winchester, a much older foundation, added to this that the boy must be able to read prick-song and sing in tune, and up to the time when competitive examination was substituted for election, the candidates had to sing one verse of a hymn, though it had become almost a farce. Certain matters were laid down as to the supply of books, ink, etc., and it was ordained that the boys must wait upon the boy-bishop in the ceremonies of Childermasse.

Colet drew up a very beautiful little catechism for the use of his school, not very unlike our own Church catechism—indeed, it is not unlikely that Dean Nowell drew upon Colet, though, of course, the part on the sacraments differs, Colet naming seven sacraments. His precepts of conduct are excellent : " To fear God and to love Him. . . . Thrust down pride ; refrain thy wrath ; forget trespasses. . . . Wash clean ; be no sluggard ; learn diligently." The catechism is followed by Latin prayers for morning and evening and for Sunday, and the Angelical Salutation ; and preceded by a little address, in which he begs " all lytel babys, all lytel chyldrene to lerne gladli this lytel treatise," and also exhorts them to "lift up their lytel white hands for him who prayed to God for them." His charge to those who taught was, " Teach that thou hast learned lovingly."

The first headmaster of Paul's was Lilly, whose grammar held the field so long, and was based on the new views of the importance of grammatical rules. Colet's own theories of the teaching of Latin were full of good sense. The examples of the best writers of antiquity, he held, were of more importance than rules : "For in the beginning men spake not Latin because such rules were made, but, contrariwise, because men spake such Latin, upon that followed the rules and were made. That is to say, Latin speech was before the rules, and not the rules before the Latin speech." Nevertheless, the putting of the cart before the horse continued, and the flogging of rules into small, dense minds was found more and more needful by such disciplinarians as Udall of Eton and Busby of Westminster, and doubtless by many an obscure pedagogue.

Later came the protest of the gentle Ascham and the wise treatise of Richard Mulcaster, already described, emphasizing the importance of training the whole child, and not his understanding and memory alone. The educational theories of the Jesuit Fathers were not unlike these, but since they had but little foothold in England, need be but briefly touched on. Like Mulcaster and Peacham, they deprecated the excessively long hours with which it was then the custom to stupefy the small brain, and made a point of taking the children much into the country. Two hours and a half in the morning, and the same in the afternoon, they considered quite sufficient for the immature mind to be kept on the stretch; and they gave one whole holiday a week in summer, and a half-holiday in winter. Much learning by heart was encouraged, and punishments were light, the cane only being used for moral faults, never for stupidity or failure in lessons.

In the seventeeth century appeared in Germany a writer for children, whose works were quickly translated into English, and soon obtained an enormous popularity in this country. John Komensky, or Comenius, as he was called in the Latinizing fashion of the day, was a

Moravian bishop, a native of Bohemia. Having been driven from his home by the Thirty Years' War, he took refuge in England, where he remained for some years, and became acquainted with Milton, with John Evelyn, and with Lord Herbert of Cherbury—all men who were interested in educational questions, and inclined to new views. He belonged to the school of German mystics, and wrote several singular books on spiritual subjects, but is best known as the author of a new theory of teaching. New in a sense it was, for it was founded on principles long lost or overlaid. And he thought it out for himself; but his aims were very similar to those of the *Colloquies, Bestiaries,* or *Elucidaria* of an earlier day.

His root principle was to follow Nature in the training of infants. Nature has given young children a quick observation and eager curiosity as to the common things around them—so new to them, though unnoticed by their elders because familiar. At the same time they have a retentive verbal memory, while they are quite incapable of sustained attention, of following a line of argument, or of comprehending rules and reasons. It is therefore a waste both of the child's capacity and the teacher's patience to approach the young mind with grammar. "Mylke for Chyldrene" proves meat for scholars rather. The child learns his own tongue, without grief and without difficulty, simply by asking, What's this? and What's that? Why not teach him Latin and French in the same way? Comenius, therefore, in his *Janua Linguarum Reserata,* or *Gate of*

Tongues Unclosed, set the child first to learn the names of common things, and little phrases on ordinary matters of gradually increasing difficulty, in parallel columns of English, Latin, and French, and not until he could speak the language with ease was the superstructure of grammar to be raised.

Some of the instructions in this book in "arts and sciences" are now quite out of date, such as the explanation regarding the stars as "lamps hanging up in the sky, which, being incessantly turned about, might by their light illuminate the darkness." But this fact does not invalidate the wisdom of his principle.

Going on, he presently discovered that words were not a wholly satisfactory medium to convey to little children a clear idea of the thing to be explained, so he thought out his *Orbis Pictus*, or *The Visible World in Pictures*—a translation of which was made by Hoole, a schoolmaster and editor of the *School Colloquies of Corderius*. In the preface of this book, Comenius sums up what he holds to constitute a true, full, clear, and solid education. "True, if nothing be taught but what is beneficial to life. Full, if the mind be polished for wisdom, the tongue for eloquence, and the hands for a neat way of living. This will be the grace of one's life, to be wise, to act, to speak." The use of the word "neat" in this connection is very singular.

In this book the Latin word or sentence is accompanied by a little picture, more explanatory than beautiful, and it is supposed to be suited to the capacity of a child from his first learning to read up to the age of six or seven. It opens with a page of quite baby sentences: "The lamb bleateth, the grasshopper chirpeth, the infant crieth, the chicken peepeth," and against each is the Latin equivalent with a little wood-cut. All sorts of common natural objects are represented, trees and flowers, birds, beasts and fishes, men and women, and the seven ages of man, just as Shakspeare describes them. We then get monsters, giants, dwarfs, and two-headed men, as well as fabulous creatures, salamanders, basilisks, and dragons. Then come all manner of trades and agricultural employments, instruments, both musical and astronomical, children's games, and, lastly, compendiums of the chief religions of the world; very difficult these last to represent pictorially. A most curious attempt is made to convey Christian theology by means of an emblem thus—

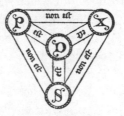

as difficult, one would think, for the child-mind to grasp as a verbal explanation would be. It reads thus round the triangle: P non est X, the Father is not Christ; X non est S, Christ is not the Spirit; S non est P, the Spirit is not the Father. Then from the corners to the centre: P est D, the Father is God; X est D, Christ is God; S est D, the Spirit is God. In this Komensky's mystical tendency comes out. Perhaps he had experience that the child's intelligence could best be reached by the visible symbol.

This seventeenth-century theorist was the forerunner of Pestalozzi, Froebel, and the kindergarten system, which follow the same principle of being guided by Nature, and, carrying it a step further, press play into the service of education. The child loves activity ; he shall be drilled and learn to sing little songs, marching round with appropriate action ; he loves to be busy with his fingers, to make mud-pies, to plait straws or string flowers together, devising chains of split daisy or dandelion stalks, or those enchanting little garlands for festooning we have all made in our time of lilac blossoms, stuck one into another. All these little propensities are to be caught and taught and trained. Instead of mud-pies he shall make little models of clay; he is given strips of coloured paper, and shown how to plait them into gay mats and baskets; he is taught to draw almost before his fat fingers can hold a pencil steady, and in the little marching songs he is not only drilled, but shows various trades by appropriate action.

Truly, there is nothing new under the sun, for we have simply got back to " Here we go round the mulberry bush," with its descriptive action ; "This is the way we bake our bread ; this is the way we wash our clothes," and so forth. As to teaching a child his letters "by way of sport and pastime" while he thought he was playing with his bricks, Sir Hugh Plat invented that in the reign of Queen Elizabeth, as we have already seen.

All this is very good, and seems wonderfully sensible. We are astonished and impressed when we are shown the working of the method in a model infant school; yet sometimes a doubt crosses the mind of the heretic whether in all this teaching to play there is not for the gain a commensurate loss; whether the child, thus tutored, thus always shown how, will not lose his initiative, his resourcefulness, his power of invention. And there is certainly truth in the observation of John Locke, that whatever you set a child to do as a task will be a task, so long as he has to do it at a set time and in obedience to an order, though it may have been hitherto his favourite pastime. The essence of lessons is the task, the essence of play is the liberty; the difference is between what the child has to do and what he does of his own accord. The value of play lies in liberty, and that of school training in the discipline of the will and the overcoming the difficulties of a repugnant task.

Komensky's immediate follower, Dr. Kinner, who wrote what he described as *A Continuation of Comenius' School Endeavours*, departed very widely from his master's principles. He, like Milton, seems to have had no conception of what a young child could be expected to learn, and treated the boy as though he had the reasoning powers of a man. His three aims, as he set forth, were piety, learning, and civil prudence. The child was to learn first to pronounce a word, then to write it, and, lastly, to be shown the natural object.

No pictures entered into his curriculum. With him grammar was the first, the chief, the whole. No wonder his book reposes in the limbo of forgotten educational curiosities.

John Locke, whose famous *Treatise on Education* appeared in the last quarter of the seventeenth century, though he wrote some forty years later than Comenius, seems to belong to an elder school. Except as regards the advantage of wet feet, he advocated no new nostrums, but his theories were laid on somewhat broader lines than those of the Moravian, who concerned himself solely with mental training. The English philosopher took the child as a whole, and considered the care of his body and the forming of his character before the development of his intellect, which with him takes the third place.

He begins with the clothes, which he would not have too warm nor heavy. He particularly advises that the feet be not too well shod nor carefully kept dry, but the child should rather be early inured to wet feet that he may not grow up tender, and pertinently remarks that we do not catch cold from getting our hands or faces cold or wet, and if we do from wet feet, it is solely because we are not accustomed to it. He urges that the feet be washed in cold water daily. The bathing of the whole body does not seem to be contemplated as an everyday habit, but was certainly practised in summer by our ancestors more than some will allow, as almost every writer on physical training, from the earliest days that the subject was written on at all, speaks of the desirableness of swimming and bathing in streams and pools, and in the old picture of water quintain referred to, little boys are represented playing in the water with no clothes on. He is particular that the clothing be not made tight, that chests may have plenty of room to expand, so important for growing boys. The plea was not unneeded in his own day, for, according to the testimony of Mrs. Earle, who has made so careful a study of childhood's garments in early America, little boys even were put into corsets in order to make their long, tight, flapped waistcoats set correctly. What would Dr. Almond of Loretto have said to this? In the sensible hygienic principles on which he built up his great Scottish school he followed very closely the old philosopher of Charles II.'s day, and in another matter too, for Locke would have his boys allowed to run about bareheaded. But that was no new thing in his time; Wykehamists never wore hats, except in the town, from the founding to quite recent days; and Endymion Porter, in a letter to his wife half a century earlier than Locke, advises her to let little George, their eldest boy, play bareheaded out of doors, "else," says he, "you will have him constantly sick." Children, says Locke, should always be allowed, when possible, to play in the open air, or, in bad weather, in some spacious hall or corridor, and should never be kept much by the fire.

Locke is no less sensible on the subject of diet. He advises that no meat at all be given while the child is in "coats," that is till he is six or seven years old, and

CHILDREN BATHING

JOHN HOPPNER

then only once a day. Milk, water-gruel, flummery, and milk-pottage he considers the wholesomest food for children, and deprecates any wine or strong drink being given them. A warning is added to take heed that servants do not give it as a treat to curry favour with young master. Another of Dr. Almond's precepts appears : children should never be allowed to eat or drink between meals, unless it were a piece of dry bread if they complain of hunger. No sweets or tit-bits at odd times. The bed, he recommends, should be hard; " rather quilts than feathers."

The training of character in his scheme must begin in babyhood. The little one should not be overmuch checked in playing, on account of the noise and fidget of his games to his elders, but should be suffered to be in a place where he can exercise lungs and limbs freely without annoyance to others. He must be made obedient from the first, but not too much abased or dejected by continual fault-finding. The use of the rod at lessons is, as with other authorities, to be entirely condemned, as tending to make the boy averse to what he should be won to. Locke also deprecates a system of rewards, for fear of teaching the child "to place his happiness in a luscious morsel or a lace cravat." Praise and esteem he holds to be a better means of encouragement, with a corresponding disapproval to follow misdoing. Therefore he would have children scolded when alone, but praised before others. He does not seem alive to the danger of this system fostering priggishness or vanity. On most points, however, his advice is most excellent. He would not have too many rules made, but good habits formed. Good manners for children, he sensibly says, should not be too punctilious, and do not consist in the doffing of a hat or the making of a leg. At the same time he holds dancing of great importance, to give children a manly and an easy carriage. A rather remarkable bit of good advice is that the tutor be not chosen for his scholarly acquirements alone, but should be a well-bred man of the world.

Unlike his successors of the eighteenth century, Locke considers reasoning, *i.e.* arguing, a mistaken system in dealing with children, who are not to be made the judges of what they should or should not do. Their natural curiosity, however, should always be satisfied, for a child craves for knowledge as for food, and their questions should never be answered chaffingly. This is wise, for chaff bewilders and perplexes the child, and makes him shut up his questions within himself. That which they cannot understand they must frankly be told is not to be inquired into until they are older.

Young folk should not be given too many toys, and those they have they should be taught to give and lend freely. They must not be encouraged to tell tales of each other, nor to run with crying complaints when they are hurt. They ought to learn to take a pride in bearing pain well, and taking hard knocks in play ; yet he would not have them chastised for crying, unless it is from temper. Caning should only be resorted to for serious faults, such as lying, stubbornness, false excuses, or cruelty. A very wise regulation provides that they

are not to be allowed to keep pets until they have
learned to be mindful in taking care of them and
supplying their wants.

As soon as the child can talk Locke considers is
the time to begin reading lessons; but at this early
age he should be "cozened," not forced into a knowledge of his letters, and the use of Sir Hugh Plat's
bricks is recommended. When this initial stage
is got over, some easy, pleasant book with pictures
should be begun, such as Æsop's *Fables* or *Reynard the
Fox.* It does not occur to this theorist, with all his
common sense, that the alphabet in front of reading is
as great a barrier as grammar in front of speaking, and
children get on much better and more easily who learn
to read little tales before they know their letters. In
this I speak from personal experience. He goes on to
observe that little children are very early capable of
religious instruction, and should get the Lord's Prayer
and the Ten Commandments by heart before they can
read them. Certain stories from Scripture, such as
Joseph and his Brethren or David and Goliath, should
be read or told them, but not the whole Bible, much of
which is unsuited or incomprehensible to a child. Next
they are to learn the Catechism. By Locke's day the
Church Catechism as we have it, compiled by Dean
Nowell, was established in the position it still occupies.

Writing and drawing are so closely connected that
Locke advises they be taught almost together—that is,
that as soon as the child can write tolerably clearly he
should begin to draw. Writing at that day was a far

more ornamental business than it has since become, and was quite one of the fine arts. French and Latin should follow, and, in his opinion, no grammar should be taught until the boy can speak the language well. He points out the quickness with which girls pick up French from a foreign governess, because they learn it conversationally, and are not puzzled and checked with rules till the tongue is accustomed to the proper expressions. It is remarkable that this is the only reference in his treatise to the education of girls, which he seems to consider of no consequence, showing that the neglect of women's education, which was so remarkable in the next century, was already setting in.

Themes and Latin verse he condemns as a waste of time. As the boy progressed, he would teach geography, arithmetic, astronomy on the Copernican system, the first six books of Euclid, chronology, and history, and further recommends that every boy be taught some handicraft, as is done in Germany at this day, and was always practised among the Jews. But by this time the subject has ceased to be a child, strictly speaking, and we may take leave of him, though our author follows him through the university and on the grand tour, and only leaves him on his entrance into the great world.

Locke evidently contemplates that the children for whom he wrote were to be brought up at home under the eye of father and mother, and this seems to have been very much the custom throughout the seventeenth century. He had himself a strong prejudice against public school education, based probably on some bitter experiences at Westminster under Dr. Busby. He could not believe that its moral dangers and the risks it afforded of ill company might be counterbalanced by its giving the boy a foretaste of the world, some freedom of choice in forming friendships, some practice in avoiding the evils he must encounter later in more serious guise, some perhaps harsh and bitter lessons, the fruits of which nevertheless could ill be spared. His home-bred youths may have turned out fitter for home than for Court or camp. As regards the training of infancy, however, his precepts are admirable, and two centuries of experience have hardly improved upon them.

CHAPTER XV

REACTION

THEORY is one thing, practice is another. Admirable as were many of the schemes of education in which the seventeenth century was so prolific, they did not bring in a millenium for the children; on the contrary, the eighteenth was in many respects a period of retrogression. With the changes in government, and the developments, religious and political, which followed, I have here no concern, save as they affected the lives of the little ones, and for them neither Commonwealth, Restoration, nor Revolution were favourable. The declension in child-life which becomes so noticeable under Anne and the Georges, set in quite half a century earlier, and is traceable as the more or less direct consequence of the great Civil War.

Much has already been said of the method of education in favour when Puritanism became rampant, and in its outcome it proved not only prejudicial to the happiness of the children, but also to their good and highest development—at least in a majority of cases. With some it tended to produce the type of character which says to all who differ, "Stand by; I am holier than thou"—a type most unlovely in childhood, but

PORTRAIT GROUP
JOHN HOPPNER

very easily induced when natural vanity is played upon. With a meek child it often crushed the spirit and lowered the vitality, while in one of a higher courage it was apt to provoke a dangerous revolt. The boy who has been brought up to think it wicked to run on "the Sabbath," and a walk in the fields on that day a high crime and misdemeanour, learns to hate Sunday, and finding himself his own master, having once broken through the strictness of home rules, thinks he may as well throw all restraint to the winds, and will outdo the young gallants of the Restoration Court in drinking, dicing, and illicit amours. We look on a few years, and we find that the training which was intended to breed a nation of saints has produced on the one hand the pharisee, on the other the rebel.

Nor was it well with the children of the Royalists; many, doubtless, of those who watched the re-entry of Charles II. into his dominions, in the midst of the acclamations of a nation mad with joy, thought the golden age was come again, and all that they so fondly looked back to in the past was about to be restored. Not so; it is easier to destroy than to rebuild, and many generations must pass before anything like the happy family life so characteristic of the first half of the seventeenth century, and so charmingly depicted in the domestic letters of that day, should come again. Or, perhaps, I ought rather to say, should become general, for there were still happy homes and happy children through the worst times; but the prevailing tone, the prevailing ideals were not good. Party spirit had cut deep into the national life, and was bearing its evil fruit. The little Cavaliers had learned, many of them, to see in any seriousness or scrupulous conscientiousness, evidence of disloyalty, of belonging to what had now become the wrong side, and a mocking spirit was fostered in them. It is not pleasant to be "underdog," neither is it profitable, and during the long days of reverse, often of exile, the boys had been neglected, left to the servants, suffered to pick up evil habits unchecked, familiarized with the devious ways of intrigue; now, when their turn had come, amid the licence they saw around them, what wonder if they grew up to think it manly to use swear-words, to gamble with cards or dice, to ruffle and pick quarrels, to hoodwink those set over them. These things were not to be rooted out in a moment because the king had come to his own again; in fact, they were only made worse, for children reflect the atmosphere about them, and the atmosphere in those days was not wholesome. Happy was it for those whose homes were in the country, in undistinguished station, free from the taint of the pervading laxity of the age.

We must not be too sweeping, however; even in the Restoration Court itself there were exquisite exceptions, such as Mrs. Margaret Blagge, afterwards Godolphin, the friend of John Evelyn, whose portrait he has drawn with such loving care. She was maid-of-honour through some of the worst of those evil days, and though bearing her part in the amusements of the Court, in masques and plays, never lost her gentle

modesty and deep religious feeling. She, alas! did not
live to bring up her own little one, but gave her life for
his. She would have been, no doubt, a devoted mother,
like her friend, Mrs. Evelyn, who lived in great retirement at Sayes Court, at Deptford, bringing up her
numerous family with rather over-care than too little.
At Penshurst and at Kirtling children were growing up
in grandmotherly care, learning nothing of the wickedness of the great world; and at Althorp the widowed
Lady Sunderland, now Mrs. Smyth, was training her
little Poppet, Penelope, and Robert, in the old wholesome ways.

A little later we get a glimpse of the children of the
Wentworth household. Embedded in the rather heavy
correspondence of Lord Strafford of the second creation,
come some charming childish letters from his little girls
and only son. It is not a little tantalizing that references
to these children should be so few, either in his regular
and constant letters to his mother—a very clever and
sprightly old lady, who, one would have thought, must
have wanted to know what her grandchildren were like—
or in those exchanged between him and his wife, whose
own epistles give the impression of a rather formal and
stately person. A letter from the little Lady Anne,
written at eight years of age, is worth quoting as a
characteristic specimen—

"DEAR PAPPA,
"I told Lady Hariote [a younger sister] that you
said as soon as she could speak you would send her A Compliment, and she said 'Thank you, Pappa.' I also told Lady

Lucy, and she desires me to give her duty to you, and says she would have writ but her nurse would not let her. Lady Hariote desires you to bring her a Baby. Pray give my duty to my Mamma and tell her that Lady Lucy's head is much better, and the lump that was in her head, and the kernels that was in her neck are almost quite disperste.

" I am your most affectionate & dutifull daughter,
"ANNE WENTWORTH."

The boy, the hope of the house, was evidently made a good deal of, and perhaps a little bit spoilt ; his spelling is somewhat wild, and does not compare favourably with that of his sister. In one of his letters there is a pleasing bit about a dormouse—

"My cousen Lee has sent me the Dor-mous But it is dead. The old Dor-mous is very well and in perfect good health. Lord Delorain and Mrs. Witworth are both dead of a fit of an Appoplex."

Little as these letters tell, they hint at simple pleasures, and an affectionate confidence between the children and their father.

Meanwhile, the fashionable beauties who flirted at Vauxhall or Ranelagh, who laughed at the plays of Congreve or Wycherly, and considered Shakspeare quite *démodé*, hardly made very good mothers. The little ones were either petted like lapdogs, fed with unwholesome sweets, decked out in feathers and fur-belows, flattered by visitors, their little naughty sayings laughed at and applauded, taught to be witty and vain, and used as a set-off to the elegance of the mother ; or, on the other hand, if they were troublesome or not pretty, they would be planted out in the cottage of the foster-mother, to grow up with her children, rude and boorish, till at about seven years old they would be suddenly taken away and sent to some "genteel Academy," where they would probably suffer much in the late rooting out of bad habits.

The spoilt child now becomes a recognized type, and seems to have persisted throughout the eighteenth century, for as late as 1783 we encounter him in the pages of *Sandford and Merton*, in the person of Master Mash, the very unattractive little aristocrat. Nor is he to be considered as a solitary and abnormal specimen, but the type of a class, for he is the ringleader in a little band of his like, and this portraiture was not considered exaggerated for a long time after, for in the preface to Dalziel's edition of 1860 it is remarked by the editor that the scene of Tommy's entry into fashionable society has been rarely surpassed for truthfulness and vividness. The modern reader is loth to believe that such odious children can ever have existed in real life, or that they would have been tolerated by their friends and relations, whom they were allowed to torment; he is inclined to hang up the portrait alongside that of Blanche Ingram in *Jane Eyre*, as the creation of class prejudice.

Spoilt children, however, there certainly were in some abundance, as is evident from many pictures and drawings of the eighteenth century. In innumerable prints of the fashionable amusements at Ranelagh, and such resorts, we see little miss and master sitting up to the supper-table when they ought to have been in bed, and clamouring at the elbow of mother or guest for tit-bits, like little lapdogs. A picture of Morland's, entitled *Wealth*, a companion piece to his *Pleasures of Industry*, depicts a couple of spoilt children rolling on the floor, quarrelling with the dog, and upsetting its saucer of food all over the rich carpet.

Discipline seemed to have oscillated between an entire abandonment of the rod and its excessive use to the point of cruelty. According to an anecdote related of Sarah, Duchess of Marlborough, it was supposed to be discontinued in English homes in the reign of George I. On one occasion, as she tells, she visited the royal nursery when the Princess of Wales, afterwards Queen Caroline, was in the act of administering wholesome chastisement, German fashion, to one of her numerous brood, who had been naughty. The little victim was roaring piteously, and the Duchess took its part, and tried to console it and beg it off. "Ah, see there!" cried the Princess, "you English are none of you well-bred, because you was not whipped when you was young." "Then I am sure you could not have been whipped when you were young," was her Grace's inward retort; "but," says she, "I choked it in."

A most painful story is told by old Lady Wentworth, mother of Lord Strafford ; a story not without parallel in our own times, and that such things could happen makes the gentle-hearted inclined to forbid the

use of whipping altogether. I tell it in her own
words—

"Hear is a strange unnaturall reporte of Lady Abergane that
she has in a pation killed her own child about seven years old, she
having been a great while whiping it, my Lord being greeved to
hear it crye soe terryably, went into the roome to beg for it, and
she threwe it with such forse to the ground she broak the scul;
the girl lived but fower howers after it."

Tales of such cruelty are happily rare in that or any
age amongst the children of the well-born; but this was
truly an evil time for those less happily placed. The
enormous advance of industrialism that was taking
place in England throughout the eighteenth century,
bore very hardly on the children, and the utilitarian
code of ethics, which for a time threatened to usurp the
place of Christianity, gave them no protection. The
coal-mining industry was making rapid strides; in
spinning and weaving, machinery was taking more and
more the place of the labour of human hands, and both
in mines and in factories there came to be tasks that
could be performed without intelligence, and with very
small strength or capacity. These, it was found, could
be done more cheaply by children, and many years of
suffering were to pass over the heads of these little
martyrs before a voice was raised on their behalf.

What were their parents doing? may well be asked.
Why, their parents in many cases were starving; for
those days, which saw the beginnings of the making of
great fortunes in trade, saw also the creation of a pauper
class which had been unknown up to the reign of

Elizabeth, but which through the Civil War and the consequent dislocation of economic conditions in the seventeenth century, and the selfish materialism of the eighteenth, was increasing at an appalling rate. When fathers and mothers had not a bit of bread to put into the children's mouths, what wonder if they snatched at the chance of earnings by the labour of those who were but infants. Better the children should toil than starve. It is piteous, it is almost incredible to read of little creatures of nine, even of six years old, toiling in mines or factories for twelve or thirteen hours a day, and hardly kept awake to fulfil their tasks. Worse even than the labours and suffering of the poor little chimney-sweeps ; far, far worse than the lot of the country children who were sent out early to weed, to pick stones from the fields, to scare birds, to keep sheep or geese, and who had often to endure extreme hardship in the winter weather, was that of these children in the mines.

The grievances of chimney-sweeps were of a much older date, as old probably as the existence of chimneys in place of a louvre in the roof for the emission of smoke. Chimneys involved the accumulation of soot, and somehow or other the soot must be got down, or it would burn, and perhaps the house with it. A man could not get up a chimney, but a small boy, with a boy's natural proclivity for climbing, could, and it became customary to apprentice quite young children, especially those who were friendless and chargeable on the rates, to this most odious industry. It was one thing for a daring boy to climb even the very highest

fir tree in daylight and fresh air, with possibly a ring-
dove's nest as a prize at the top; but to clamber in the
darkness, and in a choking smother of soot, was enough
to make a stout heart quail, and for a little timid,
underfed brat must have been absolute torture; most of
all when some cruel master would quicken his lagging,
shrinking efforts by burning straw behind him. And
yet this thing went on for centuries !

So little did people in general realize or care for the
sufferings of these poor little fellows, that when Mrs.
Montague, whose heart had been touched by an accident
befalling one of them in her own house, took to
befriending them as a class, and used to give them
a treat once a year, a fiction was invented to account
for kindness so singular, to the effect that a child of
hers had once been stolen, and was found years
afterwards as a sweep. The nineteenth century was
well on its way before legislation was invoked to
make the use of long, jointed brushes compulsory,
and the employment of children in that capacity was
forbidden.

Children's hardship and toil had lasted long before
any trace of legislation on their behalf is found on the
Statute Book. This is hardly the place to go far into
this sorrowful chapter, nor to follow in detail the
efforts of those who, all too late, sought to amend
the shocking state of things which had been slowly
growing up.

As to education, for these unfortunate infants it was
nil, and for long no one troubled their heads to give

242 ENGLISH CHILDREN IN THE OLDEN TIME

them any ; it was hardly in a flourishing condition for any children through the eighteenth century. In boys' schools for the upper classes it was becoming very perfunctory, in those for girls it almost reached the vanishing point ; for the little peasant it still flickered on feebly in the Dame School, but for those on whom the dragon of industrialism had laid its claw there was none ; they grew up little heathens or worse. The Church, which should have championed them, was supine. Throughout the Hanoverian rule a spirit of laxity seemed to have invaded it ; its priests looked on themselves as owners of a freehold rather than as trustees of a cure of souls. Pluralism was rampant. A man would ride hurriedly on the Sunday from one country village to another, to hold a service, living probably at a distance from either, and there were but few parishes where the children were gathered week by week in the church to be catechized after the good old plan.

It seemed nothing would have been done but for individual initiative. Wherever the preaching of John Wesley took root a Sunday school sprang up, and in the North a large employer of child-labour, Robert Raikes, set up schools for the instruction on Sundays of the children employed in his factories, in the year 1780. Private and often unnoted efforts were being made to supply the need, like that of John Pound, a poor cobbler of Portsmouth, who gathered the neighbours' children together in his stall on a Sunday afternoon and taught them to read, as well as giving them simple instruction in the Christian faith. With the dawn of the nineteenth century the Church awoke to her obligations in the matter; the National Society was formed, and steps taken to put the education of the children of the working classes on a sound and permanent basis. Not until 1833, when the National Society had been at work twenty-two years, did the State concern itself in the matter, and Parliament voted a grant for the building of schools for the poor.

Meanwhile in a remote part of Somersetshire Mrs. Hannah More and her sister, Mrs. Patty, had been for long devoting themselves to the attempt to civilize the little savages of the Mendip mining districts and the neglected country round about the Cheddar cliffs. The sisters had been roused to try what they could do by the distress of their friend Mr. Wilberforce, when he visited them, and going to see the romantic beauties of the neighbourhood, was beset by little beggars, and found the people hardly better than heathens. Beautiful old churches existed, built in the days when the great Abbeys of Wells and Glastonbury sent missions to outlying districts, but since the dissolution of the monasteries nothing had been done to teach or christianize the people. The livings were held chiefly by clergy at a distance, who drew the tithes and cared little what became of the people. At Cheddar the vicar was non-resident, and the curate rode over from Wells, a distance of some twelve miles, to hold one service on a Sunday. The Holy Sacrament was rarely celebrated in any of these churches more than three times a year, and Confirmations only took place at intervals of several years.

These good sisters at once undertook the labour of establishing what in these days would be called a mission in these neglected spots, Mr. Wilberforce promising to find the funds. With the sanction, in some cases the co-operation, of the clergy, they opened schools, trained teachers themselves, and, realizing that any lasting and effective influence must begin with the young, devoted their chief efforts to getting hold of the children, and bringing them up in Christian habits and principles. Good Mrs. Hannah thus describes her aims : " They learn 'on week-days such coarse work as may fit them for servants. I allow of no writing for the poor. My object is not to teach fanatics, but to train up the lower classes in habits of industry and piety. I know no way of teaching morals but by teaching principles, and of inculcating Christian principles without a good knowledge of Scripture." She would have been, indeed, astonished at the amount of subjects the educational expert of to-day expects to pour into the minds of little children of the working class.

Although, like all good works, those of Mrs. Hannah More had to run the gauntlet of persecution and misrepresentation, even at the hands of some who should have welcomed it, for the evil shepherd does not like his own work—or want of it—put to shame, yet on the whole the clergy encouraged her and gladly availed themselves of her aid, and it was very largely due to

THE COTTAGE VISIT

GEORGE MORLAND

her that the Church at last roused herself to resume her long neglected task of feeding the lambs.

The school-feast seems to have been inaugurated by these kind-hearted ladies, and several of their letters describe these functions, much the same as those of to-day; but they must have been a far greater treat to those neglected little ones, whose joys were so few, than to the pampered school children for whose patronage church and chapel outbid with buns and tea.

So highly was Mrs. Hannah thought of, that she was selected to write an educational work for a very differently placed child to those she had been most concerned with, no less a person than the hope of the nation, the little Princess Charlotte, like Andrew Borde for Princess Mary. She describes the Princess, whom she saw when visiting Lady Elgin at Carlton House, as a pretty, lively child of three years old. She says—

"She had a delight in opening draws, uncovering the furniture, curtains, lustres, etc., to show me. For the Bishop of London's entertainment and mine the Princess was made to exhibit all her learning and accomplishments. The first consisted in her repeating *Little Busy Bee;* the next in dancing very gracefully, and in singing *God Save the King*, which was really affecting, all things considered, from her little voice. Her understanding is so forward that they really might begin to teach her many things. It is, perhaps, the highest praise to say that she is exactly like the child of a private gentleman, wild and natural, but sensible, lively, and civil."

Some in these days may be disposed to think the efforts of the two sisters narrow and antiquated, but they were pioneers in dark and evil days, and it is very largely due to their initiative that the tide of reaction turned, and people awoke to consider once more, as they had done a century before, what was good for the children.

CHAPTER XVI

THE GENTEEL ACADEMY AND THE DAME SCHOOL

SCHOOLS, as was inevitable, suffered no little in the general declension of sound learning and high ideals which set in throughout the eighteenth century. The grand enthusiasms of the scholars of the Renaissance had long ago spent themselves; the delight in classical authors had become a thing academic, remote; the very word "enthusiasm" was out of favour and used in scorn, as of something fanatic, ill-bred. Scholarship had become dry, arid, pedantic, a question of words and phrases, like that of the Schoolmen in the days before the Humanists broke new ground. So the children of the upper classes—the boys, that is—were trained with a view to becoming "elegant scholars." Latin verses and the cane were the distinctive note of the day. The interest in knowledge of a new kind, in science, in invention and discovery, had not yet touched the schools.

Whereas in an earlier day all young children, gentry and peasants, boys and girls, were taught together, the separation now became more and more emphasized as the divergence between the "genteel" and the boorish, between the desired characteristics masculine and feminine, became more marked. The great public schools, with their ancient traditions, were the least affected by the changes, except that boys now went to them much later, at the age when they used to go to college, which removes them from the category of childish things. Throughout the seventeenth and eighteenth centuries private schools were springing up in great numbers, some receiving little boys of from six to twelve years of age to prepare for the great schools, some keeping till a later age those whose parents wished their sons to have more individual care, and not to be jostled in so big and rough a world as that of Eton or Winchester, Westminster or Paul's.

These private schools were, of course, liable to great abuse, more so than the monastery schools in the worst of times, since they were an unlimited autocracy, and the master responsible to no one except to parents, often at a distance. He might be an able, high-minded man, with good principles and admirable methods of teaching—or he might not. Those who know the nature of boys and the paralyzing reluctance or dread they have of speaking to grown-up people, even their mothers, of any ill-usage, can understand what unfortunate little mortals may often have had to endure at the hands of a master or an usher of cruel disposition.

The schools varied, no doubt, as much as the nature of those who kept them, but there were two leading types, the rough, hardy, middle-class school, seen at its best in Miss Martineau's story of *The Crofton Boys*, which, though fiction, unquestionably represents a well

recognized type, and at its worst in Dickens' picture—
over-coloured, we must hope—of Do-the-boys Hall—
a survival lingering on into the nineteenth century.
The other type was the genteel academy to which
fashionable mothers entrusted their curled darlings to
make modish acquaintances and study fine manners.
Master Mash and his companions in *Sandford and
Merton*, were probably educated at some such establishment.

An amusing passage in *A Book for a Rainy Day*,
by John Smith, describes how one of his treats when
he was a very little boy was being taken on a Sunday
morning to a church in High Street, Marylebone, and
allowed to stand on the pavement opposite before going
in to watch the young gentlemen from Mr. Fountayne's
Academy cross the road two and two, very gorgeously
arrayed, some in pea-green, some in sky-blue, some in
scarlet, many of them in gold-laced hats with curled
locks reaching to their shoulders. In this style we see
Master Tommy attired in the illustrations to old
editions of *Sandford and Merton*. The boys at Mr.
Fountayne's were much indulged, and favourites were
taken to the play by Mrs. Fountayne from time to time,
and the school had a great reputation in its day. John
Smith's recollections would date from about the year
1774.

A few little letters, brown with age, written in a
hand like copper-plate, and admirably spelt, on a square
sheet folded and fastened with wafers, which have been
carefully preserved for upwards of a century, give a

little vignette of a very old-established school in Winchester kept by a Mr. Richards at Hyde Abbey House, preparatory for Winchester College. This school may have been lineally descended from the Hyde School, which succeeded to the dissolution of the great Abbey; it was in the same street, and if not in the same house, in one built on or near the site. The earliest of these letters, penned when the writer was about ten years old, has a touch of home-sickness about it; he is counting the days till the end of term, and begs his mother to send him a cake. Grown older, in more formal phraseology he mentions leave-out to friends of the family in the town, and congratulates his elder sister on her engagement to a naval officer with the apposite quotation, "None but the brave deserve the fair." He says a good deal about his pony, whom he dearly loved, and on whose back he used to make the journey across the downs from Portsmouth. The old manservant, whose business it was to conduct the young master back to school, used to report, "Master Jamie kept up very well most of the way, but when we come to the Dog and Duck"—the first inn on the outskirts of the town on the Portsmouth Road—"he hauled down the flag."

Still the boy was happy enough. It was a very good school, but in those days, except in such expensive establishments as Mr. Fountayne's, schools were not the palaces of luxury they have since become; discipline was strict, and fare was plain, and since "boys will be boys," many were the shifts by which hard-and-fast rules were evaded. A favourite tale was of a gorgeous supper smuggled in by some unlawful means. When the fun was at its height, and immunity had made the revellers reckless, the footstep of "old Richards," luckily a heavy one, was heard approaching down the long passage. Into bed in a twinkling vanished the boys, taking the whole paraphernalia with them, and when the door was opened nothing was to be heard but loud and overdone snores. The boys slept two in a bed, and the one who had seized the candle, not staying to blow it out, had extinguished it by thrusting it against the back of his bedfellow. "I smell burning," said the master, and throwing back the bedclothes, revealed the whole delinquency. The cane all round was the penalty, but one hopes that justice was tender with the burnt boy and the unlucky wight who had taken the knives and forks to bed with him. If school was strict, home was all the better appreciated, and it was best so. School to be any good must be a place of discipline.

This same little boy in early childhood had a curious experience, rare in these days, common enough then— he was stolen by the gipsies. There was a fair in Portsea, and the servants having run out to see the wild beasts or something of the kind pass, left the front door open, and the child trotted out into the street. In a moment he was snatched up by a gipsy woman, who clapped her dirty brown hand over his mouth so that he could not scream, and hastened down an alley with him. She had already stripped off his little nankeen coat, and stained his face with walnut juice, and was carrying him across Southsea Common, when the child suddenly shrieked, "There's my papa!" Otherwise the father, distractedly seeking him, would not have known him.

The hero of these little adventures was the author of *Bedford's Questions for Junior Classes*, and other little books intended to simplify the teaching of the classics to small boys, which had considerable vogue for some half century. He was also the founder of Twyford School.

The education of girls suffered far more than that of boys in the general decadence of the eighteenth century; it became, in fact, a different thing altogether, being altered fundamentally in its aims as well as in its methods. The fact was that the product sought was something wholly unlike what was thought desirable in a former generation, and this arose from a complication of causes difficult to trace. The high-spirited dame of Plantagenet, Tudor, or early Stuart days, who rode her palfrey, hawk on wrist, and could manage a mettled horse, or let fly her bird with the best of them; the cultured woman who spoke two or three languages, carried on a correspondence in Latin, and took delight in reading the classics; the loyal comrade who could joyfully share her husband's perils in travel like Lady Fanshawe, or in siege and imprisonment like Lucy Hutchinson; the woman of trained capacity who found herself competent not only to rule her great family of children and servants, but to command a garrison or sustain a siege like Lady Bankes or the Countess of Derby, seemed to have passed below the horizon, and the lady who succeeded her, and was praised and admired, was of a different type altogether. Afraid to mount a horse, except on a pillion, a mode of travel formerly used only by the aged or those in weak health, clinging always to some masculine protector, fainting if a cow looked at her, shrieking at the sight of a spider or a mouse, regarding learning as unfeminine, and a blue-stocking a thing to be abhorred, her very helplessness and ignorance seemed to possess a charm, and a premium was put upon her silliness.

It has been very much the fashion of late, when women have been seeking to recover their lost heritage of learning and activity, to lay all the blame for this state of things on men as though they had deliberately contrived it, but the matter is hardly so simple. It would be tempting to explore the far-back, slow-moving causes that gradually brought it about; but that would lead us too far afield, beyond the effect upon the child of the eighteenth century. That effect was truly marvellous. We see the little romping girl caught and caged, and in a few years trained into such a mincing miss, full of sensibility and affectation, as should please the parent *in esse*, and the husband *in posse*.

The change must have come about very gradually, and is the harder to trace because we know so very little of the schools of the preceding century, scarcely more than their bare names, nothing of their inner methods, and they have to be judged solely from results. There was a girls' school at Putney kept by a certain Mrs. Bathsua Makyns, who had been governess

254 ENGLISH CHILDREN IN THE OLDEN TIME

to Princess Elizabeth, an excellent example of a well-taught child, and there were several establishments for young ladies at Hackney, for Mr. Pepys, who had an eye for a pretty girl, used to like to go to church there on a Sunday to watch the pupils file two and two into their pews. At one of these Katharine Fowler, afterwards Phillips, known to fame as "The Matchless Orinda," learned to make Latin verses; the head mistress of this was a Mrs. Salmon. At Chelsea there was a school of very good reputation for the daughters of "persons of quality," which was attended by little Anne North, the lord keeper's daughter, about the year 1680, or a little later.

The ladies of the North family kept up a tradition of learning; Dudleya in a former generation grew quite emaciated over her studies not only of Greek and Latin but also of Oriental tongues, and left behind her a very valuable collection of books, and Mary, the aunt of little Miss Nancy, was a very gifted girl, an amazingly good raconteur, and used to entertain the rest of her family with prolix romances while they plied their needles. This young lady got up a literary society amongst her sisters and their friends, and they had a badge of her designing, a sun with rays enclosed in a circle, and a motto, *autarkes* in Greek character, which they wore wrought in silver or enamel or embroidered with their own hands. The society came to an untimely end, as such things often do, on the marriage of its foundress.

Look on a few years, and education seems to have

contracted into very narrow limits. Latin and Greek were no longer in fashion because, forsooth, "much learning would only tend to excite envy in the one sex and jealousy in the other," to quote the words of Mrs. Chapone in her *Letters on the Improvement of the Female Mind*. Mathematics and the higher branches of Arithmetic were also taboo, as, according to another authority much thought of in her own day, Lady Pennington, writer of a *Manual of Advice for Young Ladies*, "the mind should not be burdened with needless application." A smattering of modern languages was taught, in most cases not more than a little conversational French and a very little Italian ; English literature was represented by picked passages from the artificial writers most in vogue, and "accomplishments" had taken the place of Art. Instead of the practical knowledge of music essential for the playing of stringed instruments or singing madrigals at sight, girls learned to strum a few show pieces on the spinet, and to sing some sentimental ballads with easy accompaniments. The drawing master set them to copy some of his own productions, usually of a romantic cast, and touched up the results for home exhibition ; or perhaps they painted flowers from nature with a multitude of fine, eye-straining touches, and an entire lack of drawing ; these were generally done on smooth cardboard for hand-screens or such domestic manufactures. To stand in front of an easel drawing freely with a long stick of charcoal would have been considered unwomanly : in fact a clever writer on the eighteenth century, whose work appears under the pseudonym of George Paston, declares her belief that at this time it was thought un-feminine to do anything well, and in consequence of this peculiar conviction a " mock-art " was invented, which at least occupied the girls' fingers and what was left of their minds. " To model well in clay would have been considered strong-minded, but to model badly in wax or bread was quite a feminine occupation. Filigree and mosaic were imitated in coloured paper, medals were made of cardboard and gold-leaf, Dresden china of rice-paper, cottages of pasteboard, flowers of lamb's-wool "— and so on through the whole dreary catalogue. Who does not know these terrible products of misguided taste? In my own family certain weird curiosities are preserved, the work of an ingenious old lady whose youth fell in the end of the eighteenth century, in which landscapes are imitated by cutting out trees, cottages, or figures in coloured paper and pasting them on to a sheet of blue cardboard to represent the sky!

Plain needlework held its ground, and little girls used to take a supply of wristbands for their brothers' shirts to be stitched at school, and still the earliest achievement was the sampler, fallen, however, from its high estate, and becoming almost confined to the letters of the Alphabet and the worker's name in cross-stitch for marking, together with some moral distich, and possibly a pyramidal tree or so to fill in the corners; but no variety of stitches, and scarcely any flowers, con-ventional or other. A little country maiden of the eighteenth century, Eliza Dawson by name, who, like

Lucy Apsley, did not take kindly to either of the feminine tastes for doll or needle, had to be won to work hers by permission to inscribe on it a favourite couplet from Pope's Homer. Such exquisite embroideries as the ladies of the Elizabethan age had delighted in were gone quite out of fashion, and the sampler having descended to the level of beadwork, presently subsided altogether.

Calisthenics and dancing were held of the highest importance, as may be gathered from the experiences of the same little Miss Dawson, who was sent at the age of eleven, after an unusually good home education, to the Manor School in York, a very highly esteemed establishment where her mother before her had been educated. The little girl, who could recite long passages from Shakspeare, and worked lines from Homer on her sampler, found that all her reading "was not to be compared with the graces the other girls had acquired at the dancing school," that " making a graceful curtsey was the chief end of human existence, and an awkward gait worse than a bad action." The Manor School, in her youthful judgment, was a place in which nothing useful could be learned : lessons were said by rote without being understood, and the girls, hampered by all manner of petty restrictions, used to bribe the servants to smuggle in clandestine dainties, and indemnify themselves for the dulness of lessons by the surreptitious reading of romances.

Dancing was a far less active exercise than it used to be in the days of galliards and corantos. The minuet with its measured movements and deep curtseys was the mode, and the calisthenics were less for developing the muscles than for teaching how to enter a room, how deep a reverence to make to this one or to that, how to present a fan, to offer a cup of tea, to get into or alight from a carriage. The children were trained to hold themselves very erect; no lolling was tolerated; and if any tendency to a round back was observed, the little victim had to wear a board or an iron frame called a "spider" strapped on like a pair of stays. The governess who had charge of the youth of Lady Brookfield, youngest of the six Miss Eltons of Clevedon, devised an ingenious but most tormenting method of teaching her to hold up her chin, by pinning a bunch of prickly holly to the front of her pinafore.

There were, of course, some exceptions, some schools in which good sense prevailed. In the seminary kept by the Miss Mores at Bristol, the elder sisters of Hannah, the books permitted for relaxation included *Don Quixote*, the *Arabian Nights*, Pope's translation of the *Odyssey*, selections from Shakspeare, and Potter's translations from the Greek Tragedians. This list speaks volumes, and shows that though the type of school we are considering prevailed, it was not universal.

But in all there was at this time a great lack of active exercise; little girls seldom enjoyed the wholesome outlet for their spirits which the playground afforded to their brothers. Sometimes they skipped with a rope or played battledore and shuttlecock, or they were taken two and two to walk, but the favourite amusement seems to have been to sit in an arbour and relate tales as in Mrs. Teachum's Little Female Academy described by Mrs. Sherwood in a very quaint book called *The Governess*. Imagine the ordinary little girl as we know her, satisfied with this as an amusement when she was let out of the schoolroom! Occasionally they were permitted the indulgence of a very artificial and highly moralized fairy-tale in which the Fairy Godmother plays an important part, rewarding virtue and chastising vice. But even such tales were considered suspect by Mrs. Teachum, who thus apostrophizes the young pupil-teacher who had been regaling the children with one: "Fairy-tales in general are an improper medium of instruction, because it would be absurd in such tales to introduce Christian principles as motives of action ; . . . all stories, therefore, in which persons are described as acting well without Divine help have a most exceeding evil tendency."

This good lady considers it more beneficial to her young pupils to be encouraged to relate their own experiences, especially their faults, and to describe the sinful way in which their parents and guardians had brought them up before they came to the Academy—an exercise, it is to be feared, tending to priggishness, if no worse. The main object of her teaching seems to have been to instil into the minds of the children a sense of depravity. How unlike Him who "took a little child and set him in the midst," bidding His disciples to become as little children !

The manners inculcated were most ceremonious :

the children curtsey on entering and on leaving a room, as well as on being presented to visitors. This respectful custom held its ground in old-fashioned families till after the middle of the last century, and was rather a pretty habit. Though the ages of the little damsels at Mrs. Teachum's range from six to twelve—little Miss Polly Suckling was so small she looked but four—they always address one another as "Miss," and are spoken to collectively by the mistress as "ladies." This was the usual custom, as we find the same thing in Mary Lamb's tale of *Mrs. Leicester's School*.

Sad to relate, these polite formalities did not avail to check the angry passions which arose in their youthful breasts when a basket of apples was to be divided equally between them, and, alack! one apple was bigger and redder than its fellows. Miss Sukey Jennet claimed it, because she was the eldest; little Miss Polly thought it should surely be given to her because she was the youngest; another because she was at the top of the class; and another because she had been so good she deserved it. Miss Henny Fret had been accustomed to cry for whatever she wanted; and the strongest girl averred she *would* have it, and proceeded to take it by force. In vain Miss Peace threw the apple of discord over the hedge, out of reach of every one; they would not be appeased. They pinched, they scratched, they bit, they tore. The fray continued till Mrs. Teachum appeared, and when the combatants were separated, in the hand of each one was found a lock of hair, a bow of ribbon, or a rag of muslin torn from her antagonist. A

"IT'S MY DOLL!"

SINGLETON

veil is discreetly drawn over the sequel. Whether they were whipped or not we are not told.

By a fortunate lapse into frivolity Mrs. Sherwood lets the reader see how these little ladies were dressed when they were taken out visiting on a Saturday afternoon—"each in a silk slip, with a lawn apron and lace tucker, and wearing a small cap with a narrow border of lace neatly quilled round it. Each of the young ladies had a rosebud and a sprig of jessamine in her bosom, and each held in her hand a silk hood and tippet, ready to put on as soon as their governess should appear." It is seen in the frontispiece that the dresses were made with short waist, short sleeves, and low necks, the skirt down to the feet, finished with a narrow frill. A simpler or more becoming dress for little girls could hardly be devised, and evidently the painters of that day thought so, for at no period were more fascinating pictures of children painted. Not only have the fashionable painters given us child-portraits of a singular charm, but Gainsborough, Hoppner, Morland, Knight, Singleton, and a host of others, employed their pencils in child-studies just for the beauty of them, to say nothing of the series of infant pictures by the prince of engravers, Bartolozzi.

But who, save as a commission, would have cared to paint the child of the next generation, with long-frilled trousers showing under her skirt, beneath which peeped white stockings and sandal shoes, given to an unfortunate habit of sticking in the mud. Her hair was neither free nor cropped, but stuffed into a net which dangled in the nape of her neck. Nor was the dress of the preceding period much more becoming, being so unchildlike, the full skirts extended over a hoop, and the long bodice stiffened with whalebone and buckram, as unsuggestive of childhood as unsatisfactory to play in. This style was worn from the days of Queen Anne to quite the middle of the century, as family portraits testify. The Little Female Academy is supposed to exist about 1770, so by that time the pretty little "Kate Greeneway" garments prevailed. The story, however, was not written till nearly half a century later. It did not hold its ground in popularity as did its author's better-known tale, *The Fairchild Family*.

A book somewhat similar in design, but of a very different tone, was *Mrs. Leicester's School*. Here we have the same formal manners and address, the same method of amusement, each of the little girls relating her own experiences for the benefit of the rest; but here the similarity ends. Spite of stiff garb, Mary Lamb's children are wholesome, simple, natural. There is no morbid religiosity, no insistence on the depravity of children; there is more direct moral than would perhaps be tolerated in the story-book of to-day, but it is healthy and true, and grows naturally out of the tale. The reader cannot but feel that Mary is drawing on her own childish experiences under the guise of fiction, more especially in the story of *The Young Mahometan*, with her browsings in the great library where her mother was housekeeper; probably, too, in *The Visit to the Farm House* and *The Effect of Witch Stories*. One or two were added by her brother Charles: an exquisite little piece of a child alone with sailors on a sea voyage is known to be his.

This school would appear to have had rather less pretension to gentility than Mrs. Teachum's; the children are of the middle class—the granddaughter of a farmer, the daughter of a poor curate, of a merchant in reduced circumstances, of a lady housekeeper, and so forth. The only one who had been brought up in a more brilliant position was a changeling, and on the discovery of her true parentage was sent to school to receive a good education, but one to fit her for a modest position in life.

It is curious to notice how very much the chasm between classes had deepened through this century: the attitude of the well-born child to the little cottager is always one either of pride or of condescension. The custom of taking a child of a lower class into the house as playfellow for little miss or master is still met with, but the poor infant thus adopted is made almost as much a *souffre-douleur* as the whipping-boy of old. The changeling just referred to, in the days of her prosperity, tyrannized over her companion, whom she believed to be her nurse's child, and patronized her when in a good humour; and one of the little girls in Mrs. Sherwood's book relates that, having the daughter of one of the servants for a playfellow, she used to beat her whenever she herself was out of temper, and was very angry at the impertinence if she dared to grumble, the nurse always taking the little mistress's part, and assuring the victim that as she was only a poor girl, and the other a gentleman's daughter, she ought to give way to her in all things, for little miss did her great honour in playing with her.

The educational opportunities of the little peasants were but narrow. So far as I know, the dame school came into existence unrecorded : it arose spontaneously, no doubt, from the very necessity of the case. The village schools, which in former days had existed in most places—sometimes in the church porch, sometimes in chantry chapels—had nearly all been swept away, and where reconstituted were altogether on different lines. The newer ones were of the grammar-school type ; there was no place in them for girls or infants. In many parishes probably the Sunday catechizing continued for a time under the new *régime*, unless let drop by the too frequent pluralist, who had no time for it ; but even if it was kept up, it was not sufficient. The peasant mothers had neither time nor ability to teach the little ones themselves, and, moreover, always wanted to get the toddlers who were big enough for mischief out of the way, so some dame who had not yet lost the mastery of her horn-book and sampler, and could cipher a bit, was glad to make a living by teaching her neighbours' boys and girls. When the dame school was about to be superseded by new efforts, it was customary to pour scorn upon it ; but undoubtedly it fulfilled a useful function and supplied a crying need, and managed by an active woman, with a motherly heart and a clear notion of discipline, was no bad foundation for the little

A DAME'S SCHOOL
THOMAS WEBSTER

peasant. When, as would sometimes happen, the dame had outlived her powers and went on with her school, though deaf and in her dotage, the results were rather lamentable and lent themselves to caricature ; but I think we may take it that Shenstone's well-known poem draws a tolerably fair portrait.

The simplicity of the subject is oddly at strife with the artificial strain in which the poet was accustomed to write, and the result is quaint—

> "Near to this dome is found a patch so green,
>   On which the tribe their gambols do display ;
> And at the door th' imprisoning board is seen,
>   Lest weakly wights of smaller size should stray ;
>   Eager, perdie, to bask in sunny day ! "

It is, perhaps, hardly needful to explain that "dome" is here used to denote cottage or dwelling-place.

> "The noises intermixed which thence resound,
>   Do learning's little tenement betray ;
> Where sits the dame, disguised in look profound,
> And eyes her fairy throng, and turns her wheel around.

> "Her cap, far whiter than the driven snow,
>   Emblem right meet of decency does yield :
> Her apron dyed in grain, as blue, I trow,
>   As is the harebell that adorns the field :
>   And in her hand, for sceptre, she does wield
> Tway birchen sprays—— "

This birch-rod comes into requisition later, and a piteous tale is unfolded of a small sinner being well chastised, while his little sister cries loudly for sympathy and indignation. When, school being over, the good dame summons her little crew to feast on gingerbread and sugar-cakes, the unhappy little mortal continues

to sob unreconciled, with one hand in his mouth, the
other tearing his hair, for he still—

"Abhorreth bench and stool, and form and chair."

He refuses to be appeased, though the dame would
fain forgive him, but—

"Scorns her offered love, and shuns to be caressed."

The school library appears to have consisted of
horn-books—

"Their books of stature small they take in hand,
Which with pellucid horn secured are ;
To save from finger wet the letters fair."

These were, moreover, adorned with "King George"
and the dragon on the back, whether in colours or in
stamped leather it does not say. These horn-books
were ere long superseded by "battledores," made of
cardboard of a similar shape, with the alphabet, numerals,
etc., printed on them, and after these had disappeared,
the name continued, for in America long after, little
narrow books of the ordinary shape with the contents
of the primer were known as "battledore" books.

The dame must have needed to be tolerably watch-
ful and alert since she was occupied in spinning while
the children said their lessons. To look through the
open door into the garden must have been tempting
to these little prisoners, and to watch the dame's hen
when she brought her little brood of chickens to pick
up the crumbs the careless little ones had dropped
while they ate their dinners, usually brought from

THE DUNCE DISGRACED
STOTHARD

home if they had far to come.   It is a pleasant picture, and this school in a Shropshire village may be taken as typical of many throughout England, which contrived to keep a faint spark of learning alive through a long, dark day.

CHAPTER XVII

THE SUPERIOR PARENT

WITH the dawn of the nineteenth century emerges the conscientious parent. The eighteenth had developed the spoilt child, and though it is true he is always with us, more or less, he was now to be taken severely in hand. Its close had been heaving with new theories and ideals, and, little as the children in England were affected by the great political changes abroad, new views of education were coming across the channel which touched them nearly. The revolutionary ideas of the Encyclopedists were permeating men's minds, and giving them new conceptions of many things, not the least of how the young should be brought up. Among these writers, Jean Jacques Rousseau, of all men least entitled to pose as censor of the domestic hearth, took the mothers of the day to task, and exhorted them as to their duty to their offspring.

Strangely enough, as some might think, the genteel academy, with its limited intellectual horizon and its cult of the feminine, had not succeeded with the domestic ideal. The young ladies, brought up on wool-work and wax flowers, had come to think proficiency in the homely arts ungenteel; motherhood served as an excuse for nerves and invalidism, and the custom of planting out new-born babies with a foster-mother had become almost universal in the class that could afford it. Strangely the new impetus came; the vague conceptions of liberty and reason that were in the air, and were to cause in France so portentous a ferment, rooted themselves in many English minds, and bore a peaceable fruit in changed ideals of life and duty. Under the new influences it gradually became quite the fashion for young married people to withdraw from the distractions of society and devote themselves to the home education of the little ones. Schools were for the present comparatively untouched; it was on the infant that attention was now focussed, and after a long dearth of children's books came a flood of literature, designed not to amuse but to instruct, and to instruct the parent quite as much as the child.

The theories of Rousseau by their novelty set men thinking, so, though to a great extent based on fallacious premises, were not without their use. He preached a return to Nature, but his was an imaginary Nature. He pictured a state of things which never had existed, and pointed back to it as the model to be followed. Along with this idea of his went the notion that Nature would teach the child by an appeal to his reason. Therefore he was not to be disciplined by obedience, taught to do blindly the things right for him because he was bid, so as to form good habits before he was able to think for himself, but should rather be left to the painful guidance of experience. Rousseau made many such suggestions as the following : Does the child break a window? Do not box his ears, but let him sit in the draught and catch cold. Does he dawdle in dressing for a walk? Leave him behind, and let him miss his pleasure. Is he greedy? He is not to be forbidden his fill of dainties, but suffered to over-eat himself and then be sick.

Actually many parents put these principles in practice, like Mrs. Ruskin, who suffered her little boy to hold his finger against the top bar of the grate that he might learn that fire would burn, and they are always represented as doing so in Miss Edgeworth's *Moral Tales.* How indignant we have all felt in our day at the cruelty of Rosamond's mamma in letting the poor little girl buy that purple jar, well knowing the disappointment that was in store for her when the "dirty water" should be emptied out; more especially making her in consequence go with a hole in her shoe, suffering with an injured foot and the loss of a day's pleasure. It was an experience dearly bought, and to pay such a price embitters a child's temper far more than a good whipping. And poor Rosamond had not deserved whipping; her fault was nothing but a small error of judgment in a matter she could not be expected to understand.

I faintly recall a story by some other author of about the same date, whose name I have forgotten, on much the same lines, relating the distressing experiences of a brother and sister called Harry and Julia, who were permitted by an equally unkind parent to do as they pleased and eat what they pleased for one whole day, the servants having instructions to deny them nothing. The results were, of course, disastrous. Another story on similar principles was *The Live Doll*, in which a little girl, having expressed dissatisfaction with her waxen baby, is permitted by her mother to adopt the child of a young widow who is obliged to go out to service, and experiment upon it, the unfortunate infant having to pay for all the whims of its little deputy-mamma. It is no wonder the story closes with its death. This is not Nature's plan, whatever Rousseau may assert; else why were children placed so completely in the hands of parents, and made more helpless than young lambs or kittens?

Neither is it wholesome for little folks to be taught to argue as those depicted in the *Parent's Assistant* argue through tedious page after page. Reason is the faculty of the mature mind. The infant obeys, he knows not why, till the sound habit is formed almost unconsciously. Locke, one of the wisest among the theorists, deprecates arguing with a boy. Obedience should come before conviction. But, unluckily, in the eighteenth century reason, though throned so high, was too often confounded with mere logic. The new views of liberty deprecated coercion even with a child, so the attempt was made, either by argument or by the appeal to experience, to convince the infant intelligence that unlimited indulgence in cakes would inevitably lead to grey powder; that the careless girl who forgot to tie her shoe would be sure to fall downstairs, and be too late for the party of pleasure; and that boys who went to slide on Sunday almost invariably fell into the pond and were drowned—though this did not always come off. Does any one seriously contend that half an hour in the corner with one's pinafore over one's eyes, a smart box on the ear, or for more grave matters a sound whipping, were not far less cruel than this "appeal to reason"?

These children of the *Moral Tales* seem never to have been corrected except by the disasters they brought upon themselves, and, unfortunately, Nature is not moral. She frequently punishes the innocent for the faults of the guilty, as when "Blue-jacket," home for the holidays, poked the calf's eyes over the paling with a stick, and when, a week later, "Blue-jacket" having departed, the cow, at large in the field, turned upon poor little "Green-jacket" and tossed him on to the dunghill. Parents have to interfere if justice is to be vindicated. Moreover, in Nature's economy blunders are far more severely visited than sins.

Another respect in which the system was at fault was in its tendency to stereotype childishness by keeping the children's attention so much fixed on themselves and their own small affairs. Imagination was deliberately starved ; there was no going out of themselves in wonder, mystery, or romance. If stories were not true—not with the high truth of poetry, but with the lesser truth of literal accuracy—then away with them! There was nothing to be learned from such. The child was taught to turn from them with contempt. The truth wrapped in the fairy tale, in the half-mythical legend, which is revealed to babes, was dropped out of sight. The child, seldom alone, always trotting about with his parents, and having all manner of natural objects and all kinds of manufactures explained to him, lived nevertheless in a contracted world, and his horizon drew in about him.

Naturally this kind of education issued in the dry materialism so characteristic of the early part of the nineteenth century. Everything was brought to the test of the senses; if sense-perception could take no cognizance of it, it was not to be believed. Everything was weighed in the balance of practical utility; if it was of no immediate, visible use, it was rejected. It was the age when science concerned itself chiefly with inventions for extending the powers of mankind by mechanical contrivance, the age also of the growth of a totally new industrialism, bringing about changed conditions in every department of life. It had its effect, of course, upon the children, and for them its eventual issue was the Gradgrind school, with its inevitable reaction.

To gather what the average child of the day was like we must turn to the story-books of the period; for where we have records of the real child it is, for obvious reasons, chiefly of the exceptionally gifted. Fiction is in this way often truer than fact. The story reflects the ordinary, the characteristic; the history records the striking, the unusual. There is no lack of material to form the picture, for, after the long dearth which followed the sporadic output of Puritan books for children, by the end of the eighteenth century the market was flooded with juvenile literature.

Mrs. Fletcher, in her reminiscences, looking back to the days of her youth, laments that in her time there were no children's books. I am not sure she was not rather to be congratulated. It is possible to have too much even of a good thing, and of anything so liable as childish literature to degenerate into trash it is easy to have more than enough. She had nothing to read, she says, but the Fables of Æsop and Gay—and old Fairy-Tales. But does not this last comprise a whole library in itself? Moreover, she had the run of her father's books, and though a modest collection, it was well calculated to form her taste: Shakspeare's Plays, the Poems of Milton, Dryden, and Pope, the *Spectator*, Hervey's *Meditations*, Mrs. Rowe's *Letters*, and a volume of Shenstone, together with some sermons and abridgments of history and geography, read and devoured, as the children of those days devoured when they had any taste for reading at all, were no bad foundation. We recall what Lamb said of "Bridget Elia," who "was tumbled early, by accident or design, into a spacious closet of good old English reading, without much selection or prohibition, and browsed at will upon that fair and wholesome pasturage." It made, he averred, and we can picture his glance resting on Mary, "if the worst comes to the worst, the most incomparable old maids."

A generation earlier, Mrs. Fletcher's Quaker aunt, Miss Hill, whose principles kept her from indulgence in fairy-lore, found the only sustenance for her imagination in childhood in Baker's *Chronicles*; nevertheless, she developed into a great reader and lover of the best in literature. Even when there was more provision for them, let the authorities say what they would, the children of independent minds chose for themselves and ratified their choice by long tradition. Three immortal works not written for them they took for their own and have kept : *The Pilgrim's Progress, Gulliver's Travels,* and *Robinson Crusoe.* With their appetites whetted by scarcity, not cloyed by superabundance, they fastened greedily upon whatever in grown-up books woke their fancy or responded to their love of the marvellous, and encountering much that they could not understand, their intelligence was on the stretch, and matured more quickly than that of children fed on tit-bits of knowledge made easy, and stories purposely written down to them.

Newbery, however, was already in the field, though perhaps his publications did not yet penetrate to the wilds of Yorkshire. He carried on the business of a bookseller, combined with that of a purveyor of Dr. James's powders and other patent medicines, at the corner of St. Paul's Churchyard. He was marvellously up-to-date in his methods ; like the grocer of to-day who advertises a present with each pound of tea, he announces "a pretty Pocket-book" at 6*d.*, but for 8*d.* will add a ball for a boy, or a pincushion for a girl. He knows how to cater for his little customers, and to set forth his wares in the most attractive light. Oliver Goldsmith was amongst those who wrote for him, and is believed to have contributed *Goody Two-Shoes* and *The Mad Dog*. The former, at least, was probably already a traditional tale ; Lamb evidently thought so from his reference to it.

Two of Newbery's publications lie before me as I write. *The Enchanted Castle*, though not dated, would appear from internal evidence to be among the earliest —between 1740 and 1750—judging by the costume in the woodcuts, the boys being dressed in long-skirted coats with flapped waistcoats and knee-breeches, the girls wearing hoops and long pointed bodices, a fashion which went out about the middle of the century. The book measures only three inches by four and a half, and is bound in the variously coloured paper which was so popular, and has now become a curiosity, embossed with a design of flowers and tinted in blotches of scarlet, yellow, dull pink, and blue. Eliza Cook sings of such—

" Talk of your vellum, gold-embossed, morocco, roan, and calf ;
The blue and yellow wraps of old were prettier by half ! "

The little volume was a most curious hotch-potch of early lessons in the alphabet and syllables, Bible stories, and moral lessons, together with scraps of geographical information, all illustrated with cuts. The bears catching the little boys who mocked at Elisha is a thrilling presentment. The information that Esau was called Lord Esau, while his brother was only Master Jacob, reads oddly, but no doubt conveyed a clear idea of the meaning of birthright. There are also some very funny conversations between some young ladies of rank and their French governess. Mademoiselle, having explained

to her pupils how vulgar and shameful a vice was
gluttony, exclaims, "You blush, Miss Harriot. What!
have you had the misfortune to commit a fault of this
kind?" To which Miss Harriot responds, "Yes, Mademoiselle. A few days ago my maid would not give me
some tea in the evening, and I cried above an hour
about it."

Enough! To quote half the characteristic and
amusing things in this tiny volume would take too
much space. The other book of Newbery's is *The
History of a Pin*, published in 1801. This is a little
larger, and bound in plain parchment. It has its
oddities, too, as when we read that though Miss Jenny
was sadly obstinate, and would not say great A when
the pin pointed to it, yet "there was no reason entirely
to despair of her reformation, for she had but just
passed the third year of her life."

Newbery's business was the precursor of Mrs.
Godwin's Juvenile Library in Skinner Street, at which
so many of Charles and Mary Lamb's books for children appeared.

A little later come a group of writers much influenced by the Rousseau ideals—Miss Edgeworth, Mrs.
Marcet, and Mr. Day—in whose work we find what I
think we may take for a tolerably faithful portraiture
of the ordinary child of nearly a century ago. Another
group, writing about the same time, and having a very
large following for half a century or more—Mrs.
Trimmer, Mrs. Barbauld, and Mrs. Sherwood—though
they wrote for children, by no means wrote so well

about children ; they had an eye to the moral effect and a very strong religious bias that tempted them to heighten the lights and deepen the shadows considerably.

Among them all, not one can approach Maria Edgeworth in her lifelike but, to a modern taste, dull delineations of good little boys and girls. She is so true to the invariable facts of child-nature as it persists from age to age, that we feel she may be taken on trust as to the special idiosyncrasies, the disagreeable little characteristics, of the particular child of a particular period. She had plenty of experience, too, on which to draw, having a multitude of small half-brothers and sisters whom she helped to educate. Her father was a man of theories on the subject of training young people, and his theories with her practical knowledge make sometimes a quaint blend. She was not without imagination, but it was the imagination which groups and makes a picture out of familiar material, not that which reveals the unseen.

In her children we see the good side of the prevailing system as well as its limitations ; her little folk have at least the foundation of discipline and obedience. Poor Rosamond, indeed, is allowed to do several silly things in order to bring judgments down upon her—which the reader feels should in justice have fallen upon her mother—but little Frank is actually forbidden to pull away the leg of the flap-table, which would have caused the collapse of the tea-tray, probably as much out of regard to the cups and saucers and the carpet as his head, which would have received a severe blow,

and, in his parents' view, a useful lesson, and he desists
at once without argument; but he has it all explained
to him at great length afterwards.

The system on which these tiny mites were instructed, though it seemed new to its promoters, was
already nearly two hundred years old, being in truth
but a fresh application of the principles of Comenius
in his *Orbis Pictus*, with its illustrations of all trades
and handicrafts, appealing at once to the child's innate
curiosity about all he sees, and to his love of pictures,
which he understands so much more easily than the
spoken word. The picture side of his method was not
so much brought forward, but the satisfying and still
further stimulating curiosity about common things was
the hinge of the whole system. Locke, too, whose
pronouncements on education were full of wisdom, had
urged that a child's questions, What's that? What is
it for? should never be brushed aside or put off with
unmeaning chaff, but answered as fully as the little
mind can bear.

In *Frank*, and in *Harry and Lucy*, questions are
encouraged, everything within their capacity is explained to them. They are shown the working of wind-
mills, water-mills, the weaver's loom, the potter's wheel.
Rosamond even goes to see a spinning-jenny, which
quite bewilders her small mind. They are also allowed
to try their hand at all sorts of things, from gardening
and bread-making, which children in all ages have
delighted in, to brick-making, building and thatching
a little hut for themselves in the garden, and trying

experiments with steam and thermometers. All these portions fascinate the children of to-day, however much the story part may bore them. All children, especially boys, love to see how things are done, still more to try and do them for themselves.

Yet, in spite of it all, Miss Edgeworth's children are undeniable prigs—intellectual prigs, just as the Puritan children of an earlier day were religious prigs. Some lack in the system fostered a self-satisfaction—a pride in limited achievement, which ought to be the last result of a study of Science, with its wide horizons and infinite possibilities. We cannot blame the children; they simply reflected the atmosphere about them. They had occasional refreshing lapses into naturalness, chiefly, I am afraid, when they were naughty. We feel sympathetic with Rosamond, when, lying too late in bed on a cold morning, she gets the string of her night-cap into a tight knot, loses her stay-lace and her pocket-handkerchief, and, irritated beyond all bearing by the cheerful virtue of her elder sister, cries three times and embarks on what she calls "a day of misfortunes." But for the night-cap and the stay-lace it might have happened this morning. Harry, too, tyrannizing over his little fat sister because she won't fetch straw fast enough for his thatching, and Lucy, crying and refusing to work any more, appeal to the reader of to-day far more than the same children pluming themselves upon their merit, as they are too frequently doing.

Very similar in tone were Mrs. Marcet's little books, designed to convey information on common things to

THE FAIR-HAIRED CHILD
JEAN-HONORÉ FRAGONARD

quite tiny children. She is much less of a story-teller than Miss Edgeworth, but her *Four Seasons* is readily understood, and liked by little tots ; and the little boy, Willy, is a more simple child, and not such a conscious paragon as Miss Edgeworth's Frank. Although the latter authoress is chiefly famous for her *Early Lessons* and *Parent's Assistant,* she is found at her best when she worked with a free hand, as in the delightful series of tales containing *The False Key, Mademoiselle Panache, The White Pigeon,* and *The Mimic.* These, though they bear a moral writ large, are less deliberately designed for instruction, and the character drawing is more vivid and crisp than in her novels. In these, it is said, she was less influenced by her father and his theories.

The characters in Mr. Day's *Sandford and Merton* seem designed by way of warning or example, and, moreover, he has too evidently the bias of the philosophical radical of his day against the upper class and in favour of the peasant. His well-born folk are so exceedingly ill-bred, most arrogant and objectionable, with the exception of Tommy's father, while not only Harry Sandford, but every one belonging to the working class down to the poor negro, who rescued naughty Tommy from the bull, are paragons of virtue. The reader wonders whether Tommy, in his girlish-looking hat and feather, carried on the shoulders of slaves, was a faithful portrait of the rich merchant's son of that day. Still more whether any society would have tolerated Master Mash and his little crew of comrades.

Surely they were but created "to point a moral and adorn a tale." The book has had an immense vogue both in its own day, and later; but one is inclined to suspect rather amongst the educators of youth, and those who had to provide presents and prizes, than with the children themselves. Persons are found to-day who assert that they enjoy it. If so, it must be as a memory of a vanished past, which casts a halo over many things better loved in the retrospect than when we had them. Did any child ever find genuine pleasure in its long-winded narrative, in which the powder is so ill-concealed by the jam?—unless, indeed, the story of the bull-baiting, which does rise to a pitch of agreeable excitement? If they did, it must have been in the dearth of matter more congenial.

Poetry, as well as prose, began now to be written expressly for children. I say began, but should rather say that the practice was revived, as the Puritan writers, Janeway, White, and John Bunyan, wrote a good deal of doggerel verse on religious topics for them. Nathaniel Cotton, the friend and physician of Cowper, comes midway between these writers and the later ones, who dealt with more secular topics. His *Visions in Verse* for children, spite of its attractive title, is severely didactic, consisting of moralizing allegories on such topics as Health, Pleasure, Friendship, Slander; not suitable, certainly, for very little ones. He had more fondness for children than comprehension of their small minds. In his *Fireside* he writes of their training—

" Our babes shall richest comforts bring ;
    If tutored right they'll prove a spring
        Whence pleasures ever rise.
We'll form their minds with studious care,
To all that's manly, good, and fair,
    And train them for the skies."

Cowper himself, though he wrote nothing expressly for children, drew his own tenderly petted
childhood in a few strokes in his *Lines on My Mother's
Picture*. We see the delicate little fellow, muffled in
his scarlet cloak, being drawn to school in such a little
carriage as is depicted in many of the cuts in *Forgotten
Children's Books*. In his day, and for some time after,
these little coaches were often drawn by dogs, as well
as by the hand, and several fascinating pictures show
these dog-curricles with small children driving them
just as they do goat-carriages nowadays. Little Master
Cowper was, however, drawn along by the servant.

With Dr. Watts and his *Moral Songs* we reach a
more direct appeal to the child mind. "Let dogs
delight" and "How doth the little busy bee" may be
laughed at in the modern nursery, but they have a
wholesome simplicity and directness, and come very
little behind Jane and Anne Taylor, whose *Original
Poems for Infant Minds* delighted many generations of
children. These are now perhaps coming into favour
again with the added charm of remoteness, a certain
suggestive scent as of dried rose-leaves and lavender
that clings about them. All their little prim moralities
do not hinder but rather enhance the genuine touches
of humour and pathos with which the two little old

284 ENGLISH CHILDREN IN THE OLDEN TIME

greenish-drab volumes abound. Some of us may have
shed a tear in our time over the *Last Dying Confession
of Poor Puss*, or Little Ann in *Turnip-Tops*.

It is, of course, impossible here to do more than
indicate a few of the leading writers for children who set
the tone for the rest. Any one interested in the subject
will find a treasure-house of information in a delightful
work by Mrs. Field, *The Child and His Book ;* here it
only concerns us as showing some of the influences that
went to the making of the child, and what it made him.
It is remarkable, when we come to reflect on it, how
the two, the child and the book, acted and reacted ;
whether the book most formed the child's taste or was
produced to meet that taste, it is not easy to say. Much
more of the same kind as has been already touched on,
showing the prevailing mode, is to be found in *Pages
and Pictures from Forgotten Children's Books*, by Andrew
Tuer, illustrated from the delightful store of old wood-
blocks belonging to the Leadenhall Press. The titles
of some of these are wonderfully lengthy and very
quaint. *The Instructor and Guide for Little Masters in
the School of Virtue and Good Manners* would seem
built on the lines of the old books of urbanity of
the fifteenth and sixteenth centuries, containing "Directions for Children and Youth to behave and carry
themselves on all occasions. Illustrated with Thirty
Copper Plates." This, to judge from its phraseology,
is one of the older productions in the volume, going
back to the eighteenth century. It contains moral
reflections *à propos* of various sports ; for instance, there

is a picture of boys trundling hoops. Miss Edgeworth
would have tried to explain how hoops were made, and
why round things would roll, but this writer thus
proceeds : " Think this to be the wheel of fortune, and
thou engaged with labour and industry to keep it turned
to thy good liking "—no bad lesson this. Against a
picture of football comes this sentiment : " Aspiring
youth, relaxed from study, disdains to indulge himself
in idleness and the chimney-corner."   But too much
energy in playing cricket is thus deprecated : " What
will it avail in such a contest to say I have conquered
Will or Tom with the loss of my life, or a broken
constitution ! "   So the chimney-corner might be safer
after all.

A book more on the lines of Miss Edgeworth is
Cobwebs to Catch Flies, for little children from three to
eight years old.   In this there is a fascinating woodcut
of a fair with the flying-boats. A small child expressing a natural desire to go in them, is reminded by his
virtuous elder that although his mother had not
forbidden them to do so, she probably would if she had
known of them, having laid an embargo on the merry-
go-round, and the lesser child submits, expressing his
thankfulness for having so conscientious a brother !
Not thus did Jackanapes and Tony comport themselves
at the fair.

The *Cautionary Stories*, as their name imports,
contain much the same moral lessons, but they are in
verse, and not without charm.   Here is a delightful
picture of a party of children straying in a lane—

" Where's Susan and Kitty and Jane,
     Where's Billy and Sammy and Jack ?
Oh, there they are down in the lane ;
     Go, Betty, and bring them all back.

" But Billy is rude and won't come,
     And Sammy is running too fast ;
Come, dear little children, come home,
     And Billy is coming at last.

" I'm glad he remembers what's right,
     For though he likes sliding on ice,
He should not be long out of sight,
     And never want calling for twice."

A lesson on vanity shows that domestic discipline had revived since the days of Sarah, Duchess of Marlborough—

" Mamma had ordered Anne the maid
     Miss Caroline to wash,
And put on with her clean white frock
     A handsome muslin sash.

" But Caroline began to cry,
     For what, you cannot think ;
She said, ' Oh, that's an ugly sash ;
     I'll have my pretty pink !'

" Papa who in the parlour heard
     Her make the noise and rout,
That instant went to Caroline
     To whip her, there's no doubt."

This chapter on moral children and their parents may fitly wind up with *The Good Girl*, and a companion picture from another publication called *The Good Boy's Soliloquy*. Ladies first—

" Miss Lydia Banks, though very young,
     Will ne'er do what is rude or wrong ;
When spoken to, she always tries
     To give the most polite replies.

BIRDSNESTING

MORLAND

> "Observing what at school she's taught,
> Turns out her toes as children ought,
> And when returned at night from school
> She never lolls on chair or stool."

Worthy of this is *The Good Boy*—

> "The things my parents bid me do
> Let me attentively pursue.
> I must not ugly faces scrawl
> With charcoal on the white-washed wall.
> I must not blow the candle out,
> Or throw the smutty snuff about."

With all these rules and regulations, founded on the appeal to Reason, Master Mash was certainly on the road to be abolished.

CHAPTER XVIII

CHILDREN IN THE COUNTRY

WHILE theorists wrangled, and the superior parent endeavoured to form himself and his offspring on the most approved models of the Encyclopedists, the children themselves played amongst the buttercups and daisies, and Nature took care of her own. The theoretic child, the over-tutored little mortal, of whom we read in the *Parent's Assistant*, might be a small, prim model, in a clean pinafore, with his hair parted in the middle, ever asking for useful information, but the real child was not always so consistent. Turn over a portfolio of drawings of that day, whether they be from the pencils of Gainsborough, Morland, Hoppner, Knight, Singleton, Bartolozzi, and you shall see a rollicking little crew, blackberrying, cowslipping, bird's-nesting, swinging on gates, blowing dandelion clocks, feeding (or teasing) the pigs and the chickens, or tearing up the lane after the travelling showman.

In one respect, at least, those little ones of an earlier day, on whom so many experiments were tried, were happier than ours can ever be, with all their indulgences, in that they had the real country to disport themselves in. Not those alone whose homes were in the country, but the dwellers in towns, even in London itself, were

288

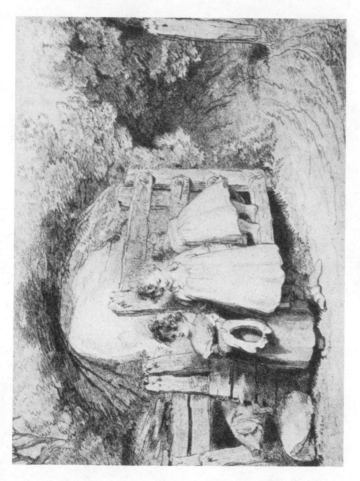

SWINGING ON A GATE
JOHN HOPPNER

within easy reach of fields, and woods, and country pleasures. Nowadays, when the great towns, with their suburbs, are so huge that it takes a railway journey to reach anything that may by courtesy be called the country, and the introduction of machinery has transformed farm-life and industry, it is not easy to realize the charm of the rural England of old. Open spaces are very well, and at least afford fresh air; but what is a park, with its hard, poor grass to play on, compared with a hayfield to tumble in, or a wood, offering its wealth of playthings to little hands? Even the seashore, with its crowds, its greasy sandwich papers and broken bottles, is no longer such a safe and entrancing playground as it used to be.

It is difficult to realize that as late as 1772 it was an easy walk from Marylebone into the country to Willan's Farm, where milk could be drunk fresh from the cow, for in Smith's entertaining *Book for a Rainy Day*, he relates that in his childhood his mother, being in delicate health, was ordered to take a glass of new milk before breakfast, and used to take him with her. He describes the route graphically: "After we had passed Portland Chapel there were fields all the way. . . . When we crossed the New Road there was a turnstile at the entrance of a meadow leading to a little old public-house; a little beyond another, leading also to fields, across which we walked to Jew's Harp Tavern and Tea-Gardens. Willan's Farm was half a mile to the south, and is now taken into the Regent's Park." Much later than this Kensington was still a country village, to be reached by a lane through fields and nursery gardens; so no doubt town children were able to spend most of their holiday afternoons in the country.

A clever little girl, whom we have seen at the Manor School in York, Eliza Dawson, known later as Mrs. Fletcher, has left a delightful record of her child-life, before she was sent to school, in the depths of the real country, as she was brought up in the little hamlet of Oxton, near Tadcaster. Her father owned the small property on which they lived, and belonged, his daughter modestly says, to the ranks of yeomen, farming on his own land ; much, we gather, what in Cumberland is called a statesman, but he seems to have been a man of some cultivation, loving books, and encouraging his daughter's literary tastes, given, too, to dabbling in political theories, a Whig of the old school. His wife had been rather above him in rank, belonging to an old Quaker family, of the name of Hill, but she died at the birth of her only child. The little Eliza was never suffered to miss a mother's care, for her father's mother, an old lady of quick temper but warm affection, a gentle and lovable aunt, and a young uncle, all came to take up their abode with the widower, and lavish unstinted petting on the little girl. She had, too, a very kind friend in an old schoolfellow of her mother's, a very accomplished and brilliant woman, who, having made an unhappy marriage, lived in great retirement in a cottage close by, and found it a great resource to cultivate her god-daughter's unusual powers. She taught the child to recite long passages from Shakspeare

and from Pope's Homer, in which she took eager
delight, partly from gratified vanity, partly from an
ingrained love of poetry—not least of that she could
hardly understand. With needlework, however, in
which Mrs. Brudenell was highly skilled, Eliza proved
but a froward pupil, for, at least in summer time, she
was never willingly indoors.

Once a threatened shadow, which she could scarcely
comprehend, crossed her sunny path, to be quickly
dispersed. A rumour arose that her father was about
to take a second wife, and her grandmother, who always
acted on impulse, without staying to assure herself of
the truth of it, took her seven-year-old grandchild by
the hand and trudged off to the house of her second
son, declaring that her pet should never submit to the
tyranny of a step-mother. Happily it proved a false
alarm, and the pair returned placably home again.

She was never lonely, and often had for playfellow
a little village girl of her own age, called Polly Bovill,
with whom she was allowed to be on terms of perfect
equality. She was never permitted to tyrannize over
her humble companion, and says, " I think she died
before I was aware there was any difference in rank
between us." She was taught kindness to her poor
neighbours. In days when tea was an expensive luxury,
her grandmother often sent her to carry her teapot to a
sick cottager. For a time two cousins came to live at
Oxton, and she was very fond of the little girl who was
six months younger than herself, and whose proficiency
—being able to read while Eliza was still learning her

letters—put her to the blush. But Eliza, though clever, was always an outdoor child. With the boy she did not get on quite so well. He was three years older, and, boy-like, rather fond of teasing little girls and putting his cousin in a passion—easily done, for she inherited her grandmother's quick temper, and most likely, as only child of the house, was somewhat spoilt.

The petted little maiden objected very much to the visits she was obliged to pay from time to time to her mother's family—her Quaker grandfather and Aunts Hill—whose ideas of discipline for children were stricter than those of her beloved granny at home, and she spent most of her time while there watching at the end of their backyard for the passing of an old cowman on his way to Oxton, whom she used to beseech to persuade her grandmother to send for her home, be it never so wet or stormy. Her journeys used to be made on an old grey mare in front of John Bovill, one of her father's tenants, and father of her little friend Polly, who used to bring a great red cloak to muffle her in case of rain or snow.

She was very fond of riding, and once, before she was big enough to be trusted on a pony of her own, her uncle took her before him on his horse after the harriers ; but her feelings were painfully chequered, the glory of being in at the death being dashed by her distress at the dying shriek of poor puss. The sports-men laughed at her and gave her the trophy, and she toiled home with it over her shoulder, half proud, yet crying all the way over its death. She never cared to go hunting again.

She seems to have had always a preference for boyish games, unlike most only girls without a brother, and she particularly delighted in playing at soldiers, having been excited to a pitch of enthusiasm by a review to which she was taken in her ninth year. Her daughter relates an amusing little trait of this taste. Having gone with her aunt for a few weeks to Harrogate, she was much noticed by a lady staying in the same hotel, being a very lovely as well as a very intelligent child. This lady often took her out in her carriage, and on one occasion, after a visit to the principal toyshop, brought her back in evident low spirits, explaining to her aunt that she was afraid from her sudden dulness the child could not be feeling well. Alone with her aunt, she unfolded the cause of her grief. "Oh, aunt, if you had seen the drums and the trumpets, and the guns and the swords in that shop!—and see, she has given me nothing but this stupid doll!"

The village where she lived was in a part of Yorkshire that boasts no special picturesqueness, but it had, says she, "a heartsome look," lying in the midst of green fields with some fine hedgerow trees shading the approach to it, and the cottages were full of comfort within, most possessing a little orchard as well as a patch of garden ground behind. The fields beyond, on the Bolton Percy side, were the child's favourite haunt, and here she sought white violets in March, or hunted for birds' nests—not to take nest or eggs, be it observed, but carefully to peep, without disturbing, and watch for the young birds to come out. Here, too, was the great cowslipping in May for the brewing of cowslip wine. But best of all her joys was the grand gathering of flowers for the garland to be hung over the door on May Day. The May-pole was already a thing of the past, but the custom of garland-making had survived, and every cottage home displayed a wreathed doorway. The last day of April was always a holiday in anticipation, and either with her cousins, if they were at Oxton, or with some of her village playmates, she was allowed to spend the whole day in the fields and coppices, Aunt Dawson providing a meat-pie and some sweets for the midday meal, packed in a covered basket, with the recommendation that it should not be opened too soon, a piece of advice rarely observed. The load of flowers was brought home at teatime, tied up in posies and fastened to an osier frame of crossed hoops, globe-shaped. I can remember years ago a similar garland, slung on a pole, used to be carried round by school-children, asking for pence.

The next good joy was the haymakers' dance and supper, which used to be held in a field close to Mrs. Brudenell's cottage, that she might play for the dancing on a barrel organ drawn up to the window. Looking back in old age to these simple pleasures, Mrs. Fletcher declares her conviction that the labouring poor had lighter spirits then than now ; not only that they had more taste for the traditional sports—the Christmas mummers, the Whitsuntide feast, or the revel at Midsummer—but they were more cheerful in their domestic

"SIT UP, PAPAGENO!"

SINGLETON

ways. She recalled the young family of John Bovill gathered round father and mother under the big walnut tree that shaded their cottage on summer evenings, " singing lustily together."

Farmhouse life always has a great fascination for children; they take the greatest interest in baby calves and colts, in pet lambs and little curly-tailed pigs, in chickens and yellow ducklings and straggling grey goslings—most of all in rabbits " of their very own." I suppose there never was a time when children did not love pets: the children of mediæval days had their Italian greyhounds, their goldfinches, their doves, as we see in many old paintings. Those whose fathers or uncles travelled afar would have marmosets, parrots, or macaws; but even the little cottagers had their kittens and their puppies, their bunnies or their white mice; sometimes, alas! "a linnet in a cage," which, as Blake averred, "puts all heaven in a rage."

The grandfather of Hugh Miller, rough sea-dog as he afterwards became, is presented in very attractive guise as a stout little boy in his sixth or seventh year, toiling alone for many miles across a dreary moor to his mother's house, a litter of puppies carried in his little kilt. He had been sent by his mother, in poor circumstances, to relations at a farmhouse to be brought up and made useful, and had been bidden to drown a litter of young pups in the pond. The child first sat down and cried; then, resolving to save his charge, tramped with them across the hills to his mother, whom he greeted with the words, "The little doggies, mither; I could na drown the little doggies." But this is the shadowed side of farm life.

One of the prettiest of the tales in *Mrs. Leicester's School* describes the first visit of a little girl of about five years old to her grandmother at a farmhouse in the country. She peeps into the barn, and is a little frightened to see a man threshing with a flail; in the farmyard she is delighted with the "little wooden houses" the hens live in, with the wee chickens running in and out, and is vastly amused with the anxieties of a hen mother when the ducklings in her charge insist on playing in the pond. The orchard seems to her a paradise, with the apple trees and pear trees and cherry trees all a-bloom, and in the grass buttercups and daisies, daffodils and bluebells which she might pick to her heart's content. Then the syllabub! a joy almost unknown to the children of to-day. Mary Lamb refers to it as to a thing understood and familiar, so I will quote Mrs. Marcet's description from her little book on the *Four Seasons*, published in 1835, feeling sure that the custom was the same as it had been for many, many years. At the close of a haymaking *fête*, sheep-shearing, or other country festivity, a favourite cow was adorned with garlands of flowers round its horns, down its back, and over its tail, and led into the field where the company was assembled. Instead of into a pail, the dairymaid, smart in cherry-coloured ribbons, milked it into a great china bowl into which wine and sugar had already been put, and the mixture, all warm and foaming, was ladled out into glasses and handed round with sweet cakes.

To return to the little Louisa: she was very happy playing in the kitchen garden, and charmed with the bees in the straw "skeps;" but it is quaint and characteristic of children that while she was in this country paradise her favourite game was to "play at London" in the wood-house, making little houses with bits of board, putting grass and daisies in the corner to represent Draper's Garden, which was all she had hitherto known of turf and trees. One cannot but see in this a reminiscence of Mary's own childhood; she, town-bred child as she was, probably did much the same on her visits to Mackary End in "pleasant Hertfordshire."

Louisa did not entirely enjoy the haymaking; it disturbed her so much to see her beloved cornflowers and moon-daisies mown down; but the sheep-shearing greatly entertained her, with the supper of roast beef and plum-pudding that followed, served on a long carved-oak table, polished with age. She and her sister were allowed to sit up till dark to see the shearers at supper, and hear the singing. She describes very charmingly, too, the everyday farmhouse supper—

"Just before the men came in from the field, a large faggot was flung on the fire; the wood used to crackle and blaze, and smell delightfully; and then the crickets, for they loved the fire, they used to sing; and old Spot, the shepherd, who loved the fire as well as the crickets did, he used to take his place by the chimney corner; after the hottest day in summer, there old Spot used to sit. It was a seat within the fireplace, quite under the chimney, and over his head the bacon hung. When old Spot was seated, the milk was hung in a skillet over the fire, and then the men used to come and sit down at the long white table."

Truly a good life, and a happy and healthy one for the children. With the changed conditions of modern life it has passed wholly away; nothing has been seen like it within the last half-century, and nothing will ever quite take its place. It was very human, and it brought the children into relation with simple working folk and with animals in a way which "Nature Study" can never replace. The woodland lore which country children, and especially gipsies, possessed almost by instinct, instead of being added to, is being rapidly stamped out by the education now bestowed. This kind of life, however, lasted on with wonderfully little change through many centuries till the nineteenth was well on its way, and the industrial revolution brought in entirely new conditions. Dame Angela Porter, taking charge of the farm at Woodhall, enjoying a visit from her little grandsons, and making them fat on dairy produce, is a seventeenth-century vignette which finds a pendant in Miss Mitford's *Mrs. Allen* in the nineteenth—

"There she sits, placid and smiling, with her spectacles in her hand, and a measure of barley on her lap, into which the little girls (her three small grand-daughters, aged five, four, and three) are dipping their chubby hands, and scattering the corn amongst the ducks and chickens with unspeakable glee."

In and out of Miss Mitford's delightful pages in *Our Village* the children flit, not made the main subject, but falling into their natural place, like flowers in a landscape,

CHICKENS
STOTHARD

so that the reader gathers half consciously the vision of what these old-fashioned country children were like ; so simple, so healthy, so hearty in their pleasures. First and foremost her pet Lizzy, the carpenter's three-year-old child, forward enough for six, big, strong—and wilful. A lovely child, with her round, laughing, sunburnt face, her big blue eyes, and curling hair. Her fond biographer sees in her a likeness to the great man of that day Napoleon, and truly she had something of his gift for commanding others.

"She manages everybody in the place, her school-mistress included ; turns the wheelwright's children out of their own little cart, and makes them draw her ; seduces cakes and lollipops from the very shop window ; makes the lazy carry her, the silent talk to her, the grave romp with her ; does anything she pleases. . . . She has the imperial attitudes, too, and loves to stand with her hands behind her, or folded over her bosom ; and sometimes, when she has a little touch of shyness, she clasps them together on the top of her head, pressing down her shining curls, and looking so exquisitely pretty ! "

A spoilt monkey, nevertheless, for when her kind friend goes to take her for a walk on a frosty morning, and her careful mother objects for fear of chilblains or sliding on the ice and coming to grief, she is heard through the closed door roaring, " I will go ! "

On a happier occasion she is taught to make a cowslip-ball. How old, I wonder, is that delightful art ? Why did not Herrick mention it in that lyric where he describes the maids going to the fields " with wicker arks to bear the richer cowslips home " ? More likely their store was intended for the brewing of cowslip wine, that delicious country dainty referred to by little Miss Dawson.. When did children first find out what cool and fragrant playthings might be made by nipping off the tasselled heads, stringing them on a long ribbon slung from branch to branch, then when the string was full, pushing them up close together, and tying them up tight? Are cowslip-balls still made, or are they to be numbered amongst the lost arts?

Miss Mitford has a warm corner in her heart for that much abused person, the country boy. She deprecates his apple-stealing, still more his bird's-nesting propensities ; still she can sympathize with the adventurous spirit that leads to both, and one of her most graphic sketches is of the half-dozen ragged varlets, following each other down the dark, smooth, liny slide, led by Jack Rapley, "the sauciest, idlest, cleverest, best-natured boy in the parish." Another pet of hers, little grave, dark-eyed Willy Brooker, six years old, she thinks would make a charming match for Lizzy at four, and the picture of the baby courtship recalls a little pair of higher rank and in an elder day, Kenelm Digby and his future wife, Venetia Stanley, who, "the very first time that ever they had sight of one another, they grew so fond of each other's company that all who saw them said assuredly something above their tender capacity breathed this sweet affection into their hearts. They would mingle serious kisses among their innocent sports."

But life was not all play, even for children in the country. Very early these little ones had to make themselves useful at home or in the fields, for in those days there was no compulsory school attendance, and if they were needed to mind the baby while mother washed, or for bird-scaring, goose-minding, gleaning, haymaking, or what not, they had to stay, and it is by no means certain they were not getting a more practically valuable education the while. Sometimes they drove a regular trade, such as rush-gathering, osier basket weaving, water-cress picking, or the selling of turnip-tops, like poor little Ann. I suppose most of us know the piteous little verses from *Original Poems*, in which she laments her hard lot in the winter—

> " Sadly cold are my fingers, all drenched with the dew,
> For the sun has scarce risen, the meadows to dry ;
> And my feet have got wet with a hole in my shoe ;
> Come haste then, and buy my sweet turnip-tops, buy."

In a very quaint book by the late Andrew Tuer, called *Street Cries*, is included a series of prints, published in 1819, of little girls driving various trades, which he calls *Six Charming Children*. One wheels potatoes in a barrow, with a little pair of scales ; another has rabbits slung on a stick across her shoulder, and cries—

> "Rabbit ! a rabbit !   Who will buy?
> The rabbit you may roast or fry,
> The fur your cloak will trim."

Little "Milk O !" with her miniature yoke and pails, looks fairly prosperous in her straw bonnet and comfortable warm coat, so too does the little strawberry-seller, but the chair-mender with her bundle of rushes under her arm has a more unkempt and gipsy-like appearance, and seems to have a task too big for her. The flower-seller, a chubby little maiden in a shady hat tied down with a kerchief, trots gaily along, her small dog gambolling beside her, and maybe singing—

"Come buy my fine roses, my myrtle and stocks,
    My sweet-smelling balsams and close-growing box!"

She belongs to summer-time when such work was lighter.

It is wonderful what industry children are capable of when thrown upon their own resources, and Miss Mitford relates a remarkable tale of Hannah Bint, the drover's little daughter, typical of many. She was but nine or ten when her mother died, and she immediately assumed the care of the house and of her two younger brothers; she fed the pigs and the poultry, and managed all the internal economy, for her father was often absent for days together, with his dog Watch, fetching or taking herds to great distances. When she was about twelve a severe rheumatic attack crippled her father entirely, and they would have had nothing to depend on but the pittance he received from a benefit club, but for the exertions of this little girl. She went to the great cattle-dealer in whose service her father had lost his health, and begged from him a cow. Half-touched, half-amused by the child's earnestness, and wondering how she would succeed, he presented her with a fine young Alderney. Thereupon she repaired to the lord of the manor, and undertook to pay the rent and keep her father off the parish, if she might graze her cow on the common, and he not only granted

"MILK O!"

her request, but greatly reduced the rent. Actually this child of twelve succeeded in establishing a regular dairy business, and making it pay, added to it a trade in eggs, poultry, and honey, and got her father, who still retained the use of his hands, to learn how to make mats and baskets with the assistance of the elder boy, who collected the rushes and osiers. How many children of to-day, even could they leave school at twelve years old, could do as much ?

Miss Mitford has given so graphic a description of the successive stages through which the village girl passes, I cannot do better than quote it—

"The first appearance of the little lass is something after the manner of a caterpillar, crawling and creeping upon the grass, set down to roll by some tired little nurse of an elder s. ter, or mother with her hands full. There it lies—a fat, boneless, rosy piece of health, aspiring to the accomplishments of walking and talking ; stretching its chubby limbs ; scrambling and sprawling, laughing and roaring. There it sits in all the dignity of the baby, adorned in a pink-checked frock, a blue-spotted pinafore, and a little white cap, tolerably clean and quite whole. One is forced to ask if it be boy or girl ; for these hardy country rogues are all alike, open-eyed, weather-stained, and nothing fearing. There is no more mark of sex in the countenance than in the dress.

"In the next stage, dirt-encrusted enough to pass for the chrysalis, if it were not so very unquiet, the gender remains equally uncertain. It is a fine, stout, curly-pated creature of three or four, rolling about amongst grass or mud, all day long ; shouting, screeching—the happiest compound of noise and idleness, rags and rebellion, that ever trod the earth.

"Then comes a sunburnt gipsy of six, beginning to grow tall and thin, and to find the cares of the world gathering about her ; with a pitcher in one hand, and a mop in the other, an old straw bonnet with ambiguous shape, half hiding her tangled hair ; a tattered stuff petticoat, once green, hanging below an equally tattered cotton frock, once purple; her longing eyes fixed on a game of base-ball at the corner of the green, till she reaches the cottage door, flings down the mop and pitcher, and darts off to her companions, quite regardless of the storm of scolding with which her mother follows her runaway steps.

"So the world wags till ten; then the little damsel gets admission to the charity school, and trips mincingly thither every morning, dressed in the old-fashioned blue gown, and white cap and tippet, bib and apron of that primitive institution, looking as demure as a nun, and as tidy; her thoughts fixed on buttonholes and spelling-books—those ensigns of promotion; despising dirt, base-balls and all their joys.

"Then at twelve the little lass comes home again, uncapped, untippeted, unschooled; brown as a berry, wild as a colt, busy as a bee—working in the fields, digging in the garden, frying rashers, boiling potatoes, shelling peas, darning stockings, nursing children, feeding pigs—all these employments varied by occasional fits of romping and flirting, and idle play, according as the nascent coquetry or the lurking love of sport happens to preponderate; merry and pretty, and good with all her little faults. It would be well if the country girl could stand at thirteen. Then she is charming. But the clock will move forwards——"

And here we must leave her, for with the grown girl we have nothing to do.

Warton's picture of peasant children, in his Ode, *The Hamlet*, written some half century earlier, is very like all this in tone, though with far less detail. Describing the cottage of the "hind," he goes on—

> "Their little sons who spread the bloom
> Of health around the clay-built room,
> Or through the primrose coppice stray
> Or gambol in the new-mown hay;
> Or quaintly braid the cowslip twine
> Or drive afield the tardy kine;

BLACKBERRYING

HAMILTON

> Or hasten from the sultry hill
> To loiter at the shady rill ;
> Or climb the tall pines gloomy crest
> To rob the raven's ancient nest."

Meanwhile Wordsworth was regarding children with "larger, other eyes," the eyes of a poet, seeing deep things, contemplating the mystery of childhood, "trailing clouds of glory," or "moving about in worlds not realized." He has captured some of those strange, half-conscious visions of infancy which schooldays have wholly effaced from the minds of most of us. He can still call up his own mysterious delight in the rainbow ; he sees himself chasing butterflies with his sister, and the remembrance brings back so much in its train that he calls the insect " Historian of my Infancy."

Like Bishop Earle, he has noted the prime characteristic of childhood, its imitativeness : the picture is vivid and true for all time ; the six-year-old boy so intent on his play that he is—

> " Fretted by sallies of his mother's kisses,
> With light upon him from his father's eyes.
> See, at his feet, some little plan or chart,
> Some fragment from his dream of human life,
> Shaped by himself with newly-learnèd art ;
> A wedding or a festival,
> A mourning or a funeral ;
> And this hath now his heart,
> And unto this he frames his song :
> Then will he fit his tongue
> To dialogue of business, love, or strife :
> But it will not be long
> Ere this be thrown aside,
> And with new joy and pride
> The little actor cons another part."

But this is childhood in the abstract; abstract, too, is that visionary little maiden, formed in Nature's school, at once sportive and serious, listening to the becks that prattle and the winds that sigh and whisper through the fells till—

> "Beauty born of murmuring sound
> Shall pass into her face "—

and that other little Lucy—"the sweetest thing that ever grew beside a human door"—who met so tragic a fate. These were ideal children; with them our poet was in sympathy; but it is with the sense of a sudden jarring descent to earth we find him trying to play the superior parent. Even in *We are Seven*, sweet as is its picture of the little girl, taking her little porringer to eat her supper beside the graves of her young brothers and sisters, lying there so still, it is impossible not to resent the stupid denseness of the man with his reiterated question—every child at least resents it. Still more objectionable is the father who torments his five-year-old son for a reason for his preference for Kilve by the seashore, as if a creature of that age could be capable of giving a reason; till the child, goaded to desperation, casts his eye about in search of help, and catching sight of the golden vane, cries—

> "At Kilve there was no weather-cock,
> And that's the reason why."

CHAPTER XIX

TRANSITION

ROMANCE was not wholly banished, as the Mrs. Teachums and the superior parent would have wished, but was coming to meet the children once more, her eyes like stars, her hands full of gifts. The sensible infant, nurtured on hard fact, the small moralist who had been taught to be good because it paid, was not to be the last exponent of the English child. Already, while the flood of little improving books was at its height, there were signs of something more wholesome, more human. Two of the best writers of the century, alien in spheres of work, alien in sympathy, were at one in the insight into the child-mind which genius gives. Sir Walter Scott, commenting on the "good-boy" stories of his day, writes—

"The minds of children are, as it were, put into the stocks, like their feet at the dancing school, and the moral always consists in good conduct being crowned with success. Truth is, I would not give one tear shed over Little Red Riding Hood for all the benefit to be derived from the history of Jemmy Goodchild. I think the selfish tendencies will be soon enough acquired in this arithmetical age, and that, to make the higher class of character, our own wild fictions—like our own simple music—will have more effect in awakening the fancy and elevating the disposition than the colder and more elaborate compositions of modern authors and composers."

And this is what Charles Lamb said of the priceless stories, told when the world was young, at a later day when they were in danger of being shelved—

"*Goody Twoshoes* is almost out of print. Mrs. Barbauld's stuff has banished all the old classics of the nursery. The shopman at Newbery's hardly deigned to reach them off an old exploded corner of a shelf when Mary asked for them. Mrs. Barbauld's and Mrs. Trimmer's nonsense lay in piles about. Knowledge must come to a child *in the shape of knowledge*, and his empty noddle must be turned with conceit of his own powers when he has learnt that a horse is an animal, and Billy is better than a horse, and suchlike ; instead of that beautiful interest in wild tales, which made the child a man, while all the while he suspected himself to be no bigger than a child. Science has succeeded to poetry no less in the little walks of children than with men. Is there no possibility of averting this sore evil ? Think what you would have been now, if, instead of being fed with tales and old-wives' fables in childhood, you had been crammed with geography and natural history."

A delightful little boy, Hugh Miller, grandson of the child who saved the puppies, born more than a hundred years ago, and brought up in a remote corner of Scotland, has recorded his own earliest intellectual experiences in *My Schools and Schoolmasters*, and they fully bear out this. To discover that the toilsome road of the horn-book led to the ability to read the story of Joseph and his brethren for himself was a revelation to him, and a new world opened to him in the wonderful narratives of David and Goliath, Samson and the Philistines, Elijah and Elisha. Would he have felt the same had he made their first acquaintance, watered down in the manner of Mrs. Trimmer in her *Scripture Histories*, and her imitators in the *Peep of Day* or *Line upon Line?* Soon he added to

KITTENS
HAMILTON

these precious stores a little library of small paper-
bound chap-books, which he kept in a box about nine
inches square, large enough, he observes, to contain a
great many immortal works—*Jack the Giant Killer*,
and the *Yellow Dwarf*, and *Bluebeard*, and *Sindbad the
Sailor*, and *Beauty and the Beast*, and *Aladdin and the
Wonderful Lamp*, and other like treasures. And these
early browsings in the fields of romance by no means
unfitted him to become an explorer in the paths of
science and an eminent geologist. He is quite as
severe as Lamb on the flood of improving books for
children, which, when he was a man grown, threatened
to swamp the ancient favourites. "Those intolerable
nuisances, the useful-knowledge books," says he, "had
not yet arisen, like tenebrous stars, on the educational
horizon, to darken the world and shed their blighting
influence on the opening intellect of the youth-hood."

This brings to mind a story told in one of Mrs.
Hannah More's letters. A little girl from one of the
"threepenny semi-genteel schools" was asked by a
gentleman what she was studying. "Oh, sir," was her
reply, "the whole circle of the sciences." "Indeed!"
said he. "That must be a very large work." "No, sir ;
it is quite a little book. I bought it for half a crown."

Elia's "imperfect sympathy" with Scotchmen could
hardly have resisted the appeal of Hugh Miller's
appreciation of Homer—

"Old Homer wrote admirably for little folk, especially in the
Odyssey, a copy of which—·in the only true translation extant, for,
judging from its surpassing interest and the wrath of critics, such I

hold Pope's to be—I found in the house of a neighbour. . . . Next came the *Iliad*. With what power, and at how early an age, true genius impresses! I saw, even at this immature period, that no other writer could cast a javelin with half the force of Homer. The missiles went whizzing athwart his pages, and I could see the momentary gleam of the steel, ere it buried itself deep in brass and bull-hide."

At this very time Lamb was bringing out *The Adventures of Ulysses* for children, and since children cannot read it in the original Greek, it was a task well worth the doing ; for though Hugh Miller thinks they could not have it in a better version than that of Pope, it may be doubted if the glorious simplicity of Chapman, which Lamb closely followed, is not better adapted, both to the child-mind and to the directness of the old Greek story, than Pope's smooth and polished couplets. But let that pass. We all have a tenderness for the form in which a new tale was first unfolded to us. Most vividly Lamb sets before the imagination of the children, for whom he wrote, the succession of immortal stories—Polyphemus, with his horrible one eye in the middle of his forehead ; Circe and the Swine ; Nausicaa washing her brothers' garments and playing at ball with her maidens ; the meeting of Telemachus and his father ; Ulysses drawing the bow ; and the slaughter of the suitors of Penelope—wisely refusing to soften off some of the harsher features of the narrative, as some of his critics would have had him do. But why, oh why, does he leave out the death of Argus at his old master's feet? Was it too harrowing? Truly, it always sent us to bed in tears.

If Shakspeare is not to be read at first-hand by children, then they could not make his acquaintance better than in Lamb's *Tales from Shakspeare*, which Charles wrote for the Juvenile Library in conjunction with his sister Mary. They are well chosen and beautifully told, yet there seems no reason—not equally valid against Bible stories—why children should not read many of the plays in the original. As with the Bible, children do not understand, and are not interested in, the parts unsuited for them, unless, indeed, an unwholesome curiosity has been fostered by injudicious hints and forbiddings. Be that as it may, the Lambs' book is a store-house of delightful stories, and excellent to put into the hands of a child who is to be taken to see a Shakspeare play for the first time.

Another book which the brother and sister wrote together, a small volume of poetry for children, is much less known than it deserves to be. It never seems to have attained such wide popularity as many other things of the kind less worthy; perhaps because it was less obviously didactic than the fashion of the day demanded. The moral is never obtruded, though it is there, and of the truest and purest. There is a sweet simplicity, childlike rather than childish, which especially characterizes the verses which Mary contributed. *Baby's First Tooth*, the description of the breeching of a little boy, almost as graphic as that in Lady North's letter, and the story of an innocent and fearless little fellow sharing his bread and milk with a snake in the woods, are amongst the prettiest where it is hard to choose.

This old maid and old bachelor, who had not even any small nephews and nieces to awake a vicarious parental feeling, had more insight into the child mind than a great many excellent folk who were devoting their whole energies to the production of what they deemed for the children's good. Elia, indeed, in his article on *Married Folk*, pretended that other people's children bored him. But we know better; the tenderness of his *Dream-Children* betrayed him. How that passage on the death of John goes home to the heart of a child who has lost a comrade—

" How when he died, though he had not been dead an hour, it seemed as if he had died a great while ago, such a distance there is betwixt life and death ; and how I bore his death as I thought pretty well at first, but afterwards it haunted and haunted me ; and though I did not cry or take it to heart as some do, and as I think he would have done if I had died, yet I missed him all day long, and knew not till then how much I had loved him. I missed his kindness and I missed his crossness, and wished him to be alive again to be quarrelling with him (for we quarrelled sometimes), rather than not have him again."

Meanwhile a wild singer, further removed than even Lamb from the proprieties of the *Cautionary Stories* and their like, was singing both to and about children. William Blake had in him much of the eternal child, of the grave innocence, of the freakish fancy. To the former belongs the description of the Charity Children at St. Paul's—

TRANSITION 313

> "O what a multitude they seemed, these flowers of London town,
> Seated in companies they sit, with radiance all their own :
> The hum of multitudes was there, but multitudes of lambs,
> Thousands of little boys and girls, raising their innocent hands."

In the other vein is *The Child and the Piper*—

> "Piping down the valleys wild,
> Piping songs of pleasant glee,
> On a cloud I saw a child,
> And he, laughing, said to me,
>
> "'Pipe a song about a lamb.'
> So I piped with merry cheer.
> 'Piper, pipe that song again.'
> So I piped: he wept to hear."

A modern writer has touched the same note—

> "Come away, O human child,
> To the waters and the wild ;
> With a fairy hand in hand,
> For the world's more full of weeping
> Than you can understand."

Though he is unique, and, like the greatest, has no date, Blake has more in common with the modern writer for children than with him of the eighteenth century. In his verse for childhood he seems to touch hands though but lightly with the Lambs amongst the earlier, with Robert Louis Stevenson among the later, writers of children's poetry. Stevenson has something of the quaint simplicity, a touch of the elvish fancy, which make Blake seem half a child himself as he writes; but his fascinating volume belongs to the modern child.

He was a Scotchman, and Scotland—whether, thanks to the Celtic temperament, or to its remoteness from

Gradgrind influences, not impossibly to its comparative poverty—was keeping alive a spirit that in the England of the early nineteenth century bade fair to be smothered. For in these years a whole new tract of country was being opened to the youthful imagination in the *Waverley Novels.* Nothing quite like them had ever been seen before. The old romances were full of things which children could not understand, and some which, perhaps, it was better they should not. But here were stories written in simple, forcible, graphic English, easily to be followed by a child of nine or ten, full of the high romance of chivalry, of the swift narrative of adventure, the continual happenings that appeal to the opening intelligence of youth, of an absolutely pure and wholesome morality without a touch of the didactic ; written, moreover, for men and of manly concerns, so that the child's mind was led on and expanded. Hannah More had complained of much of the child-literature that was becoming so profuse, that it had a tendency to " arrest the understanding and protract the imbecility of childhood." Scott's novels had the very opposite effect. We are told they are losing in popularity with the young in our own day. Is this because they are used as tasks, and papers set in them ? or because of the weakening of the mental digestion of our generation ? Perhaps from both causes combined.

When Sir Walter wrote purposely for children, he could do it well, and did not write down to them. The *Tales of a Grandfather,* which he designed to make his little grandson acquainted with the history of his own

PLAYMATES

GEORGE ROMNEY

country, have many of the most delightful qualities of his novels. They only differ from history for grown-up people in that the broad, salient outlines, and the events that appeal to a child's mind, are brought into prominence, while obscurer matters of politics which may be studied later are briefly passed over. The way in which these tales are told emphasizes strongly his opinion on the value of romantic reading for children. That had been his own nurture. When he was a little lame boy at his grandfather's farm at Sandy Knowe, living among the sheep, his delight was in the wild old Jacobite tales and ballads of the countryside, sometimes listened to by the winter hearth, sometimes from the lips of an old shepherd, beside whom he used to spend the long summer days. In this lonely life he grew to be friends with the storm and the thunder; for once when a dairymaid, who used to carry him out to the field and fetch him again, had forgotten him and left him alone in a sudden thunderstorm, she found him, on her return, clapping his small hands and crying, " Bonny ! bonny ! " at every flash. He loved the history of Josephus, too, which he heard his grandfather read aloud, and drank in romance at every pore. He was such an eager child, and so loud in talking of what pleased him, that the long-faced parson, Dr. Duncan, used to say of him, " One may as well try to talk in the mouth of a cannon as where that child is."

Scotch children would seem to have been more high-spirited, more original, less tutored, than their contemporaries in England. Scott's little favourite,

Maidie Fleming—"Pet Marjorie," as he called her—was as quaint a specimen of precocious intelligence as you could find. Gifted as she was, and in all simplicity aware of it, she was a thorough child, both in looks and in nature. Her chubby round face, bright eyes, and close-cropped hair were not the attributes of the ideal prodigy, nor were the utterances of her odd little mind. She had her own opinions on many things, and expressed them forcibly, but quite without the self-conscious virtue of the Edgeworth children. For some time she was taught at home by her mother, with several brothers and sisters all a little older than herself; but when she was six, a grown-up cousin, struck with her unusual ability, begged to take her to Edinburgh and educate her in that intellectual city. Her little letters home and the journal which she kept are a wonderful mixture of precocity and childish fun and wilfulness.

She had a generous temper, shown in a story told of her when she was only five. Running with her sister ahead of the nurse, they were called back because of a dangerous mill-stream close to the path. Marjorie heeded not, but ran on, tripped and fell; and her sister, a little older, saved her by snatching at her frock. The frock was torn, and the old nurse, always a little hard on Isabella, proceeded to "give it her" for spoiling the little one's clothes; but Marjorie flew at her, crying, "Pay Maidjie as much as you like, and I'll not say one word; but touch Isy, and I'll roar like a bull!"

This old nurse was quite a character, and there is an amusing account of her showing off Master William, the youngest boy, saying the Shorter Catechism at nineteen months old. He could answer correctly enough to the query, "Wha made ye, ma bonnie man?" and to the three next, but to the question, "Of what are you made?" not even a fist shaken in his face could get out another answer than "Dirt." "Wull ye never learn to say dust, ye thrawn deevil?" with a cuff, was the inevitable close of the performance.

The devil plays a considerable part in Marjorie's confessions. On one occasion she writes in her diary—

"I confess I have been very more like a little young divil than a creature, for when Isabella went upstairs to teach me religion and my multiplication and to be good and all my other lessons I stamped with my foot and threw my new hat which she had made me on the ground and was sulky and was dreadfully passionate. . . . She never never whips me so I think I would be the better of it and the next time that I behave ill I think she should do it."

A little later she records the sad fact—

"Yesterday I behaved extremely ill in God's most holy church. . . . It was the very same divil that tempted Job tempted me I am sure, but he resisted Satan, though he had boils and other misfortunes which I have escaped."

Religious education at that day, especially in Scotland, was a severe business, and sermons very long, and this child was but six!

Quick as she was, she had an honest hatred to the multiplication-table. "The most devilish thing," she remarked, "is eight times eight and seven times seven; it is what nature itself can't endure." Her great delight was in history and in poetry, especially the latter, a great deal of which she used to get by heart, and soon tried to imitate. Those were the days in which a daily task from one of the best poets used to be set, and though it was hard, it was surely better for the growing mind than the baby verses, pretty though they may be, which the children learn to repeat after babyhood should be past. It is a mistake to think that children do not love what they do not understand. They like the vagueness which they feel in poetry beyond them, and ear and taste are formed by being used to the best. Marjorie was none the worse for having to make an effort to learn Gray. She says in her journal, "I get my poetry now out of Gray, and I think it beautiful and majestic, but I am sorry to say I think it is very difficult to get by heart."

We must not linger over Marjorie's lessons, nor over her own quaint poetical effusions with their funny rhymes and their wonderful promise of originality. Before she was eight years old her love of history and poetry met in the composition of a long poem on Mary Queen of Scots, which, in spite of childish diction, has here and there a true poetic thought, as in the line—

> " Elizabeth said she would her keep,
> And in her kingdom she might sleep."

Poor little poetess! It will never be known what she might have blossomed into. At eight years old the after effects of measles cut short her little day, and she goes down to posterity as the pet of the great romancer, who, it is related, used to carry her off from Mrs. Keith's house, wrapped in his plaid, to spend a winter evening with him, and recite scenes from Shakspeare to him till she brought the tears to his eyes.

Far away in the south another gifted child of Scottish descent, but English upbringing, was foreshowing what his future tastes were to be. Little Tommy Macaulay, in his home on Clapham Common, was engaged at eight years old on the composition of *A Compendium of Universal History.* His mother said that he had succeeded in giving a tolerably connected view of the chief events in the history of the world on about a quire of paper. He, too, tried his hand at poetry—" in emulation of Marmion." At three years old he was an omnivorous reader, and a parlourmaid in Mrs. Macaulay's service used to recall how he would sit on the table beside her while she cleaned the plate, dressed in a little nankeen frock, expounding to her out of a volume as big as himself. He did not care much for toys, but loved to go for a walk, talking and telling stories to his mother or nurse all the way.

He must have been a droll, old-fashioned little person, as his remarkable memory enabled him to reproduce exactly words or phrases he had read, with more or less appropriateness. One day Mrs. Hannah More, calling on his parents, was amused at being received by a little slim, fair boy of four, who said he was sorry his parents were out, but if she would step into the parlour he would bring her a glass of old spirits! Being asked what put such an idea into his head, he replied, " Robinson Crusoe always had them."

His costume when taken to Orford to be shown to

Lady Waldegrave affords a glimpse of the dress of a little boy at the beginning of the nineteenth century. He wore a green coat—probably what we should now call a tunic—with red collar and cuffs, a broad frill, and white trousers, nothing like so pretty or convenient as the preceding fashion for small boys of the "skeleton suit" with a large collar.

These all are exceptional children, standing out from the common herd, but the new century was bringing in a new literature, the realistic, in which the children were depicted, not as their mentors thought they ought to be, but as they really were; neither as patterns nor yet gibbeted as awful warnings, but painted with their own idiosyncrasies, with their trifling faults and follies, their small virtues, their limitations; tiresome, lovable little mortals, much as we know them now, allowing for differences of environment. Miss Yonge is usually credited with bringing in this school of fiction, but though she certainly carried it further and won for it an enormous popularity, it arose with Miss Martineau. The character-drawing in *Feats on the Fiord*, in *The Settlers at Home*, most of all, in *The Crofton Boys*, cannot be surpassed. It is curious that while with Charlotte Yonge and Catherine Sinclair the modern child appears, Anne Mozley, writing about the same time, or a very little earlier, draws unmistakably the Early Victorian child as the type had existed for a quarter of a century before—longer than that, indeed, for the pages of *The Fairy Bower*, with the young people appearing in the drawing-room before a dinner-party or making their entry with the almonds and raisins, as used to be the custom when people dined at five or six, would have been quite appropriate any time back to the days of Queen Anne. The formidable Mr. Everard, terrifying his little god-daughter with mythological questions, recalls Dr. Johnson at the house of Dr. Hawkins, the learned author of the *History of Music*, noticing and "fondling in his way" the latter's little daughter. Miss Letitia, in her somewhat acidulated memoirs, records this with more pride than pleasure. He was fond of children, but probably his great ungainly figure and loud pompous voice frightened them. She was more at ease with Oliver Goldsmith, who taught her to play at Jack and Jill with two bits of paper, and made orange pigs for her.

To return to *The Fairy Bower ;* the story perhaps does not amount to much, but the characterization of the various contrasted groups is wonderfully clever. The quiet little heroine brought up in seclusion with her widowed—but unusually natural and human—mother; the quick, clever town children who had had their wits rubbed bright by being much noticed by their parents' visitors ; the cousins who had been "brought up on a system," forbidden even to see cards or dancing, and were the most self-righteous little prigs ; more especially the background of grown-up people—it is all so vivid, it seems to plunge the reader back into the society of sixty years ago and more. It might be far more truly described as *A Looking-glass for Children*, than the old work of that name.

Country stories are at all times so rife, it is interesting sometimes to see how the town children lived and were amused, and a very old-fashioned book of slightly earlier date, called *A Month's Vacation*, gives a very lively account of "the manner in which a Juvenile Party passed their time in Baker Street, with an Entertaining Description of the Principal Places of Amusement they visited in London." Since June the 18th was celebrated at Vauxhall as a Gala night in honour of the battle of Waterloo, it cannot have been earlier than 1816, but the costumes in the illustrations point to a date not much later. Mr. Taylor, the gentleman at whose house the little party were visiting, is depicted in a top-hat of antique fashion, a frock-coat, and gaiters; an elder boy wears the same. The next boy is in an Eton suit, with an oddly shaped hat, larger at the top of the crown, and with a shiny peak and strap; just such an one is shown on a boy trundling a hoop upon a bit of Derby china of at least a hundred years ago. The smallest boy rejoices in a skeleton suit and a muff.

Mr. and Mrs. Taylor conducted their little guests first to the Menagerie at Exeter Change in the Strand, where they saw an elephant ringing the dinner-bell with his trunk, and visited the lions in their cage, being specially impressed with Nero, a very aged lion who had been twelve years in captivity, and whose roaring was tremendous. Another day they were taken, together with the little ones and the nurse, to a box at Astley's. The picture shows the Ring, with a man riding on a bare-backed steed, waving two flags, and being baited by the traditional clown. The visit to Vauxhall took place in the evening, for the grounds we learn were illuminated. There was a juggler who greatly pleased the boys, and in the Rotunda the Fantoccini (puppets) acted *The Babes in the Wood.* A hermit was to be seen in " Fingal's Cave," and on their way round to inspect him they came upon a Cosmorama, from its name probably a moving panorama with views from all quarters of the globe, for still it was very much the fashion to blend instruction and amusement.

The Play and the Pantomime were as popular then as now, and the latter quite as funny. Charles Lamb has recorded the solemnity with which in early youth he accepted the "clownery and pantaloonery" of the first Pantomime he witnessed. That is characteristic of a young child ; it is all quite real and serious to him ; the sense of the comic comes later. He was but six when he was taken to Drury Lane to see *Artaxerxes*, and felt himself transported bodily to Persepolis—and into the Book of Daniel. Walter Scott was the same age when he saw his first play, and realized it quite as keenly. It was *As You Like It*, and the child was so scandalized at the quarrel between Roland and Orlando that he screamed out loud, " Why ! ain't they brothers ? "

But we have reached the threshold of the Victorian Age, and with that this little study should end, for hardly yet do we call it the Olden Time.

CHAPTER XX

LITTLE CHILDREN UNDER GREAT MOVEMENTS

SO with the changing centuries the children change. Looking back over the way we have travelled, as the course of history unfolds, it is curious to notice how the lives of children have been affected in one great epoch after another. Outside influences have acted upon them in various ways, and, moreover, children, like little mirrors, reflect faithfully their environment.

The coming of Christianity was the beginning of a new order of things; the Church gathered the little ones into her fold, and taught, disciplined, civilized them. Schools were amongst the prime activities of the early Church. The consolidation of the Kingdom, perfected under Alfred, brought in a new conception of education as part of the national life, and what had been scattered and half destroyed by the Danes was set up again and inspired with fresh vigour. With the conquest came a very different condition of affairs, and the children suffered as those of conquered countries always do, and as the little Finlanders suffer at this day, in having a language foreign to them imposed upon the schools, which must have made learning a

JUVENILE NAVIGATORS
GEORGE MORLAND

toilsome thing for them for many generations. What the Wars of the Roses did for them has been almost obliterated, for records that deal in any way with childhood at that day are so sparse. Civil war, however, must have left deep traces on the lives of the little ones, as it did so lamentably at a later day, in homes broken up, houses ruined or burned, lands confiscated, children left orphans; and doubtless many perished unrecorded in those hard, rude days.

The Renaissance, with its marvellous advance in knowledge and enthusiasm for learning, did not have an effect altogether favourable on the teaching of little children, applying to them a method of study only suited to the mature mind. Far more serious—nay, disastrous—were the results of the Reformation on them; for the dissolution led to the forcible closing of all the Chantry schools and those attached to the monasteries, and the founding or re-establishment of Grammar Schools in many or most of the towns out of the confiscated funds was no compensation for the stamping out of the parish schools throughout the country districts; and we probably have Henry VIII. and his advisers to thank for the fact that we are so behindhand in the teaching of young children, especially those of the poor.

For children more fortunately placed came an interval of peace between that distracted time and the Great Rebellion. Home life flourished in tranquillity and leisure, and all the arts that adorn and beautify the home blossomed; moreover, fathers began to take a more personal interest than heretofore in the little ones and their unfolding powers of mind and body. The earliest manifestations of Puritanism were by no means unfavourable to home nurture, but its later and more grotesque developments—not to call them distortions— bore very hardly on the children. Little Mr. John Langham at five years old reciting the Assembly's Shorter Catechism, and questioning his sister of three on the state of her immortal soul, or Mistress Lucy Apsley at four rehearsing the sermons she had listened to, pulling her playfellows' dolls to pieces, and exhorting her mother's maids, reflect but too faithfully the atmosphere about them, and the long war brought mischief in its train to both sides. The relaxation of all discipline that followed invaded even the nursery and the school-room, and the spoilt child comes into prominence, though doubtless he had existed before.

Look on a little, and the growing materialism and indifferentism of the eighteenth century, and its utilitarian spirit, come out in the " rational" child, who argues every question, and is taught to obey not from respect to authority, but because he is convinced he will entail greater disagreeables on himself by having his own way. With the dawning of the nineteenth century come new ideals, new enthusiasms, and an immense quickening of care for children, together with a new interest in childhood *per se*, which, could we follow it, would lead to the modern child as we have him now.

And through it all the essential elements of childhood

persist: the new theorists can tell us little beyond what Vaughan with the insight of the poet, Bishop Earle with the keen observation of the satirist, Mulcaster with the practical experience of the schoolmaster, have told us long ago about the child. One thing stands out marked—and to many minds strange—that we can have travelled so far and learnt so little. We are still in the experimental stage, and may well ask ourselves, are we truly any wiser than Mulcaster or Dean Colet?—or to go further back, than King Alfred or good Bishop Ingulphus? We are gentler in our methods now than were the pedagogues of the Renaissance, but hardly more so than those just named. We are much more moderate in the use of the cane than they were in the schools of the eighteenth century; yet sometimes a doubt may cross the mind whether it were well to put it so wholly on the shelf, especially if with it we have put on the shelf also the respect for authority, the reverence for what was wise and great and good that was among the fairest graces of childhood.

But for the difference in discipline the children of to-day seem to have far more in common with those of the seventeenth century than with the little folk of any later period : they are, as those children were, the playthings and delight of their parents. Priggishness is nowadays the anathema of childhood; the new child laughs at the demure little budding divine of the end of that century, and no less at the infant philosopher of the early nineteenth ; except as curiosities he cannot read their books. The pert nimble-witted page of the Elizabethan dramatists is not nearly so far off from him, nor even the Saxon schoolboy, with his little Latin lessons, and his rewards of figs or almonds for saying them well ; but it is with the little Sidneys and Boyles, Verneys and Porters that our children feel most at home. It is only when childhood casts off its simplicity and masquerades in artificial garb, that it is cut off from the natural freemasonry of child with child that binds the ages together.

It is good both for children themselves and those who train them to look back sometimes to the childhood of other days ; they may learn some strange and unexpected lessons. No one who had read much about the children of our forefathers could give utterance to the sentiment so often heard, especially on the lips of those who praise the past indiscriminately, that the little folks of to-day are so precocious ! If there is one thing that distinguishes the modern child from all who went before him, it is his extraordinary immaturity and backwardness, compared with the development of his ancestors at the same age. " Forward," indeed, he often is, but it is in the other sense. Boys and girls, especially girls, will thrust themselves into notice, make their voices heard at table, rush at their elders, pull them about, call them by their Christian names, act as if they thought themselves—as, indeed, they have been taught to do—the principal persons in the company ; but in knowledge, sense, capacity, self-command, they are years behind their forefathers.

What boy of five can speak Latin ? far less would weep, like little Richard Evelyn, because he was thought too young to read the Greek dramatists ? He, of course, was a prodigy, but the speaking of Latin is frequently referred to as a by no means uncommon accomplishment at that age : in the sixteenth and seventeenth centuries it was customary to teach a child to read as soon as he could speak, and to read Latin concurrently with English. It was quite usual for a boy to be ready for the university at twelve, or from twelve to fourteen, at which age with us they are only beginning at a public school. Not only in knowledge but in character they ripened faster : the prevalence of youthful marriages may have hastened an early maturity, but we must not imagine when we read of the marriage of a little maiden of twelve that she was the nursery child we look for at that age; probably she was much what a girl of eighteen, just leaving school, would be now.

With us many things have tended to prolong the age of childhood. The enormous increase of the things to be learned, keeping either boy or girl much longer in a state of pupillage ; the great absorption in games, narrowing the children's interest in actual life ; and not least the flood of children's books, filling the mind with childish things, and keeping it from caring for the wider interest of real literature, so that in very truth our riches have tended to poverty. Perhaps, too, the pre-occupation of the adult with childhood in itself, as if it were something more than a mere phase leading to manhood, but almost as if children were a race apart, has helped to this result.

I have observed, as doubtless many have done, that whereas in the old days boys and girls, too, were eager to be grown-up, to be thought older than they are, now the contrary feeling is gaining ground ; they are unwilling to leave school, reluctant to take up the responsibilities of life, by no means eager to play their part in the world. Many rejoice at it, thinking that it shows that children are happier than they used to be. Possibly this is so, and a happy childhood is good ; but, after all, childhood is not the end but the road, and the best child is he who is soonest and most completely ready to be a man.

But it is not with the modern child, save by way of contrast or comparison, that I have to do ; yet, perhaps, if that important personage will deign to peep into the nurseries of his ancestors, he may glean from many ages many qualities that are worth his adoption ; the eager, adventurous spirit of one age, the courtesy of another, the loyalty of the little cavalier, the obedience of the little Puritan, the thirst for knowledge that distinguishes one period, the love of romance and mystery that pervades another, and withal the reverence that adorned all until these latter days.

And herewith I take leave of the long procession of children of the olden time, commending them to the sympathy of their little descendants with the hope that the children of to-day, as well as those who love and study them, may find them as pleasant company as I have done.

INDEX

331

PRINTED BY WILLIAM CLOWES AND SONS, LIMITED, LONDON AND BECCLES.